ויקרא | LEVITICUS

A PARSHA COMPANION

ויקרא | LEVITICUS

A PARSHA COMPANION

Rabbi David Fohrman

AlephBeta PRESS

מגיד
MAGGID

Leviticus: A Parsha Companion
First edition, 2024

Aleph Beta Press
EMAIL info@alephbeta.org
WEBSITE www.alephbeta.org

Maggid Books
An imprint of Koren Publishers Jerusalem Ltd.

PO Box 8531, New Milford, CT 06776-8531, USA
& PO Box 4044, Jerusalem 9104001, Israel
www.maggidbooks.com

Book design by Cory Rockliff
Volume design by Estie Dishon

ISBN 978-1-59264-677-7 (hardcover)

A CIP catalog record for this title is available from the British Library

Printed and bound in the United States

The *Parsha Companion* series
is reverently dedicated by

Ronny & Toby Hersh

in memory of their parents

אברהם בן אהרן הלוי ז״ל
אסתר בת אברהם יהושע ז״ל

Abraham & Esther Hersh *z"l*

שמואל משה בן פסח יוסף ז״ל
חיה רבקה בת צירל ז״ל

Moshe & Rivka Zytelny *z"l*

and the many among their family
who perished in the Shoah

About Our Parents

Our parents surmounted great tragedy and hardship to live exemplary lives. They loved us, nourished us, and sacrificed much to help us flourish and become committed Jews. In their example, we saw sacred values of the Torah brought to life. We live in the shadow of their deeds.

ABRAHAM AND ESTHER HERSH hailed originally from the Carpathian mountains. They were both survivors of Auschwitz, and they met after the war in a displaced persons camp in Germany. Shortly thereafter, they made their way from the ashes of Europe to the Land of Israel, where Abraham fought in Israel's War of Independence. He was a fierce lover of both the land and the Torah of Israel. Together, Abraham and Esther lived difficult lives but, through it all, somehow always maintained a deep faith in Hashem. Their strong values — commitment to family and to Judaism, and an abiding love of the State of Israel and the Jewish people — made powerful impressions upon their children.

RABBI MOSHE AND RIVKA ZYTELNY made their way from Europe to America. Toby's father was, in his younger years, a yeshiva bachur in Kletzk. Before Lakewood was a gleam in the eye of history, he became a close student of Rabbi Aharon Kotler, and a *chevrusa* of his son, Rabbi Shneur. He escaped the ravages of war by heading, with his yeshiva, first to Siberia and then to Kazakhstan, where he met his wife, Rivka. The couple moved from Kazakhstan to France — and all this time, despite war and constant upheaval, Rabbi Aharon remained like a father to him. To this day, Ronny and Toby cherish letters in their possession that Rabbi Aharon sent to Rabbi Moshe in France, advising him on major life decisions. Eventually, Rabbi Moshe and Rivka came to America, where he rejoined his rebbe and yeshiva in Lakewood. There, he became part of an unlikely success story, as he helped reestablish a vibrant center of Torah on new and distant shores. All in all, Moshe was the only one in his entire immediate family to survive the war. Together, he and Rivka raised seven children.

Our parents lived through harrowing times and emerged with a steely, strengthened faith; they sacrificed much to pass on their vibrant heritage. We remember them with love, and are honored to carry their legacy forward.

Ronny & Toby Hersh

The Leviticus volume of the *Parsha Companion* is dedicated by

Alan and Fran Broder

Dr. Hillel and Chayi Cohen

in honor of our children: Ari, Rebecca, Talia, and Josh,
May we be *zocheh* to continue to witness…

כִּי יְדַעְתִּיו לְמַעַן אֲשֶׁר יְצַוֶּה אֶת־בָּנָיו וְאֶת־בֵּיתוֹ אַחֲרָיו וְשָׁמְרוּ
דֶּרֶךְ ה׳ לַעֲשׂוֹת צְדָקָה וּמִשְׁפָּט

A special thank you to Rabbi Fohrman for sharing his endless insights on the parsha, and whose *divrei Torah* enhance our Shabbos table on a weekly basis.

Avram M. Cooperman MD, the Cooperman and Weiss Families

in loving memory of
Philip and Lillian Cooperman
Gerald Mark Cooperman

Mark and Erica Gerson

Chaim and Livia Jacobs and Family

in memory of our marvelous mother,
MRS. LOLA MAPPA, *A"H*;
her warmth, kindness and selflessness overflowed to her family,
friends and every person she touched.

Harry and Eta Klaristenfeld

in memory of our dear grandfather
צבי יוסף בן ,אליעזר אשר
who was the epitome of והגית בו יומם ולילה;
and our dear grandmother
יהודית בת שמואל זאנוויל,
the quintessential עזר כנגדו.

Yaron and Lisa Reich

in memory of Lisa's beloved parents,
Ernie and Shirley Weiner, *a"h,* who would be *kvelling* from
Rabbi Fohrman's prodigious and illuminating Torah insights.

Donny and Arielle Rosenberg

in honor of Miriam Latova,
avid consumer of Aleph Beta videos and Torah,
superb teacher, and wonderful role model to our children.

Yanky and Aliza Safier

in honor of our dear brother-in-law,
Rabbi David Fohrman,
who uses his unparalleled knowledge and endless devotion
to inspire others to learn, think, and know.
May Hashem give you the strength
to keep up your incredible work.

We gratefully acknowledge the following patrons who, with generosity and vision, have dedicated individual volumes of this *Parsha Companion* series:

BEREISHIT

Tuvia Levkovich *a"h* & Barbara Levkovich

SHEMOT

Daniel & Jamie Schwartz

VAYIKRA

Alan and Fran Broder

Dr. Hillel and Chayi Cohen

Avram M Cooperman MD,
the Cooperman and Weiss Families

Mark and Erica Gerson

Chaim and Livia Jacobs and Family

Harry and Eta Klaristenfeld

Yaron and Lisa Reich

Donny and Arielle Rosenberg

Yanky and Aliza Safier

BAMIDBAR

Dr. Bruce Wayne Greenstein
& Ms. Monica Patricia Martinez

DEVARIM

Andrew & Terri Herenstein

We also wish to acknowledge

Legacy Heritage Fund

for its generous support to help
make this series of books possible.

LEGACY HERITAGE FUND

Contents

Some Words of Appreciation

LEVITICUS BRINGS US TO the halfway point — and more — in this five-volume series of *Parsha Companions*. I'm happy to be able to use the arrival of that propitious moment to give thanks to those who've partnered with me in bringing this volume, and the series thus far, into being.

Ronny and Toby Hersh are the patrons of this five-volume series of books. Ronny and Toby have dedicated the series to the memory of their parents, Abraham and Esther Hersh *z"l* and Moshe and Rivka Zytelny *z"l*, whose own personal stories were great journeys in their own right. I am honored that this series of volumes bears their name.

I would also like to acknowledge the Legacy Heritage Fund for its generous support to help make this series of books possible. The foundation focuses much of its effort on supporting Jewish education in innovative and trendsetting ways. I am honored that the Legacy Heritage Fund has chosen to include this series of books among the many worthy projects they've chosen to support.

This particular volume of the series (essays on Leviticus) has been generously sponsored by a wide group of patrons. Together, they've made the research, development, and publication of this volume possible. They are:

- Alan and Fran Broder
- Dr. Hillel and Chayi Cohen
- Avram M. Cooperman MD, and the Cooperman and Weiss Families
- Mark and Erica Gerson
- Chaim and Livia Jacobs and Family
- Harry and Eta Klaristenfeld
- Yaron and Lisa Reich
- Donny and Arielle Rosenberg
- Yanky and Aliza Safier

I am privileged to count all of you not only as supporters but as friends, as well. Your support of my work means a great deal to me. May these pages serve as a worthy and lasting credit to the lives you've sought to honor in the words of your dedications.

I want to also acknowledge those who have dedicated other volumes in the *Parsha Companion* series: Tuvia Levkovich *z"l*, and Barbara; Dan and Jamie Schwartz; Dr. Bruce Wayne and Ms. Monica Patricia Martinez; and Andrew and Terri Herenstein. Sadly, Tuvia, patron of the Genesis volume, has passed away since the publication of the volume that bears his name. May the thanks of those who've benefited from his generosity continue to nourish his soul in the Land of the Living.

* * *

An old adage tells us that not everything that you think, should you say; not everything you say should you write down; and not everything you write should you publish. The process of taking thoughts and turning them into something worthy of publication is daunting, and, gratefully, I've had a good deal of help in that endeavor. Let me introduce you to those who've helped shepherd these words into the volume you hold in your hands:

First, Matthew Miller, Rabbi Reuven Zeigler, and the rest of the team at Koren/Maggid have been wonderful to work with. They are proudly bringing a new generation of original Jewish thought to the public, one beautiful book at a time. We are all enriched by their efforts.

Shoshana Brody (from Aleph Beta) skillfully edited many of the essays and designed the graphics and charts that grace these pages. Joining her were Immanuel Shalev, Sarah Penso and Evan Weiner, who also lent their talents to this work (broadly speaking, Immanuel helped see the forest not just the trees; and Sarah and Evan made sure the individual trees got their fair due as well). Ari Levisohn, as well as Rabbis Eli Raful and Elinatan Kupferberg contributed valuable research. Adina Blaustein oversaw the overall production and kept the various moving parts… well, moving. We are grateful to the team at Koren, overseen by Caryn Meltz, who transformed the manuscript into a book, including Estie Dishon, Tani Bayer, Rachelle Emanuel, and Debbie Ismailoff. Thanks as well to Cory Rockliff, who designed the series' overall aesthetic.

Many of the ideas in this book on Leviticus had their *own* genesis, as it were, in parsha videos I created with the help and support of the amazing team at Aleph Beta (you can find those videos at www.alephbeta.org). I want to take this opportunity to acknowledge, with gratitude, those behind the scenes who have, over the years, helped to transform Aleph Beta from a mere idea, to a fledgling startup, to a viable, going concern: its founders, board of directors, and officers, past and present. They are Etta Brandman, Alan Broder, David Hamburger, Jeff Haskell, Josh Malin, David Pollack, Donny Rosenberg, Robbie Rothenberg, Dan Schwartz, Kuty Shalev, and Steve Wagner. I want to thank, as well, the manifold subscribers of Aleph Beta, who each support our work in ways great and small, and provide us with meaningful feedback, appreciation, as well as a dose of constructive criticism. It is a privilege to take this journey through Torah along with you; having you by our side gives us the drive and motivation to continue.

I want to also take this opportunity to recognize three men, each of whom is no longer with us; all three played an outsized role in nurturing my development over the years. My father, Moshe Fohrman, *z"l*, passed away when I was quite young, but he taught me so much about life, people and relationships in the short years we had together; his love and influence continue to pervade my work. My stepfather, Zev Wolfson, *z"l*, a man of towering accomplishments, took me under his wing, believed in me, and helped me thrive. LeRoy Hoffberger, *z"l*, a bulwark of the Baltimore Jewish community, became a dear friend and mentor. Roy and I first met when he attended a class that I taught at the Johns Hopkins University; he took a keen interest in my work and ultimately helped give it life by creating the Hoffberger Foundation for Torah Studies. The love of all three I shall carry with me as long as the One Above deigns that I walk the earth.

Finally, I want to acknowledge my family. My wife, Reena, has given me her unfailing love and support, and has partnered with me in the greatest endeavor of my life — raising seven delightful children: Moshe, Shalva, Avigail, Shana, Yael, Ariella, and Avichai. All have helped shape this book in ways great and small, for they, together with my three sons-in-law, Yosef, Boruch, and Moshe, really are *my* "parsha companions." Many of the ideas contained in these pages were born, shaped, or refined in animated discussions with them around the Shabbos table. I treasure those moments: Learning Torah with my family is a constant opportunity to talk about things that matter deeply with people I care about the most — and what could be better than that?

Rabbi David Fohrman

Woodmere, NY
September 2023

Introduction

How Many People Put Leviticus on Their Summer Reading List?

LEVITICUS, OR VAYIKRA, AS we call it in Hebrew, is a tough book to read. Ask your average person on the street what books they pick up for light summer reading, or even "heavy reading" — deep thought and inspiration — and not many will point to Leviticus. So, how should we approach this book? In it, we read of animal and meal offerings, *tumah* and *taharah*, ritual purity and impurity. Its laws seem related to a world hardly familiar to us. Do you need to be a priest living many, many centuries ago to really appreciate Leviticus?

Thus relevance is one issue that confounds the mind of the contemporary reader of Leviticus. But that's not the only issue. Another problem we confront when opening Vayikra is the simple fact that this book seems so different from what's come before it in the Torah. Because, let's face it: Genesis and Exodus had a really good story going: God develops a relationship with a family of humans, but they eventually become enslaved in Egypt, until the Lord frees them from bondage with signs and wonders. Hollywood has made quite a bundle out of telling that story, from *The Ten Commandments* to *The Prince of Egypt*. But then along comes Leviticus, and rudely interrupts the narrative flow of the Torah. It introduces the reader to a series of seemingly arcane precepts, and the reader can be excused for feeling somewhat befuddled. It seems almost like a bait and switch. How exactly, the reader wonders, does Genesis and Exodus prepare me for this third book, Leviticus? Or, to put the same question differently: How, if at all, should my experience of Leviticus be enlightened by having read Genesis and Exodus first?

The volume you hold in your hands is an attempt to grapple with these questions.

Everything You Need to Know about the Torah You Learned in Kindergarten

To some extent, each essay you are about to encounter navigates its own path in finding overarching meaning in the pages of Leviticus. But still, I think, some words can be said about the general approach I'll be trying to employ. If you've read the first two *Parsha Companion* books in this series, you'll note that I use a kaleidoscope of close-reading techniques to try and get at some core ideas in biblical text, and this new volume on Leviticus is no exception. In this volume, though, I'll be using a particular technique a bit more heavily. I'm speaking here of a tool we might call *intertextuality*.

Intertextuality is actually just a fancy name for something very simple — a basic, Sesame Street–style game we might call: *Where Have We Heard These Words Before?* Readers of previous volumes in this *Parsha Companion* series will be familiar with the game because, well, you've already played it — but at the risk of boring the seasoned reader, let me reintroduce the rules of the game. They go more or less as follows.

Say you're making your way through one of the Torah's stories or sections of laws. As you read, you come across an unusual phrase. But then you stop and ask yourself: *Where have I heard these words before?* It strikes you that you *have* seen that phrase before. You flip through some pages and there it is. That phrase showed up thirty chapters before, in another story altogether. Sure, the context is entirely different, but the unusual phrase — it is undoubtedly exactly the same.

If that was the end of the matter, you wouldn't really think anything of it. Coincidences happen all the time. The phrase appears here in Story A, it appears there in Story B — no big deal. But here's the thing: No sooner do you resume reading, than it happens again: A few lines later in Story A you come across *another* unusual phrase. You consult a concordance just to make sure, and, wouldn't you know it, the only other time this second phrase is used in the Torah … is thirty chapters ago, in that very *same* Story B.

Then, as you continue to read story A, it happens a third time. And then a fourth.

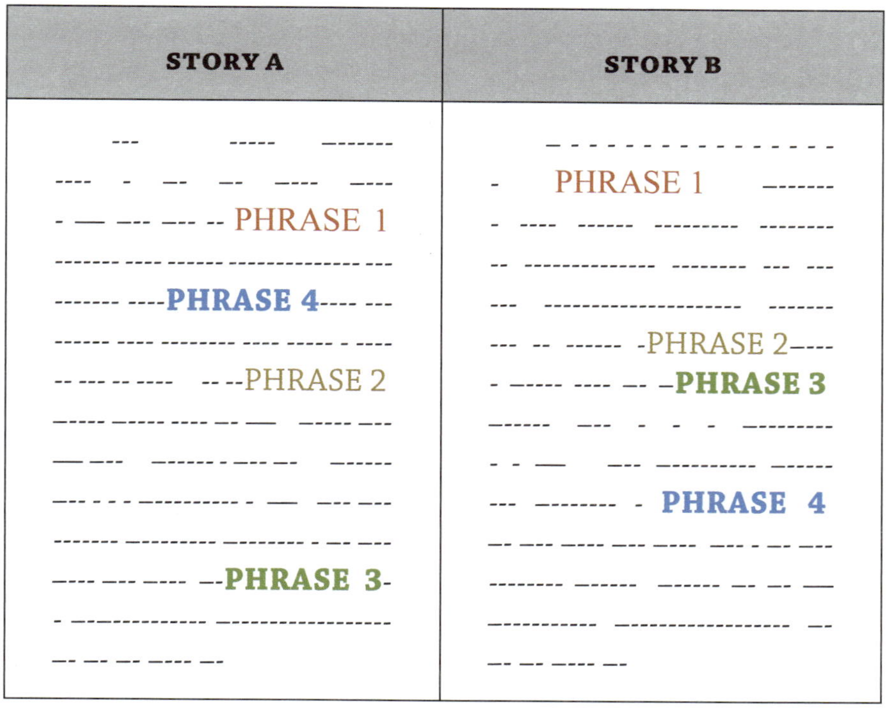

When this kind of thing happens once or twice, you can just raise an eyebrow and chalk it up to a coincidence. But four or five times, or even more? At a certain point, you stop ascribing these correspondences to mere coincidence. As different as story B seems from story A, the reluctant reader needs to conclude that the author wants you to somehow link these texts. In these cases, I'd suggest that the Torah is actually creating a unique kind of commentary on its own text. It is almost as if you, the reader, are being asked to take story B gently in your hands and overlay it onto story A. Story B is to become a kind of lens through which you can view story A, or vice versa.

Which is remarkable, right? Because imagine someone came to you and asked you for a new commentary they could use when going through the Torah this year. They'd already been through all the classical commentaries. One year they used Rashi, another Ramban, and another, *Ha'amek Davar*. They were interested in something revelatory, but authoritative; something that felt new, but was steeped in our tradition.

Well, what if you pointed them to the oldest commentary of all? Older than Ramban, Rashi, or even Onkelos or Midrash. What if you pointed them to…the Torah *itself*. You could justifiably do that, because that's really what's happening with these intertextual connections. The Torah is using its own text to create an intricate web of commentary within its own pages.

Stereo Vision

Intertextual commentary like this gives us the ability to perceive surprising layers of depth in biblical text. And I'm not using the word "depth" metaphorically here. Because stop for a moment and think about how depth perception works for us humans. We have two eyes. *Ever wonder why we have two of them?* It's not just a matter of having a spare just in case something goes wrong with the first one. Two eyes grant us an ability to encounter depth. They allow us to perceive a world unfold before us in three dimensions.

How does that work? Well, being set apart from one another by a centimeter or two, our two eyes occupy two different vantage points in space. Each therefore looks out on the world using a slightly different vantage point than the other. Yet for some strange reason, we don't have the perception of "seeing" two different things. We don't have double vision, at least not if our brain is doing its job. Our brain seamlessly merges the input from each of our two eyes, creating a single image out of the dual input. And when this occurs, miraculously, the sensation of depth is created. That single image appears rich and three-dimensional.

Two slightly different pictures, merging into one. That is how our sensation of depth gets created. That's how it works with two eyes. And that's how it works, I'd like to suggest, with two texts. The Torah takes advantage of the magic of stereo perception in order to allow us humans to transcend what appears to be the inherent "flatness" of text. Text seems to be just two-dimensional words on a piece of paper. But by seeing two connected texts together, by coming to perceive how Text A plays off of Text B, the Torah's words begin to leap off the page. We learn to see the Torah in something akin to three dimensions.

Internet 2.0

The kind of thing I'm talking about is not a rare occurrence in biblical text. Indeed, intertextual patterns linking various texts to one another don't just appear once or twice in the Five Books of Moses. They are *everywhere.*

And if you really stop to think about it, that has surprising implications for the information potential contained within the Torah.

You know, the Talmud famously tells us that the Torah is nearly infinitely deep. The Sages almost tease us by telling us: הֲפֹךְ בָּהּ וַהֲפֹךְ בָּהּ דְּכֹלָּא בָהּ — *Delve into it and delve into it, for all is in it.*[1] But the modern reader, skeptical by nature, may doubt that maxim. How can the Torah be *that* deep, you wonder to yourself; after all, it has a finite number of words. How much information can anyone — even God — really integrate into a finite, given number of words? The Torah might be profound, but can it really contain almost infinite realms of wisdom? This talk seems like the stuff of fantasy.

But it's not fantasy. Because what if the Torah is not just asking you to read its stories and laws as isolated chapters? What if it is asking you to see the links between them? The … *hyperlinks* between them. What then? You and I are used to thinking of hyperlinks as a feature of the modern-day wonder we know as the internet. But what if hyperlinks are not new inventions of the human mind, but very old inventions of the Divine Mind?

I would suggest to you that the latter possibility is in fact correct. More than that: The Torah's sophistication when it comes to the use of hyperlinks may well dwarf that of modern-day, early-twenty-first-century technology. For consider the way we use hyperlinks on a modern-day internet site. When your cursor hovers over that little blue underlined word, what happens when you go and click on it with your mouse? Well, you are magically transported to some new place on the internet. That's what a hyperlink does; it takes you to a new location. But what if a hyperlink could do more than that? *Much* more than that?

What if instead of just *taking* you from point A to point B, a hyperlink created a window from point A *from which you could view* the information in point B? You would be able to survey point B from the perspective of point A. And what if point B wasn't just linked to point A but to three, four, or five other points? Each of these hyperlinks would open a different window on point B? You could see point B simultaneously from all these different perspectives. Well, talk about really understanding point B! The information potential in *that* kind of interconnected web would be astounding.

---

1 *Pirkei Avot* 5:22.

And you might say to yourself: That's the stuff of science fiction. We can't actually engineer a system like that. Even with an investment of billions of dollars, it would be impossible to create anything like that. We lack the technology to engineer it. I hear you. But what if I told you that a system like this already exists — and has existed for three thousand years; that the Torah itself is this kind of interconnected web? That, in just a few words, is my claim. Long before electricity was invented, there was the Torah — an astonishing, hyperconnected web of texts, each shedding light on the other. The stereo effect I described above is not a onetime phenomenon. It is a feature of the system. At the highest levels of understanding, it is part of how the Torah is meant to be read.

It Isn't New. It's Old.

If this kind of analysis sounds new to you — it isn't as new as it sounds. Certainly, neither I nor any other modern scholar is the one who first came up with this. I would argue that the oldest type of biblical commentary we know, the commentary found in Midrash, is replete with this kind of analysis. Sometimes the Midrash is overt about it, sometimes it is covert. But the Sages of the Midrash understood well the inherent interconnectedness of texts, and they used this understanding to great effect to illuminate larger vistas of meaning. The teachings of the Midrash might often be cloaked in allegory, but they are profound. And they are based, in large part, on a core understanding of the fundamental unity of the Five Books of Moses.

Those of you who aren't masters of the Midrash, but who have picked up the Genesis or Exodus volumes in this series, already have a sense of the ubiquity of intertextual patterns in biblical texts. But in this volume, more of this kind of reading is to be found. In Leviticus, I've leaned on this mode of analysis to try to grapple with, at least implicitly, the two issues I raised at the start of this introduction:

- The casual reader finds Leviticus barely relevant to the modern reader.
- The casual reader finds Leviticus to be an outlier in the Bible, a book seemingly disconnected from the story line of Genesis or Exodus.

My feeling is that a key to grappling with the first of these issues lies in successfully confronting the second. So let me say for starters: If there is one thing that I hope the volume you now hold in your hands shows you, it is that Leviticus is *deeply* connected to the books that precede it. The reader who reads Leviticus and plays the deceptively simple *"where have I heard these words before"* game, will find that Leviticus comprises a veritable treasure trove of intertextual connections. In law after law, passage after passage, Leviticus is picking up on threads in Genesis and Exodus, and weaving these threads into rich tapestries of meaning. Indeed, contrary to first appearances, Leviticus is emphatically *not* a book that stands alone. It is part and parcel of an organic whole that we call the Torah. Its laws are inseparable from the stories that precede it. And once you begin to see how that is true, the meaning — and yes, even the contemporary relevance — of its laws and precepts, starts to jump out at you in unexpected and dramatic ways.

This volume represents my attempt to give you a taste of the richness that the mysterious text patterns of Leviticus offer us. As you read, I hope that you, too, will be struck with some of the same wonder that I myself feel when coming across these links. And I hope that this wonder will excite not just your mind, but will touch your heart and soul as well.

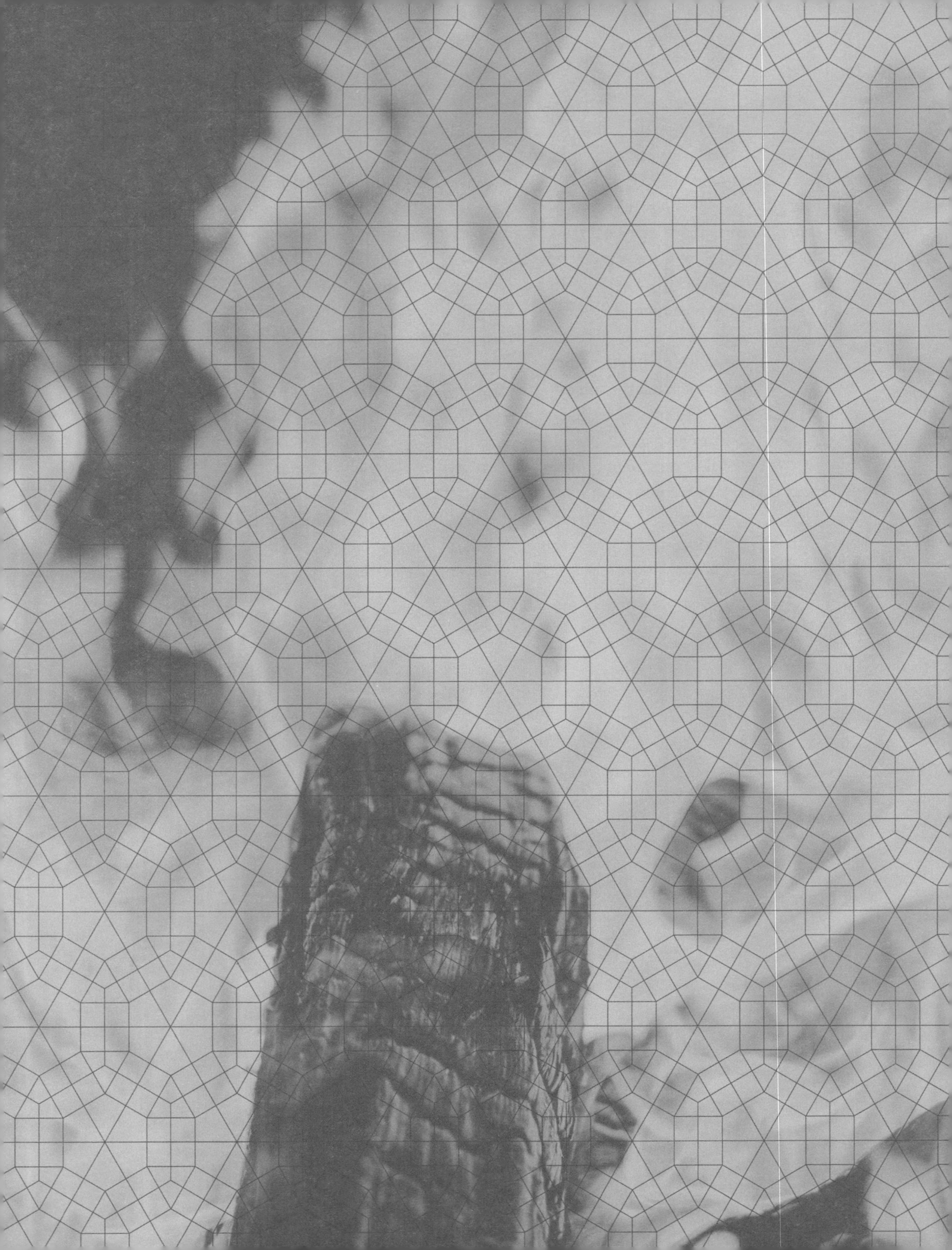

VAYIKRA

A Peek into the World of Offerings

דַּבֵּר אֶל־בְּנֵי יִשְׂרָאֵל
וְאָמַרְתָּ אֲלֵהֶם אָדָם
כִּי־יַקְרִיב מִכֶּם קָרְבָּן
לַיקֹוָק מִן הַבְּהֵמָה
מִן הַבָּקָר וּמִן הַצֹּאן
תַּקְרִיבוּ אֶת קָרְבַּנְכֶם:

Speak to the Children of Israel and say to them: When any of you presents an [animal] offering to God, he shall choose his offering from the herd or from the flock.

LEVITICUS 1:2

VAYIKRA I

A Peek into the World of Offerings

Is There a Matrix Here?

OF ALL THE ASPECTS of Judaism described by the Torah, perhaps none seems as alien to modern sensibilities as the notion of *korbanot*, especially animal offerings. For thousands of years now, prayer has taken the place of these offerings as a prime way of serving the Almighty. And yet, such offerings are ubiquitous in the book of Leviticus. Full chapters of the Torah are devoted to laws and regulations that describe and govern them. How should we, in our day and age, relate to these chapters? Should we merely gloss over them and move on, wait for the Messianic Age when such offerings might emerge from dormancy in some shape or form? Or what?

I'd like to suggest that these offerings remain instructive to us, today. Even if they no longer define our practical actions, the spiritual themes that animate these offerings offer us some important truths. How might we see those themes?

Let's take a moment to briefly review the main types of offerings the Torah describes, and then we'll be better positioned to launch our exploration.

The basic types of the Torah's animal offerings are introduced to us in the first four chapters of **Parshat Vayikra**. More or less, the text tells us of three categories.[1] These are:

---

1 See Rambam, *Hilchot Ma'aseh HaKorbanot* 1:2. There is, technically, a fourth type of offering as well, a specialized form of sin offering known as an *asham*. An *asham* is brought when someone is unsure whether they have transgressed a prohibition for which a *chatat* would otherwise be warranted. This is known as an *asham taluy* — an uncertain *asham*. Additionally, in a handful of specialized prohibitions, the bringing of an *asham* is mandated as well. The latter is known as an *asham vadai* —

- The *olah*
- The *shelamim*
- The *chatat*

How might we translate these terms?

Some render an *olah* as a burnt offering, but that's not a very literal translation of the term. A more precise translation might be: "that which is offered up." *Olah* is an apt description for this particular offering since, by law, it is to be entirely offered up to God, which is to say, it is entirely consumed upon the altar:

Leviticus 1:9

וְהִקְטִיר הַכֹּהֵן אֶת הַכֹּל
הַמִּזְבֵּחָה עֹלָה אִשֵּׁה רֵיחַ
נִיחוֹחַ לַיקוָה:

The priest shall offer it all upon the altar; it is an *olah* — an offering by fire, of pleasing fragrance to God.

Our next category of offering, the *shelamim*, is often described as a peace offering, or alternatively, a wholeness offering. Indeed, *shelamim* seems related to the words *shalem* or *shalom*, which mean that which is whole and at peace, respectively. As opposed to the *olah*, which is entirely offered on the altar, the meat of a *shelamim*, according to the Torah, is meant to be shared: Some of it is eaten by the Kohanim, the priests in the Temple, some is offered on the altar, and most of the offering is consumed by the owners of the animal themselves.[2]

The third main type of animal offering is the *chatat* — the sin offering, many of whose laws are detailed in Leviticus chapter 4. This particular offering is brought by someone who has inadvertently transgressed

---

a certain *asham* (ibid. 1:6). Because of its conceptual similarity to the *chatat* (the sin offering) we won't treat the *asham* separately in the body of this essay.

(Unlike the *olah*, *shelamim*, and *chatat*, each of which is introduced and whose sacrificial process is detailed independently at the beginning of the parsha, the *asham* appears at the end of the parsha and relies on the description of the *chatat* for its procedures. See Lev. 5:14–26.)

2 See Lev. 7:15–16, and Rambam, *Hilchot Ma'aseh HaKorbanot* 10:7.

certain prohibitions in the Torah.[3] *Chatat* offerings come in different varieties — but when it comes to the standard type of *chatat*, a salient feature of the offering is that some parts of its meat are offered upon the altar, but the rest of it is eaten exclusively by the Kohanim. The meat is not consumed by the owners at all.[4]

This is the very briefest of sketches. Other important distinctions exist between the three types of offerings, too, but this will be enough to get us started. Having reviewed a bit about each offering, let's try to get some further context by considering an intriguing question: Do these various types of offerings first burst forth out of nowhere, here in the book of Leviticus, or do they have earlier roots in the Torah, too?

By way of explanation: As far as the halachic parameters of these offerings are concerned, these are introduced to us here, in the book of Leviticus: It is here that we learn about their "whats," "hows," and "whens." But we've been introduced to these offerings before, in some shape or form. Or at least the prototypes for these offerings. Long before Leviticus, back in the narrative sections of the Torah, we find stories in which either these kinds of offerings appear, or at the least, situations exist that seem to call for these kinds of offerings. I think if we go back to these stories and situations, by reaching back into the distant past, we may learn something crucial about the "why" behind each offering, helping us understand what these offerings might still mean to us today.

So let's ask: What episodes in the Torah, if any, might serve as the earliest historical touchstones for each kind of offering?

---

3 Not all inadvertent transgressions create liability for a *chatat*, but when the misdeed is significant enough, then a *chatat* offering is brought (see Rashi on Lev. 1:4, and especially Ramban, there). Note that a *chatat* differs significantly from an *olah* or *shelamim* in the sense that, for the most part, when an individual brings an *olah* or *shelamim*, he or she does so voluntarily. The *chatat*, however, cannot be brought "voluntarily" (i.e., it can't be brought in cases of transgressions where it is not mandated by the Torah; see Mishna Chullin 2:10 and Menachot 91b).

4 See Rambam, *Hilchot Ma'aseh HaKorbanot* 7:1–2. The above generalizations apply to standard *chata'ot*, known technically as the *chatat ne'echelet* (the *chatat* that is consumed). Certain unusual *chata'ot*, known as *chata'ot hanisrafot* (burned sin offerings) are not eaten even by Kohanim.

Antecedents for the *Chatat*: Where Does the Idea of Sin Start?

We will start with the *chatat*, the sin offering. What is the earliest notion of sin or transgression that we find in the Torah? That question would seem to take us back to the earliest of all stories, and land us squarely in the Garden of Eden. God had placed us in a veritable paradise and had allowed us to eat of all its wonderful trees, save one. And we ignored the trees we could have eaten from, and made a beeline for the one tree that was off-limits, the Tree of Knowledge of Good and Evil.

In English, we have a synonym for the word sin: transgression. Think about that word. Its very structure connotes a kind of violation of boundaries. The Hebrew equivalent, *aveirah* — from the root *alef-vav-resh*, crossing-over, suggests as much. What does boundary crossing have to do, exactly, with the idea of sin?

Well, consider humanity's situation back in the Garden. By virtue of God's commands concerning those trees, there were now two domains in the world, one human and one divine:

Genesis 2:16–17	מִכֹּל עֵץ הַגָּן אָכֹל תֹּאכֵל: וּמֵעֵץ הַדַּעַת טוֹב וָרָע לֹא תֹאכַל	Of every tree of the Garden you should eat, yes, eat; but as for the Tree of Knowledge of Good and Evil, you must not eat of it.

The human domain, as God describes it in that verse, contains virtually all the trees in the Garden. *Here are all these wonderful trees. You may — indeed, you should — eat from all of them and enjoy them.* But there's one tree on the other side of the boundary: The Tree of Knowledge of Good and Evil. It is as if God, the Master of the Garden, is saying: "There is something about that tree that needs to remain Mine. Everything else I give to you. But that's the tree in the Garden which I reserve for Myself."

I want to suggest that this notion of boundary crossing isn't limited to humanity's first sin, the choice to eat of the forbidden fruit. It is, in at least a subtle way, a feature of all sins. The world is an environment God has placed us in, we generally have free rein — but there are certain actions that God has restricted, almost as if God is saying, "This is still part of My domain; don't cross this yellow tape over here." And every sin involves an improper crossing of that yellow tape — a failure to respect a boundary that was important, a wrongful transgression, or trespassing into someone else's domain. In this way, all the Torah's prohibitions can be seen as expressing a little piece of the Garden, a little piece of the forbidden fruit, as it were.

How does one atone for an illegitimate act of crossing boundaries? How does one make up for not showing the respect you should have shown? The answer would seem to be: by showing the other that you regret having ignored the boundaries, and are trying to make up for having done so. And it is through this lens, perhaps, that we can interpret the idea of the *chatat*.

If humanity's first transgression involved an act of consuming something on the other side of that yellow tape — *people ate things they weren't supposed to eat* — a *chatat* creates an inverse of that: Humans give back something of their own to the Divine, for God, as it were, to consume. This is brought home to the owner of the offering when that owner observes Kohanim quite literally eating the meat of an animal he or she previously owned. The tit-for-tat is right there for the owner to see: *I consumed something of God's and benefited from it; now people who represent God (Kohanim) are consuming something of mine and benefiting from it.*[5] By offering to take something from *my* side of the boundary and using it to

5 Technically, something similar is true for an *olah*. Like the *chatat*, it is consumed by the Divine, at least in the sense that it is offered entirely on the altar. But the *chatat* is visibly eaten by humans representing the Divine Estate in a way that the *olah* is not. My argument is that with regard to a *chatat*, the owner is well aware that the Kohanim will be eating the meat, and there is a tangible sense of providing a this-worldly benefit to God and His agents as a way of providing restitution for the transgression committed. However, the energy of the *olah* is different: It is not so much "I consumed and benefited; now You, God — or your agents — please go ahead and consume and benefit"; instead, offering an *olah* entails the visceral experience of watching something that, by rights I would consider my own, disappear entirely from the world, as it is brought absolutely into God's World. This, I'll argue below, is an entirely different kind of experience. It is less about recompense than it is about absolute surrender.

recompense God for any benefit illegitimately gained, I am signifying my desire to rectify matters.[6]

The *Shelamim*

The ideas we see expressed through the *chatat* — of respect, or non-violation of boundaries — are important values to be upheld in humanity's relationship with God, but they are not the *only* important values. Indeed, another quality, one which balances out respect, is equally vital, and this seems to be where the *shelamim* comes in. Let's take a moment to examine the earliest references we have to *shelamim* offerings.

The somewhat longer name **Parshat Vayikra** uses for a *shelamim* offering is a *zevach shelamim* (Lev. 3:1), and the first time we have an instance of this sort of offering actually being offered seems to be when the Children of Israel sealed their covenant with God at Sinai with *zivchei shelamim* (Ex. 24:5). If we go back even further in biblical history, for the

---

6 One might, perhaps, object to the notion that a *chatat* atones for a lack of respect on the grounds that a *chatat* is offered only for inadvertent transgressions. In response, I would argue that lack of respect is, in truth, a feature of all transgressions, inadvertent or willful — and the difference between the two is just a matter of degree. In other words: When we *intend* to transgress a command in the Torah, when our lack of respect comes with premeditated malice — in that case, an offering is not appropriate, and can't offer atonement. The lack of respect is too blatant. But when our transgression is inadvertent, a product of carelessness more than anything else, then the Torah mandates that we offer a *chatat*.

Another objection might be raised as well: If, in fact, a *chatat* is only offered for an inadvertent transgression, it seems odd that the story of mankind's sin in the Garden of Eden would serve as a touchstone for the *chatat*. For that first sin, seemingly, was anything but inadvertent. The first humans were instructed not to eat from the tree, and they chose, quite willingly, to transgress that command. This is an intriguing little trouble spot for this theory, which suggests that we may not have fully arrived quite yet at the historical antecedent for the *chatat*. While the notion of sin, one could argue, is born in Eden, the first case of *inadvertent* sin would seem to come elsewhere, somewhat later in biblical history. In the next essay on **Parshat Vayikra**, a part 2, of sorts, to this essay, we shall unravel the implications of this little problem, which, as it happens, may well add some dimension and depth to our discussion of the antecedent of the *chatat*. Interested persons are advised to keep reading.

first instance of an offering known as a *zevach* at all, we will find ourselves looking at another sealing of a covenant — this time, between Jacob and his father-in-law, Laban (see Gen. 31:54).[7] Something about this kind of offering seems connected to the making of a covenant.

Why would the sealing of covenants be associated with this particular type of offering? The name of the offering might provide us a clue. The word *shelamim*, as I mentioned before, is a version of the word *shalem*, which means either peace or wholeness. There is, indeed, a kind of wholeness that comes about through a covenant. A covenant both creates, and defines, a new relationship between two parties. Before a covenant, there was just me and you, two entirely separate beings. But after a covenant is struck between us, there are really three parties: You, me, and ... *us*. A new "we" has been created in the bond struck between us. A new "wholeness" has come into the world.

There are, of course, different kinds of "we's." Some covenants establish trade agreements or business corporations. An agreement like this is transactional in nature, and so the "we" it creates exists primarily at a financial level. But there are more profound levels of "we", too, such as those struck in love. The kind of "we" they create, through the institution we know as marriage, is a new family.

Whenever a new "we" gets made — certainly when the "we" is loving and sublime, but even when it is more superficial and transactional — we intuit that there is cause for celebration. When Jacob and Laban sealed their covenant at Gal'ed, even though they didn't quite part on the best of terms, still, Jacob and Laban's family feasted together to mark the occasion (see Gen. 31:46). And at the more sublime end of things, Israel feasted at Sinai when their covenant with God was created (see Ex. 24:11).[8] When we make covenants we sit down and feast; we celebrate the new wholeness that is being brought into the world.

---

7 See Rabbi David Tzvi Hoffman ad loc., who suggests that the *zevach* brought by Jacob was a prototype of a *shelamim* offering; see also Bechor Shor; cf. Rashi, as understood by Mizrachi, who does not view Jacob's *zevach* as an example of an offering at all.

8 The feast the Torah describes at Sinai can be seen as the meal that celebrated what God had proposed to Israel at Sinai: a kind of marriage, as it were, between the Divine Being and a nation that God had committed to treasure as His own (see Ex. 19:5–6, where the proposal for just such a union is laid out).

Shelamim and Sharing

We might say then, that a *shelamim* offering — the offering whose very name denotes celebration of wholeness — evokes a different energy than respect. It is an offering that, interestingly, still has something to do with a crossing of boundaries — but not in a transgressive way; rather, in a good way. A *shelamim*, perhaps, evokes sharing, a value that is at the core of all covenants. Fittingly, sharing governs how the *shelamim* is supposed to be consumed. Part is eaten by the owners of the offering, and part is given to God on the altar. So, to put this in terms of the model of domains we introduced earlier: If people have their domain and God has His domain, a *shelamim* might be a way of saying, "Could we share? Maybe I could have a part, and You'll have a part — and we will go forward … together."

The *Olah*: From Noah to Abraham

On to the third category, the *olah*.

The very first recorded *olah* was brought by Noah immediately upon his exit from the ark (Gen. 8:20). The next recorded *olah* in the Torah was the offering Abraham readied himself to give in the story we know as the Binding of Isaac, or the *Akeidah*:

Genesis 22:2

וַיֹּאמֶר קַח נָא אֶת בִּנְךָ אֶת יְחִידְךָ אֲשֶׁר אָהַבְתָּ אֶת יִצְחָק וְלֶךְ לְךָ אֶל אֶרֶץ הַמֹּרִיָּה וְהַעֲלֵהוּ שָׁם לְעֹלָה עַל אַחַד הֶהָרִים אֲשֶׁר אֹמַר אֵלֶיךָ:	Take your son, your special one, the one whom you love, Isaac, and go to the land of Moriah, and offer him there as an *olah* on one of the mountains that I will point out to you.

What commonality, if any, exists in Noah and Abraham's offerings? I would suggest it is the notion of "awe."

Consider Noah and his particular, unique vantage point on life at the moment he brought that *olah*. He and his family had just survived the Flood. Upon leaving the ark, Noah gazed at a new world. In one sense, it was a world that was his for the taking: God had blessed him and told him to be fruitful and multiply, asking him to fill the earth with his progeny. But in another sense...*was it really his at all?*

Noah witnessed God acting as the Master of Creation, deigning to destroy His handiwork entirely, and to start fresh with a new world. The notion that mankind owns this world in any ultimate sense would seem laughable to Noah in the aftermath of the Flood. Noah, more than anyone else in history, must have been acutely conscious that the earth can never really be possessed by a human. It is a realization that on some level, not only Noah can intuit but we can, too: All of us, in our quieter moments, can look at the earth upon which we tread and realize that it outlasts us; we don't really own earth. If anything, at the end of our lives, the earth takes us back and it is it that "owns" us.

This sensibility is what we mean by awe. Or, to put it in the language of domains we spoke about earlier — an *olah* is neither about transgressing domains nor about sharing them; it is about a renunciation of the idea that I really have a domain at all. That is, an *olah* says: *In truth, there is no "my domain and Your domain"; it is all Your domain.* In recognition of this, Noah punctuated his entry into the new world with an *olah* — an offering given *entirely* to God.

Abraham's *Olah*

The next recorded *olah*, that of Abraham, evoked a similar stance. For in the *Akeidah*, God asked Abraham for the one thing in life that we might instinctively say is most *surely* his: his child, Isaac. *If anything is mine it must be that.* And yet, in the *Akeidah*, it is precisely *this* that Abraham is asked to give back to God. In complying with God's request for this *olah*, Abraham was really saying: "Even that which *seems* most mine in this world, I cannot in good conscience withhold from the Master of the Universe. He can lay claim over *all* that seems to be mine."[9]

---

9 Or, to put it slightly differently, in order for Abraham to have made sense of the *Akeidah* from a moral standpoint, he must have seen God as even more deeply Isaac's parent than Abraham himself. For this reason, God is within His rights to ask for Isaac back: The ultimate parent, as it were, is asking for custody of the child. The language of the angel who puts a halt to the *Akeidah* suggests as much: עַתָּה יָדַעְתִּי כִּי יְרֵא אֱלֹקִים אַתָּה וְלֹא חָשַׂכְתָּ אֶת בִּנְךָ אֶת יְחִידְךָ מִמֶּנִּי — "Now I know that you are in awe of God, for you did not **withhold** your son, your only one, from Me"

The *Olah* Vis-à-Vis the *Shelamim*

In summary, if the *shelamim* is about sharing, the *olah* is about surrender. Surrender and sharing are in *some* ways the same — they both entail a merging of domains — but they work in very different, almost opposite, ways. When I share, I give to you and you give to me. I have to have a space that's mine, you have to have a space that's yours, and then we can each give something we can share. Awe is something else entirely. It is the surrender of my domain to yours. It is a recognition that there is, and always has been, one domain only: *Yours*.

To put this in terms of relationships, we might say that sharing, or the love that arises from it, is in some ways similar to awe. Both evince the quality of adoration, and nowadays, if we aren't careful, we can slip into using the two words almost interchangeably: We sometimes might casually say, "I am so in awe of you" almost as a synonym for "I love you so." And yet, awe is, in truth, a very different quality from love. Love, characterized by giving, is a relationship of equals: I give to you, you give to me. And so we meet in love on a level playing field. Love, at least of the romantic variety, implies a certain prizing of the individuality of the other. I must be "I," with a real sense of separateness and independence, in order for me to be able to give to you, or for me to be able to receive from you. If we each have that independence, then we can share. When it comes to awe, though, all this changes. I *don't* see myself as your equal, separate and independent. If I am truly in awe of you, I see you as completely above and beyond me; independence is the last thing on my mind. Awe compels me to abandon my sense of separateness in the face of your overwhelming presence.

Yirah: A Relationship Between Sight and Awe

The Torah presents the *Akeidah* as an episode in which Abraham is said to have demonstrated awe of the Almighty. At the climax of the *Akeidah*, an angel addresses Abraham and tells him: עַתָּה יָדַעְתִּי כִּי יְרֵא אֱלֹקִים אַתָּה —

(Gen. 22:12). Abraham's passing of the *Akeidah* test is cast in terms of his willingness not to "withhold" the child from the Parent who wants Isaac with Him.

"Now I know that you are **in awe of** God"[10] (Gen. 22:12). But the careful reader will note that this is not the first time the text of the *Akeidah* uses that particular word. It has appeared earlier, albeit in a different form.

Interestingly, one of the three-letter combinations that appears over and over again in the story of the Binding of Isaac is *yod-resh-alef*.[11] Earlier in the story, though, this combination of letters meant something else. It invariably meant "to see." By way of example:

Genesis 22:4

בַּיּוֹם הַשְּׁלִישִׁי וַיִּשָּׂא אַבְרָהָם אֶת עֵינָיו **וַיַּרְא** אֶת הַמָּקוֹם מֵרָחֹק׃	On the third day, Abraham lifted his eyes and **saw** the place from afar.

But at the end of the *Akeidah*, the same combination of letters suddenly means "to be in awe of," as in the verse we saw above. The Torah thereby seems to be signaling a connection, of sorts, between the experience of being in awe, on the one hand, and seeing, on the other.

What is the nature of this connection? Well, think, for a moment, of something that might leave you awestruck. And now consider how sight might affect that experience. Let's say you *see* that something from up close. Would you say that you are *more* likely to feel awestruck by it, or *less* likely?

The answer probably is: it depends.

Some things leave me with a sense of awe on account of deception or illusion, like a magic trick, for example. I may find myself staring, with mouth agape, at a magician who pulls the card I've picked out of an unsliced orange, but the magician will never perform the trick twice. He or she will never do the trick for me in slow motion. Because *if I observe it too closely I won't be in awe of it anymore.* We can rightfully, then, call this

---

10 An alternative translation: "Now I know that you fear God." Both awe and fear have a certain commonality — seeing oneself as small in the face of something much larger or more powerful than oneself, except that fear includes the perception of threat in a way that awe does not.

11 Note: These *yod-resh-alef* combinations are not always permutations of the same root. In the first example, given above (awe), the *yod* is part of the root; however, in Genesis 22:4, quoted here, the same letter combination means "to see," the root is different *resh-alef-chet* and the *yod* is a prefix.

fake awe. The awe is illusory, for the closer I see the thing, the more diminished my sense of wonder.

With true awe, however, the reverse is true. *The closer I see the thing, the more profound my sense of wonder.* Consider a human cell. View it under your average high-school-grade microscope, and it looks like no big deal. There's a little dot for a nucleus, some cytoplasm around it, and a little round cell membrane to hold it all together. But now look at it under an electron microscope, where each atom is the size of a tennis ball, where the cell as a whole seems to extend for miles, and where the manufacturing capacity of the system dwarfs that of New York City — and suddenly a sense of boundless wonder emerges. With true awe, the closer you look, the more speechless you become.

Awe, Sight, and God

And so it is with God, the Master of the Universe. For the most part, in this world of ours, God remains safely out of sight. Indeed, the Almighty is invisible to the human eye. A good thing, too, because the Torah tells us that a human being cannot truly see the Presence of God and survive the experience. But this invisibility also fosters certain illusions. We can, if we are not careful, overplay our hand in the world. We humans dominate other forms of life and are stewards of this planet, but we can easily succumb to the hubristic notion that we have ultimate power, that our "I" is entirely self-sufficient. That is a fiction made possible by God's being so difficult for us to perceive.

Other fictions are more subtle — like the notion that we can meet God on level ground, as it were, as if we were two co-equal, independent beings. Yes, we, like God, are beings possessed of free will, and hence, a certain kind of equality exists between us and the Master of the Universe — enough equality, perhaps, that the notion of our having a relationship with God characterized by love and mutual giving is not completely laughable. But the closer one comes to actually encountering God — the closer our brush with transcendence — the less our sense of independence becomes possible to maintain.

It is for that reason, maybe, that *yirat Hashem* is, perhaps, a double entendre. The phrase can be read as "awe of the Almighty," on the one hand, and "seeing God" on the other. To encounter God as if one could see Him right there before you is to feel dumbstruck with awe. It is to feel a sense that my "I" is fragile and as nothing in the face of Your Everything. And *that* is the energy of the *olah*: *The notion of boundaries, of my having my own domain, is an illusion.*

A Matrix

Looking back, then, on these three offerings — the *chatat*, the *shelamim* and the *olah* — we can see them, perhaps, as emblems of three stances we might carve out in our relationship with God. Moreover, we might say that these stances build on each other. The starting point, the most basic stance in my relationship with God, is that of respect. Most basically, I am called upon to stay in my lane. Enjoy your domain; partake in the world — but don't transgress God's domain. Have some respect. Honor that which God places off-limits for us human beings, His guests in the universe. And if you *do* transgress, the notion of respect calls upon you to recognize that and seek to rectify things. The emblem of this is the *chatat*.

Once I master respect, another possibility opens up for me. I can participate in a covenant with God. I can be in a "we" with Him. I can give to Him, and hopefully, He can give back to me. I can seek wholeness and love with Him.[12] The emblem of this is the *shelamim*.

And then, another possibility begins to open up: The visceral, rarified truth of the *olah*. Occasionally, for all of God's invisibility, I feel as if I can glimpse His Presence. I can feel *awe* with respect to God. In moments of awe, I see my own separateness as illusory; the notion that I have anything at all I can call my own is laughable. In moments like these, I surrender entirely to the Divine. It is here that a human being feels compelled to offer an *olah*.

I'd like to close with a word about love and awe.

It seems to me that although both are desirable, there is an inherent tension — almost a paradox — between the ideals of love of God and awe of God. One might, perhaps, envision the two almost as if they were a kind of alternating current in electricity: A human being in relationship with

---

12 Without respect, love collapses. If one cannot muster respect for the boundaries that separate them from their beloved, one is doomed to violate the being they purport to love. One's drive to create a "we" will end up extinguishing the other independent "I." For a further elaboration of these ideas, see the author's *The Hidden Structure of the Ten Commandments*, a video presentation available at alephbeta.org.

God needs to somehow alternate between love and awe, seesawing between them. Of the two stances, love is the more ubiquitous one. For the bulk of our time here on earth, we see ourselves as individuals, possessed of free will. Hence, we see ourselves as cultivating a bond of affection with the Divine and as giving to and receiving from God, in the context of that bond. But every once in a while, a deeper recognition pierces us, and we become taken with a sense of awe. Indeed, moments of awe toward the Divine are generally less common than moments of love. The sense of surrender and loss of self-inherence in awe, if maintained over the long term, might well imperil the sense of individuality that is necessary to assert oneself, and achieve things, in our day-to-day world. Thus, at some point, we retreat from being overtaken with awe, and move back toward the stance of "sharing" and love — only to veer into awe again when we find ourselves so moved. The catalyst may be a sense of personal crisis or difficulty, or nothing more out of the ordinary than a particularly reflective walk in the woods. But in those moments, the bottom falls out of our sense of independence and strength, and our stance toward God veers into awe and surrender.

It is natural for a human to shuttle between the two in their relationship with God.

Respect, Love and Awe: Three Stances, Three Offerings

We may not have these three offerings anymore. But we do experience the stances they represent. All of us do. Together, they form a matrix of possibilities that we each seek to navigate as we develop our own, personal relationships with the Master of the Universe.

VAYIKRA II

The *Chatat* and the Garden, Revisited

IN THE PREVIOUS ESSAY, I suggested that three of the most basic kinds of animal offerings detailed in Parshat Vayikra — the *olah, shelamim,* and *chatat* — have antecedents in the narrative sections of the Torah, and that the antecedent for the *chatat* — the sin offering — might come from the very first sin ever discussed in the Torah, namely, Adam and Eve's decision to partake of the forbidden fruit, back in the Garden of Eden. However, my sense is that there actually is more here than first meets the eye. In this follow-up essay, I'd like to explore with you more deeply the question of whether there is a more compelling antecedent for the *chatat* in the Torah's narratives — and if there is, what the implications of the existence of this antecedent might be.

To be sure, there is something attractive about seeing the Tree of Knowledge story as the ground from which the *chatat* offering springs. It seems intuitive that the Torah's spiritual response to sin, as formulated in its *laws,* might somehow draw upon the first example of sin in the Torah's *stories.* And yet, much as we might be tempted to simply accept this proposition on the basis of our intuitions, we are forced to acknowledge some inconvenient objections that might be raised against it.

An Inconvenient Omission

First, wouldn't it be peculiar for a story to serve as a touchstone for the laws of a *chatat* offering ... when the story itself doesn't actually speak of such an offering? Indeed, throughout the entire story of Adam, Eve, and the Tree of Knowledge, we never find the first humans seeking to atone for their sin, much less actually bring an offering to God in order to effect such atonement. By contrast, when it comes to finding an antecedent for the *shelamim* in the Torah's narratives, we were successful in identifying actual biblical stories where an honest-to-goodness *shelamim*-style offering was brought on an altar — at Laban and Jacob's covenant, for example, and at the covenant between God and Israel at Sinai. Similarly, we found concrete antecedents for the *olah*, too: Examples of actual *olah* offerings being brought in the Torah's stories — in the case of Noah after the Flood, and in the case of Abraham in the *Akeidah*.[1] But the *chatat* would then be an outlier. If we look only to the Garden of Eden as its antecedent, this would be the only major type of offering whose touchstone comes from a story where no *chatat* was brought whatsoever. A bit odd, no?

But it's more than just odd. For it's not just that Adam and Eve fail, in the wake of their misdeed, to bring an offering that is technically known as a *chatat*. Even more essentially, they are missing the soul of the *chatat*, as it were: *regret*. Adam and Eve never seem to express remorse for what they've done. That feeling of remorse, that acknowledgment of having sinned, is an integral part of the *chatat*. Indeed, halachah mandates that, as part and parcel of the sacrificial service, the person bringing a *chatat* needs to express this recognition in an act of *viduy*, confession.[2] How, then, could it be that the story from which the *chatat* in some way is supposed to derive, tells neither of an actual *chatat*, nor the signature intentions that are meant to lie behind one?

Moreover, the idea that our experience in the Garden somehow foreshadows the *chatat* runs into trouble on still other grounds. For the Torah makes clear that a *chatat* offering is designed to atone only for *inadvertent* misdeeds (see Lev. 4:2), and yet, the story of mankind's sin in the Garden of Eden was anything but inadvertent. The first humans were instructed not to eat from the tree, and they chose, quite willingly, to transgress that command. So if Adam and Eve, by virtue of their willful intent, wouldn't even have been eligible to bring a *chatat* had they lived in the right period of history (i.e., in an age where such offerings were legally mandated), it is hard to see how their experience could be a touchstone for this kind of offering.

---

1 In the case of the *Akeidah*, of course, no actual *olah* was brought in the end, for an angel of God retracts the command to offer Isaac on the altar. But in the story, an *olah* is clearly sought by God, and even in the end, a ram is offered as an *olah* instead of Isaac. Hence, we might well argue that the *Akeidah* can meaningfully serve as a touchstone for the *olah*.

2 See Rambam, *Hilchot Ma'aseh HaKorbanot* 3:14–15

The Garden as Prelude

All of the above suggest that if the Torah does contain a historical antecedent for a *chatat* offering, we may not yet have fully arrived at it. What about our intuition that the story of humanity's first sin would be a logical place to find the roots of an offering designed to provide a religious response to sin? Well, that supposition might not be entirely wrong; it might just be *incomplete*. Perhaps the story of the *chatat* begins in Eden ... but doesn't *end* there. In other words, maybe there's a continuation to the story that we still need to talk about.

What I am suggesting is that the story of the forbidden fruit is larger than we think it is. The ending of the story *seems* to come when the first humans are expelled from Eden. But what if the story actually continues ... with the very next events the text of the Torah tells us about? That would mean humankind's first story *begins* in the Garden, but *ends* with the conclusion of the next episode — that unfortunate meeting in the fields between Cain and Abel, when one brother ended up standing over the lifeless body of the other. If that were true, maybe this entire composite story ends up being the antecedent for the *chatat*.

That's an interesting possibility. But before we discuss the repercussions of such a theory for understanding the *chatat*, let's ask: Is the basic supposition here really true? Is the Cain and Abel episode really to be viewed as the natural continuation of the Tree of Knowledge story?

I want to suggest that there are good reasons for believing that this is true. A number of textual considerations seem to point in this direction. As a matter of fact, why don't I issue this as a challenge to you, dear reader. Crack open a copy of the book of Genesis and spend a few moments reviewing first the story of Adam and Eve, and then the follow-up events involving Cain and Abel. As you do, take note of anything in the second episode that reminds you of the first. Can you find any repeating themes?

Indeed, such themes abound, suggesting the connection between them is real. Here's a small sampling:

- Both Adam and Cain hear the divine question *Ayeh*? Where are you?
  - » Adam heard this question asked about himself.
  - » Cain heard God ask it about his brother.
- Both Adam and Cain express fear and hide from God.

- Both Adam and Cain, in the wake of their respective misdeeds, are condemned to experience difficulty farming the land.[3]
- Both Adam and Cain suffer exile.

So the stories really *are* uncannily similar. But truthfully, they aren't *merely* similar. A progression seems to be at work here, too. Every element in the first story… seems to become more intense in the second:

- *Missing Persons*
  - » In the Garden, God sought the whereabouts of a temporarily missing person (Adam).
  - » In the story of Cain and Abel, the person He seeks (Abel) is gone for good.
- *Hiding from God*
  - » In the immediate aftermath of his sin, Adam hides from God momentarily.
  - » Cain, on the other hand, intuits that he will spend his life hiding from God.
- *Toil*
  - » Adam will have to wrest bread out of the ground "by the sweat of his brow," but at the end of the day, he will have his bread.
  - » Cain, on the other hand, is told that even if he works the land with mighty toil, it simply won't produce anymore what it once did (see Gen. 4:12).
- *Exile*
  - » Finally, Adam and Eve leave paradise to build a new home elsewhere.
  - » Cain, on the other hand, must not only leave home; he is cursed in that he is told he will always be a wanderer. In other words, he won't be able to call *any* place "home" (see v. 13).

It seems that we can say more than just that the two episodes are connected. The second episode actually seems to build on the first. This "intensification of consequences" that we've seen as we go from the Adam and Eve story to the Cain and Abel story suggests that… humankind's

---

3 Moreover, Eve is told she will experience toil (*etzev* — literally, "sadness") with respect to childbirth; Cain is told he will experience toil (*itzavon* — literally, also "sadness") with respect to cultivating the fruits of the ground.

failure in Eden somehow set the stage for the terrible conflict between Cain and Abel. It is almost as if you could place the two stories — Adam and Eve in the Garden, and Cain and Abel — on successive rungs of a ladder: What one *starts*, the other *finishes*.

But what, exactly, is it that gets started in the Tree of Knowledge story and is completed in the Cain and Abel story?

The answer is: sin.

The Gateway to Evil

Here's a proposition for you to contemplate: What if the act of eating the forbidden fruit is not *truly* to be thought of as an act of sin?

Yes, I know that's counterintuitive. The Almighty is undoubtedly angry with the first humans for their actions, and indeed, they are even expelled from Eden as a result of their disobedience. But still, disobedience is not quite the same as committing a sin or transgression, is it? Indeed, of a being who does not yet understand the concept of good and evil — a being who has not yet eaten of the tree — one can rightly ask: Is he or she *really* capable of committing a *sin*?[4]

As if to prove the point, consider God's reaction to Adam and Eve eating the forbidden fruit. Isn't it interesting that although God seems *angry* with the humans for eating from the tree, the Almighty never actually tells the humans that they have sinned or transgressed, at least not in so many words? That omission is all the more striking, because, in the very next story, God *does* mention sin. Quite explicitly. To be sure, right before Cain strikes his brother, the Almighty talks to Cain and speaks openly to him about the idea of sin. Moreover, consider the word God uses to

4 Seemingly, this concept of sin, of actively doing something morally wrong — *that* only really kicks in if I understand that my act of disobedience is… something evil or wrong. But if that understanding is somehow itself wrapped up in the fruit of the tree, then, seemingly, Adam and Eve didn't yet have that understanding before they chose to partake of its fruits. This apparent paradox is one I addressed at length in my book *The Beast That Crouches at the Door* (Maggid Books, 2021). Here I present a somewhat different approach to the issue than I did there.

describe sin to Cain. It is a term that has become familiar to us. Believe it or not, that word is … *chatat:*[5]

Genesis 4:6–7

וַיֹּאמֶר יְקוָה אֶל קָיִן לָמָּה חָרָה לָךְ וְלָמָּה נָפְלוּ פָנֶיךָ: הֲלוֹא אִם תֵּיטִיב שְׂאֵת וְאִם לֹא תֵיטִיב לַפֶּתַח חַטָּאת רֹבֵץ וְאֵלֶיךָ תְּשׁוּקָתוֹ וְאַתָּה תִּמְשָׁל בּוֹ:	God said to Cain: Why are you angry and why has your face fallen? Is it not the case that if you do well, then you can lift up [your face]. And if you don't do well — then, **sin (*chatat*)** lies crouching at the door. Its desire is unto you, and yet, you can rule over it.

What if the story of Adam and Eve and Cain and Abel really *was* to be viewed as one long story: a first episode that creates the potential for sin (eating from the Tree of Knowledge of Good and Evil), followed by a second episode in which that potential for sin comes into actuality? In the latter episode one brother strikes another dead, and sin comes into the world as a concrete and terrible reality. As the composite story draws to its conclusion, God speaks about sin to the person contemplating an act of wrongdoing. And maybe, just maybe, that discussion God has with Cain about *chatat* is the antecedent for the *chatat* offering, delineated in **Parshat Vayikra**, which bears the very same name?

It seems a tantalizing possibility.

---

5 What is particularly striking about this is the grammatical oddity. The standard word for sin would be *chet*, not *chatat*. The word *chatat* is rather rare and is seldom used by the Torah other than to describe the offering brought for sin, the *chatat*. The unusual use of the word here in the Cain story, to connote what is apparently humanity's first sin, is therefore remarkable.

Indeed, what makes its use here even more striking is the fact that the Cain and Abel story is also the episode in which the idea of offerings first appears. Abel brings an offering to God, and so does Cain. While neither was a *chatat*, and while both offerings were brought before Cain sinned in killing his brother, the fact that the term *chatat*, which seems to presage a kind of offering, just happens to appear in the story that introduces the reader to the very idea of offerings, leaves one wondering if there is something about the *chatat* of which God speaks to Cain, and the *chatat* that later appears in the Torah as a kind of offering.

The Line Between Malice and Accident

If we accept this proposition, some questions we left hanging above would seem to fall away. Humanity's first story *does* presage the *chatat* offering, after all. For not only is the composite "Tree of Knowledge and Cain and Abel" story an example of the first sin in the Torah, it is also an example of the *kind* of sin for which one expressly brings a *chatat* — namely, an act of *inadvertent* wrongdoing.

By way of explanation, recall that a *chatat* is brought only for an inadvertent act of sin. Premeditated transgressions can't be atoned for with a sin offering. So let's consider Cain's killing of Abel. Was it deliberate or accidental?

At first blush, many of us might just assume that Cain killed Abel with malice aforethought. It feels like the Torah is telling us the story of the world's first murder — and murder is a wanton, intentional, malicious thing. But if we pause and carefully consider the evidence, it starts to become hard to sustain this view. First of all, let's just acknowledge that, to this point in time, nobody had killed anybody before. Nobody had ever even *died* before. So Cain couldn't have known how, exactly, to bring about his brother's demise, even if that were something he was aiming to achieve.[6]

Moreover, the way God deals with Cain in the aftermath of his killing his brother resonates with the way the Torah later treats an act of *inadvertent* manslaughter. Cain is exiled, condemned to live a life on the run (Gen. 4:13). He is also given a mark, of sorts, to protect him from anyone who might seek to kill him in vengeance (see v. 15). These consequences seem to foreshadow the way the Torah treats an inadvertent killer: the text later tells us (see Num. 19:2–7) that such a killer is to be exiled, and may hide in a city of refuge to seek protection from those who might seek to kill him in vengeance for the death he caused.

All told, then, it seems as if Cain's killing of his brother was something akin to manslaughter. It was a wrongful death, to be sure, but there must have been a kind of inadvertence about it. And still, while we might regard

---

6 On some level, then, when Cain responds to God's question: "Where did your brother go?" with the answer: "I don't know," he wasn't lying; he really *didn't* know. Before striking Abel, death couldn't have been anything more to Cain than a vague intellectual abstraction. But after striking him, Cain was left to ponder the import of his deed: Abel seemed to be gone. Where? No one could know.

Cain's act of killing inadvertent, that's not quite the same as saying it was an accident. For while Cain might well have been surprised at what happened to his brother after he struck him — he still *did* strike him. What he did was still wrong. Indeed, his blow against his brother is perhaps the first act in the Torah that can unambiguously be called a sin. Cain, living after the story of the Tree of Knowledge, had the requisite moral understanding to *know* that what he was about to do — inflict violence upon his brother — was wrong, even if, tragically, he didn't know exactly what that violence would cause.

So the *chatat* of the Cain story starts to look more and more like the sin for which we try to atone, later in the Torah, through a *chatat* offering: An act that was wrong, avoidable, but still, there was something inadvertent about it. And perhaps that shouldn't come as much of a surprise. For the "Tree-Cain" composite story is perhaps *the* paradigmatic story of transgression, realized.

The Beast That Crouches at the Door

Now to be sure, the *chatat* of which God speaks to Cain doesn't *actually* refer to an offering. But still, by the Almighty using in His speech the selfsame rare and exact word that, in **Parshat Vayikra**, comes to mean sin offering, the text seems to be revealing that the two are related. Somehow, whatever God was talking to Cain about appears to be a meaningful precursor to the *chatat* of the book of Leviticus.

So, let's ask ourselves: What, exactly, *was* God talking to Cain about? Here are the key words of God's speech:

Genesis 4:7

לַפֶּתַח חַטָּאת רֹבֵץ וְאֵלֶיךָ תְּשׁוּקָתוֹ וְאַתָּה תִּמְשָׁל בּוֹ:	**Sin (*chatat*)** lies crouching at the door. Its desire is unto you, and yet, you can rule over it.

Much ink has been spilled trying to figure out what this verse means.[7] But for our purposes, one interpretation of God's words to Cain is especially

7 I offered an interpretation of these words myself in *The Beast That Crouches at the Door* (Maggid Books, 2021). The *Chizkuni*'s interpretation offers an alternative way

illuminating. It is a reading put forth by the thirteenth-century French commentator known by his work, *Chizkuni*. Under the *Chizkuni*'s reading, the enigmatic *chatat* about which God speaks to Cain indeed becomes a powerful lens through which to view the offering which, in the book of Leviticus, will end up bearing the same name.

Let me take you through God's speech to Cain as I think the *Chizkuni* would have us read it.

The *Chizkuni*'s Interpretation

Cain is about to confront Abel with clenched fists. He is suffused with anger and jealousy toward his brother. And at that moment, God addresses Cain.

Consider that moment. It is rife with danger. The possibility of violence hangs in the air. And what makes the situation all the more explosive is the fact that the potential perpetrator of violence, Cain, has no true understanding of either his immense power or the stakes that are at hand. Remember, no one has ever killed anyone before. Cain is walking blind into a situation whose true gravity he can't even begin to foresee.

It is precisely this, the *Chizkuni* argues, that God seeks to warn Cain about:

הֲלוֹא אִם תֵּיטִיב שְׂאֵת וְאִם לֹא
תֵיטִיב לַפֶּתַח חַטָּאת רֹבֵץ

Is it not the case that if you do well, then you can lift up [your face]. And if you don't do well — sin (*chatat*) lies crouching at the door.

Genesis 4:7

The *Chizkuni* interprets the word *chatat* not so much as sin, but as...the consequence of sin. The Master of the Universe is speaking to Cain about the possibility that irreparable consequences would flow from his actions. Which makes the next thing that God says to Cain particularly poignant:

---

of looking at God's speech, one that I will explore here. On another plane entirely, the novelist John Steinbeck spent most of an entire book — *East of Eden* — contemplating the meaning of this one biblical verse.

Genesis 4:7

וְאֵלֶיךָ תְּשׁוּקָתוֹ וְאַתָּה תִּמְשָׁל בּוֹ׃	His desire is unto you, but you can overpower him.

Whose desire is "unto Cain"? we might ask. As the *Chizkuni* understands it, God was talking here about Abel. He is telling Cain that Abel is drawn to him and wants to reconcile. Ironically, as the *Chizkuni* sees it, this is precisely the thing that gives Cain the power to kill his brother. Abel will draw close to his brother in an unguarded way, and therefore, *you*, Cain, have the power to "overpower him." *You can use Abel's brotherly love against him.*

The particular tragedy of the story of Cain and Abel, as *Chizkuni* seems to paint it, is that Cain weaponizes Abel's brotherly desire to connect with him. He uses it as a lure.[8]

As the *Chizkuni* would have it, God was telling Cain about all this...before the fact. God was telling Cain that Abel's love and innocence is the latter's point of vulnerability, and that if Cain is not careful, he may end up exploiting his brother's love, and the end product of that exploitation will be to inflict upon Abel a harm so grievous, so final, that Cain himself cannot begin to grasp its enormity. It is as if sin is lying in wait for Cain, entrapping him, getting ready to pounce. It seems like Abel will be the victim of Cain's malice, and in some ways he is, but Cain is also a target here. His rage will entrap him, and will be his own undoing.

---

8 The text seems to suggest as much with these words: וַיֹּאמֶר קַיִן אֶל הֶבֶל אָחִיו וַיְהִי בִּהְיוֹתָם בַּשָּׂדֶה וַיָּקָם קַיִן אֶל הֶבֶל אָחִיו וַיַּהַרְגֵהוּ — "And Cain said to Abel, his brother. And then, when they were in the field together, Cain rose against Abel, his brother, and killed him" (Gen. 4:8).

The first part of this verse seems to be a non sequitur, for the text tells the reader that "Cain said to Abel," but then doesn't tell us what he said. The sense of the text is that there was an interrupted conversation here. Cain *began* speaking to Abel but then stopped, and rose up against him in violence instead. Seemingly, there was an opportunity to talk things through, which was the premise for inviting Abel out for a walk in the field. But the conversation barely gets started when Cain's violence short-circuits it. All told, then, the conversation ended up being little more than bait to draw Abel into close contact with Cain, a proximity Cain used to inflict mortal harm upon him.

The fact that Abel's love would be used against him makes the reality of Abel's demise, in retrospect, all the more tragic and abhorrent. One day in the future, Cain may well be overcome with revulsion at what he did in a fleeting moment of anger. But by then it will be too late. He will already have been entrapped, imprisoned in a lifetime of regret, unable to do more than look back mournfully on the consequences of his own impetuosity.

Indeed, consider God's words carefully:

לַפֶּתַח חַטָּאת רֹבֵץ	*Chatat* lies crouching at the door.	Genesis 4:7

It is a remarkable turn of phrase. God seems to describe the searing regret Cain might one day feel as if it were some sort of powerful beast, lying in wait for him. It is crouching, ready to spring. It is seeking, in a word, to ambush him.

The Ambush of Regret

What exactly did God mean with this metaphor? How exactly would sin ambush him? It is here that we arrive at the essential, tragic character of inadvertent misdeeds, the kind for which the Torah will mandate a *chatat* offering. For inadvertent sins really *do* ambush us. They are a product of careless disregard. They happen when we don't correctly size up the stakes of our actions and instead recklessly veer into wrongdoing.

It turns out that inadvertent sin has a certain quirky quality to it: How we judge the gravity of a careless act changes quite a bit with the passage of time. *Before* we acted, maybe we didn't fully appreciate the gravity of our actions. We didn't understand how indelible they might become, how very difficult to reverse. And so we were less careful than we otherwise might have been.

But all that is before. What about after?

When we are in the "after" of a wrongful thing, our attitude toward it tends to change dramatically. Once it is too late to take back what we've done, the full gravity of our actions begins to sink in. And from this flows regret: *If only we had known....* We feel that somehow, we were caught by surprise. We have been ambushed by our own actions.

And that, I think, was precisely what the *Chizkuni* is telling us God was trying to talk to Cain about. *Chatat* lies crouching at the door. Your jealous anger toward your brother can ambush you. Right now you're in the "before" of wrongdoing, so you can't imagine what your anger might unleash. But that will eventually change. There will eventually be an "after."

When Abel's lifeless body lies on the ground; when Cain has to admit to himself, and to God, that he doesn't know where the self that used to be Abel has gone (v. 9) — it is *then* that the true consequence of Cain's actions begins to sink in. And it is then that Cain himself professes to be overwhelmed. Cain tells God that his act was so outrageous וְהָיָה כָל מֹצְאִי יַהַרְגֵנִי — "anyone who finds me will kill me" (v. 14), as if, somehow, all living beings, man or animal, would unite in vengeance against him in collective revulsion for his brother's wrongful death.

In light of this, Cain says to God, simply:

Genesis 4:13

גָּדוֹל עֲוֹנִי מִנְּשׂוֹא	My sin is greater than I can bear.[9]

At the outward, physical level of things, when Cain invited Abel out into the fields, it was Cain who ambushed Abel. But at the deeper, spiritual level of things, it was Cain who ambushed himself.

---

9 It is interesting that Cain speaks of sin differently here than God did. Previously, before his act, God had warned him about *chatat* crouching at the door. *Chatat*, from the word *chet*, is generally associated with inadvertent wrongdoing (and of course, it becomes the name for the offering meant to atone for inadvertent transgression). Cain, though, uses a different word: מִנְּשֹׂא גָּדוֹל עֲוֹנִי — "My *avon* is greater than I can bear." An *avon* is typically seen as a willful act of wrongdoing, a sin more serious than a *chet*. The discrepancy between the two words may be less of a contradiction than it is a reflection of time. God was speaking to Cain before the fact. After the fact, though, Cain is overwhelmed with the burden of what he's done. He ascribes to his actions an exaggerated sense of gravity once he views them in retrospect.

Cain's *Chatat* as the Antecedent of the *Chatat* Offering

The maddening thing about all this is that the whole reason God spoke to Cain about *chatat* was to help him understand it. It was to warn Cain of the dangers of carelessness before it was too late. And it didn't work. Cain became history's first victim of the great discrepancy between the way a careless act looks *before* you do it, as opposed to *after* you do it. By the time Cain came to understand the truth, it was too late to undo what he had done.[10]

Like it or not, there is a little bit of Cain in all of us. Who hasn't acted, at one time or another, in a way they later came to regret, when the true cost of a carefree act finally makes itself painfully clear? Who hasn't felt ambushed by a sense of regret that, before the fact, they never quite anticipated they would ever feel? What would we pay to get just a few fleeting moments of our lives back so we could replay them with greater seriousness?

Later in the Torah, the text seems to validate this very sense of anguish when it names the offering precipitated by inadvertent sin a *chatat*, after the great unanticipated sin of which God once spoke to Cain. It is almost as if the Almighty is offering us a way, of sorts, to redeem the feelings that Cain must have felt — that sense of being ambushed by overwhelming remorse in the aftermath of a careless but fateful misdeed.

The path toward redemption starts, as it turns out, with a symbolic act of recognition. When one offers a *chatat*, one shows they understand that they have violated another's boundaries, and they are now seeking — symbolically at least — to give something back from their own side of the fence.[11] Moreover, one shows that they are beginning to change

---

10 Later in this volume, I will come back to the story of Cain and Abel once more. Toward the end of this volume's essay on **Parshat Kedoshim**, I will revisit some of these themes — especially the manifold ways in which Cain and his actions are exquisite teachers of what *not* to do.

11 Indeed, such recognition is an integral part of the sacrificial service itself. As we mentioned earlier, every *chatat*, by Torah law, must be accompanied with *viduy*, confession or acknowledgment of the sin on the part of the one bringing the offering. Without that, the symbolic reciprocity of the *chatat* is an empty gesture. See Rambam, *Hilchot Ma'aseh HaKorbanot*, 3:14–15.

in a positive way. The very act of bringing a *chatat* shows that we now regard with some sobriety an act we once approached in too carefree a way. That, in and of itself, is redemptive. For if acting carelessly was wrong because we, like Cain, casually failed to reckon with our own responsibility for impetuous actions — well, when one offers a *chatat*, one demonstrates the opposite: that an act done inadvertently is *still* one for which I will take responsibility.

We no longer have *chatat* offerings today, but we can still avail ourselves of the lessons that such offerings imply. We too can wrestle with our sense of being ambushed by remorse when, at least in hindsight, we treat with more seriousness a casual wrong we once inflicted. We can try our level best to make up for such wrongs by fixing the damage we've done when we can. And when, despite our best efforts, we can't — we can at least show, symbolically but soberly, that we know we've improperly violated another's boundary.

If we do that, we've taken an important step forward. We've assumed at least some degree of responsibility for an act that would be more convenient to simply shrug off. And in so doing, something wondrous can happen: The equal and opposite burden we are carrying — that of undying remorse, that of wishing a moment of our lives back so we can fix the unfixable — can suddenly seem just a little bit lighter, a little bit more possible to bear.

The Four Who Offer the *Todah*

אִם עַל תּוֹדָה
יַקְרִיבֶנּוּ וְהִקְרִיב עַל
זֶבַח הַתּוֹדָה חַלּוֹת
מַצּוֹת בְּלוּלֹת בַּשֶּׁמֶן

If he offers it for thanksgiving, he shall offer together with the sacrifice of thanksgiving unleavened cakes with oil mixed in.

LEVITICUS 7:12

TZAV

The Four Who Offer the *Todah*

PARSHAT TZAV INTRODUCES US to the *korban todah*, which we might call a "thanksgiving offering,"[1] and in these pages, I want to talk about something the Rabbis of the Talmud tell us about the *todah*. In Tractate Berachot (54b), the Sages identified four types of people who are expected, perhaps even required, to bring this kind of offering.[2] While most of the four seem similar to one another, one seems ... rather different. And that difference, I think, is telling. To understand why, I want to introduce you to one of my favorite little games, one I first learned back in my Sesame-Street days, when I was maybe six years old: *One of These Things Is Not Like the Others*!

The way things used to go back on Sesame Street, *One of These Things Is Not Like the Others* was a very simple game: The screen would split into four boxes, each encasing a single item. The music would then begin to play and you, the viewer, would try to decide how three of those things were very similar, but a fourth just didn't seem to belong.

The Torah seems to beckon us to play *One of These Things Is Not Like the Others* quite a bit. We often find the text grouping a bunch of things together, but, at face value, while *most* of those things seem united by a certain commonality, one of the elements doesn't really seem to fit. It seems not to belong. In a moment, we will play a round of the game using the four people who, according to the Sages, bring the *todah*, that thanksgiving offering. But before we do, allow me to let you in on a little secret: in my experience, more often than not, the outlier really *does* belong; it's just that you haven't yet figured out how or why.

What I'm suggesting is that sometimes, by including an apparently anomalous member of a group, the Torah is challenging you to think

---

1 The *todah*, technically speaking, is a particular kind of *shelamim* offering (see Lev. 7:12).

2 The degree of obligation is a dispute among *Rishonim*; see Rashi on Menachot 79b and Rambam, *Hilchot Ma'aseh HaKorbanot* 9:5.

carefully about the underlying nature of the group: What, *really*, is the common element that unites all the parts? When one of the elements doesn't seem to fit, that signifies to you that, sure, maybe you *think* you know the underlying commonality that unites the group, but you don't. Not completely. You're ever so slightly mistaken in your understanding. To solve the puzzle, what you need to do in these situations is shift your understanding of the nature of the group. Sometimes, just by a little bit. Usually, when you're willing to go out on a limb and do that, all the elements will suddenly fit.

A Study in Outliers: The First Tablet of the Decalogue

Let's try a little practice round, just so we can hone our skills. Let's try *One of These Things Is Not Like the Others* with ... the first tablet of the Ten Commandments.

Here you are, looking at the five precepts that comprise the first tablet of the Decalogue. As you do, you seem to pick up the beginnings of a common theme. You might have even learned about that theme back in grade school. It would seem, as you begin to read the commands on the first tablet, that you are looking at a series of *mitzvot bein adam laMakom,* commands that govern the relationship between mankind and the Almighty.

But now let's test the theory to see if it's really true.

Sure enough, the first four seem to fit perfectly. The first command is: "I am the Lord, your God." It is immediately followed by "Do not have any other gods before Me." Right after that we get: "Don't take My name in vain," followed by "Honor the Sabbath to keep it holy." All these precepts clearly govern the relationship between people and God. They are, indeed, *mitzvot ben adam laMakom.* So far so good. Everything fits the pattern. But, there's an outlier, for there's still one more precept left on this first tablet, and it just doesn't seem to belong. That precept is: "Honor your father and mother."

Clearly, our parents, wonderful as they might be, are merely human beings like ourselves. So what is *that* command doing as part of this group? Honoring our parents seems to govern our relationship with other human beings; what is it doing engraved on a tablet that supposedly focuses exclusively on our relationship with God?

The answer is: *Maybe we got the nature of the overall category wrong.* Maybe the commonality in the commands on the first tablet isn't mitzvot between man and God, but something a little more subtle than that. Can we refine our understanding here?

Well, let's see: On that first tablet, we seem to have four commands that address our relationship with God, and a fifth that addresses our relationship with parents. Rather than assume that the fifth is anomalous, let's search for an underlying common denominator between God and parents.

A moment's reflection turns one up. *They are both your creators.*[3]

Yes, that's right — *creators,* in the plural. We human beings have both a heavenly Creator *and* earthly creators. And the first tablet of the Decalogue adjures us to honor them both.

We can begin to see, now, how a very simple, almost childlike game can, when applied to biblical text, yield a surprising depth of understanding. Consider, for example, how this new understanding impacts our understanding of that fifth and final command on the first tablet. It brings the rationale for *why* we honor parents into sharper focus. We don't honor them because they're smarter than we are, or because they have more life experience than we do — or even because they're nicer people than we are. Indeed, Jewish law proclaims that one is duty bound to honor one's parents even if they are not very wise, and, believe it or not, even if they're not so nice.[4] We honor our parents because...they are our creators: because they are partners with God in bestowing upon us the mysterious gift of life.[5] We owe them a debt of gratitude that we can never fully repay, and for this, we honor them.

---

3 See Kiddushin 30b, *Tur, Yoreh De'ah* 240.

4 Rambam, *Hilchot Mamrim* 6:11; *Shulchan Aruch, Yoreh De'ah* 240:18; see, however, *Tur, Yoreh De'ah* 240.

5 Indeed, in light of this, it does not seem coincidental that, in the Decalogue itself, the text promises long life to the one who fulfills the mandate to honor their parents (see Ex. 20:12). While it is unusual for the Torah to explicitly promise a reward for the fulfillment of a particular command, in this case, the reward serves almost as a commentary on the command itself: When one honors one's parents, one is acknowledging the importance of those who are the very ground of our being. Thus, in granting that honor, we are retroactively nourishing the roots from which our own lives have sprouted forth, thus allowing our being to flourish more thoroughly.

Who Brings a *Todah* Offering?

All in all, *One of These Things Is Not Like the Others* may be a simple game to play, but it isn't simplistic; it can yield decidedly profound fruits. So if you would, please join me in playing a round with reference to something that appears here in **Parshat Tzav** — the four kinds of people who, according to the Sages, are obliged to offer a *todah*, or thanksgiving offering.

Rashi, citing a talmudic statement in Tractate Berachot (54b), tells us who those four kinds of people are. They are four souls who underwent difficult circumstances and survived. Rashi lists them as follows:

- יוֹרְדֵי הַיָּם, those who survive a perilous ocean journey
- וְהוֹלְכֵי מִדְבָּרוֹת, those who traverse a desert and survive
- וְחוֹלֶה שֶׁנִּתְרַפֵּא, someone who falls gravely ill and survives
- וַחֲבוּשֵׁי בֵּית הָאֲסוּרִים, those who are imprisoned but ultimately freed

So... *which one of these things is not like the other?*

Well, let's look for a common thread, and then we will be able to see the outlier. What, at face value, is the common denominator between these four people?

Illness as a Different Kind of Endangerment

Three of the above seem to pretty neatly converge around a common theme. An ocean and a desert, for example, are certainly foreboding places to find oneself (although for strangely opposite reasons: The former has too much water to support life; the other, too little). A dungeon is another inhospitable place, a place where someone is cast away and basically left to live the rest of their life in squalor, or left to die. Those who successfully traverse a sea or a desert, or were locked away in a dungeon and lived to relate their experiences, were plunged into an environment that doesn't readily support human life and somehow survived anyway.

So, had the list comprised only those three kinds of people, things would be simple enough: One could summarize the Talmud's teaching as follows: If you traverse a place inhospitable to life and you live to tell the tale, you ought to give thanks. But here's the rub: The list comprises four kinds of people, not three. There's an outlier here: the example of grave illness.

Illness is not really an "environment" in the way a desert, ocean, or dungeon is. Sure, it's true that someone who survives a terrible illness did find themself in exceptional danger, just as the other people on the list. But still, it wasn't because they were in a space that didn't support life. You can be ill at home, and you're in a perfectly fine place — you just have other things to worry about. Seemingly, this one out of the four seems just a bit off-kilter. It doesn't quite seem to fit.[6]

Or maybe it does.

Illness and Displacement

I'd like to propose that all four here *do* fit into a single category. Moreover, seeing how this is so makes quite a difference, for it can offer us a subtle insight into the nature of grave illness. It can help us perceive why the experience of a serious health malady can be so terribly frightening.

Why is being terribly ill so frightening? I would suggest it isn't just because such illness threatens us, that we might succumb and die. Look, we all die, eventually. And so, in some strange but comforting way, the possibility of death is something we are forced to learn to live with. No, the fear of illness comes from something else besides just fear of death. And the Sages, in connecting being gravely ill with these three other elements, are helping us see what that is.

A perilous sea voyage, a vast unforgiving desert, and the unknown darkness of a dungeon — there is something about being in these places that, in a deep way, shares a quality with being gravely ill. There is an angst associated with illness that has something to do with ... place.[7] Indeed, illness, over and above everything else it might feel like, is also profoundly

---

6 One might object that the four can in fact be united quite simply around the general idea of endangerment, and that the notion of place should be disregarded as a red herring. And that's possible. I can't disprove that contention. Nevertheless, the fact that three out of the four seem to unite around a narrower commonality suggests that the idea of place may be important, and the fourth example may unexpectedly relate to the idea of place as well. It just requires us to expand our notion of place.

7 Indeed, the source the Talmud cites for the "four who must give thanks" is Psalm 107, a psalm that describes a terrifying place. It tells of people וַיַּגִּיעוּ עַד שַׁעֲרֵי מָוֶת, who have "reached the gates of death" (v. 18). The notion of being saved from a

disorienting. To be sick is to feel, deep down, like one is living in an environment that's inherently inhospitable to life. It is just that this time, that environment is not external to yourself but internal: It is *one's own body.*

When our own body turns on us, when it becomes akin to foreign terrain, when it becomes fundamentally inhospitable to our living spirit — it is then that we're no longer at home in our own skin, and *that* is the scariest thing of all. All told, the four who give thanks experience a profound commonality. They are four who have recovered from the fright of living in an alien space. And when this happens, the Talmud is telling us, one must give thanks.

Celebrating Thanks with Others

Understanding this truth about the commonality of the four who offer a *todah* can help us understand something else unique about this offering. The Talmud (Menachot 77b) tells us something striking about a *todah* offering: It is accompanied by an extraordinary surfeit of food, no less than forty loaves of bread.[8] This leads one to believe that the meal that accompanies the *todah* is meant to be shared by an abundance of people. We might wonder why. Seemingly, the answer is that there is something about expressing thanks — thanks for salvation from fearsome circumstances — that makes us long for togetherness and the company of others.[9] What underlies that instinct?

---

place of terror, a place where death beckons, feels common to the four who must give thanks.

8 The Talmud derives this exegetically from Lev. 7:12–13, taking each of four kinds of *challot* mentioned in these verses to represent a set of ten loaves: אִם עַל תּוֹדָה יַקְרִיבֶנּוּ וְהִקְרִיב עַל זֶבַח הַתּוֹדָה חַלּוֹת מַצּוֹת בְּלוּלֹת בַּשֶּׁמֶן וּרְקִיקֵי מַצּוֹת מְשֻׁחִים בַּשָּׁמֶן וְסֹלֶת מֻרְבֶּכֶת חַלֹּת בְּלוּלֹת בַּשָּׁמֶן. עַל חַלֹּת לֶחֶם חָמֵץ יַקְרִיב קָרְבָּנוֹ עַל זֶבַח תּוֹדַת שְׁלָמָיו. — "If he offers it for thanksgiving, he shall offer together with the sacrifice of thanksgiving unleavened cakes with oil mixed in, unleavened wafers spread with oil, and cakes of choice flour with oil mixed in, well soaked. This offering, with cakes of leavened bread added, he shall offer along with his thanksgiving sacrifice of well-being."

9 Indeed, consider the modern custom of Thanksgiving dinner. It is, perhaps, the most traveled time of year for a reason. Intuitively, families reach for togetherness and community when they say thanks. Incidentally, the folklore surrounding the origin of the American custom of Thanksgiving is strikingly similar to the ideas

Perhaps it has to do with the ideas we've been talking about. When we give thanks, we acknowledge not just that we were saved; we acknowledge the terror of what we were saved *from*. In the case of the *todah* offering, we survived being somewhere fundamentally alien to life — a notion that is not only scary, but isolating. If I can't trust my surroundings or my body — usually the most familiar of things — I feel profoundly alone. In offering the *todah*, we give thanks that we are back home; we are back in the community of humanity. We are grateful for human connection, something that eluded us when we felt we were flirting with the abyss.

I wonder then, whether this might, ever so slightly, change our perception of exactly what we are doing when we visit the sick. We aren't just bringing with us words of good cheer or even of hope. We aren't just bringing cookies or balloons. One of the deepest comforts we can offer, over and above anything we say or do, is the mere fact of our human presence, and our willingness to connect. Indeed, the Talmud (Nedarim 39b) teaches that one who visits the sick has the potential to heal them just a bit. In the words of the Sages, the visitor can "take away one sixtieth" of the afflicted person's illness. And the reason this is true, perhaps, is because of this aspect of illness we've been talking about: Coping with sickness is more than just the biological task of living through a difficult malady. It is also the spiritual and emotional task of coping with the feeling that one is like a stranger in one's own body. And *that* is something the visitor, with their loving touch, smile, or mere presence, can help ameliorate. Indeed, one isn't truly a stranger, even if they walk unfamiliar terrain, if they have company on their journey.

---

sketched out by the Talmud concerning the "four who must give thanks": In 1621, Pilgrims at the Plymouth Plantation celebrated their survival of a harsh winter and terrible sickness by sharing their abundance with those around them, in a great feast attended even by the neighboring, indigenous peoples.

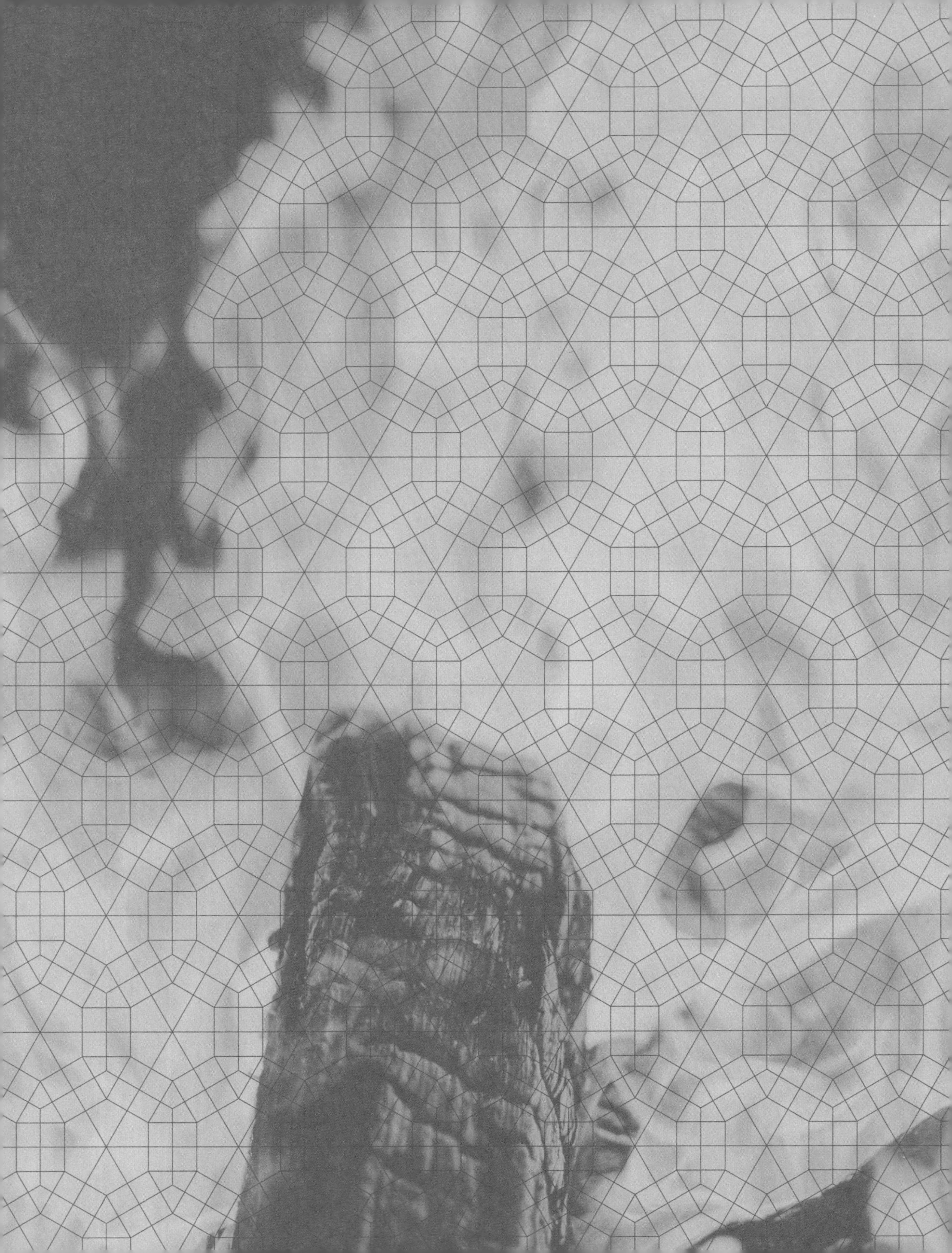

SHEMINI

The *Chatat* That Masqueraded as an *Olah*: A Study in Grief

וַיִּדֹּם אַהֲרֹן׃

And Aaron was silent.

LEVITICUS 10:3

The *Chatat* That Masqueraded as an *Olah*: A Study in Grief

PARSHAT SHEMINI TELLS OF a climactic triumph made bittersweet by the accompaniment of a devastating loss. The people of Israel, en route to the land of Canaan, consecrate a *Mishkan*, a Tabernacle, to God. But just as the consecration ceremony achieves its zenith, it is marred by a pair of tragic deaths. Two sons of Aaron, Nadav and Avihu, bring incense before God in a way they weren't commanded to. In response, a blaze erupts from within the innermost, most sacrosanct part of the *Mishkan*, and Nadav and Avihu are killed in the flames:

וַתֵּצֵא אֵשׁ מִלִּפְנֵי יְקֹוָה וַתֹּאכַל אוֹתָם וַיָּמֻתוּ לִפְנֵי יְקֹוָה:	And fire came forth from the Lord and consumed them; thus they died, before God.	Leviticus 10:2

Less well known, though, is something that transpires just after this. Right after the deaths of Nadav and Avihu are recorded, we hear about a certain *chatat* — a sin offering — that was brought. Somehow, a dispute erupts between Moses and the surviving sons of Aaron, Elazar and Itamar, over whether the service for this *chatat* was executed properly. Moses becomes upset at Elazar and Itamar, accusing them of wrongly allowing the meat of the offering to be burnt. Aaron, their father, comes to their defense and offers a rationale for their actions — an argument that, in the end, Moses accepts, and the incident draws to a close.

An Arcane Debate

Why must we hear about this little episode? Comparatively speaking, it seems of trivial importance. Big things are happening. The *Mishkan* is being consecrated. The ceremony is marred by the deaths of two children of the High Priest himself. Shock hangs thick in the air. And for some reason, the Torah follows all that up with ... what? An arcane debate, subsequently resolved, that some leaders got into over the granular details of sacrificial law? Why do I need to hear about that debate at all? And why do I need to hear about it right *now*?

A Story Behind a Story

I want to suggest that this apparently obscure dispute between Moses, Aaron, and his sons might have a larger significance. To see what that might be, I want to come back to something I talked about in **Parshat Vayikra**: a framework for understanding the relationship between three of the Torah's most basic types of animal offerings — an *olah*, a *shelamim*, and a *chatat*.

One of those offerings, of course — the *chatat*, or the sin offering — is right at the crosshairs of that arcane dispute between Moses and the surviving children of Aaron:

Leviticus 10:16–17

וְאֵת שְׂעִיר הַחַטָּאת דָּרֹשׁ דָּרַשׁ מֹשֶׁה וְהִנֵּה שֹׂרָף וַיִּקְצֹף עַל אֶלְעָזָר וְעַל אִיתָמָר בְּנֵי אַהֲרֹן הַנּוֹתָרִם לֵאמֹר: מַדּוּעַ לֹא אֲכַלְתֶּם אֶת הַחַטָּאת בִּמְקוֹם הַקֹּדֶשׁ כִּי קֹדֶשׁ קָדָשִׁים הִוא וְאֹתָהּ נָתַן לָכֶם לָשֵׂאת אֶת עֲוֹן הָעֵדָה לְכַפֵּר עֲלֵיהֶם לִפְנֵי יְקוָה:	Moses inquired about the goat of the *chatat*, and it had been burned! He was angry with Elazar and Itamar, Aaron's remaining sons, and said, "Why did you not eat the *chatat* in the sanctuary? For it is most holy, and [the Almighty] has given it to you to bear the guilt of the community, and to achieve atonement for them before God."

The meat of the *chatat* was supposed to have been eaten by the priests, these sons of Aaron — but instead, they burned it and did not partake of it.[1] To understand why, at that moment in time, what happened to that meat mattered so very much, I want to take you back to that paradigm we spoke of back in **Parshat Vayikra**.

There we contrasted the *olah* and the *chatat*. An *olah*, you will recall, is an offering that, by Torah law, is meant to go entirely up to God — hence, its name *olah*, which means "go up." A *chatat*, by contrast, is not meant to be burnt entirely on the altar; part of its meat is consumed by the Kohanim. But the contrast between the two kinds of offerings doesn't end there. When it comes to the basic significance of each, there is a certain kind of tension between an *olah* and a *chatat*. And that tension can be traced all the way back to the earliest antecedent of each offering.

The *Chatat*: Taking a Trip Back into the Garden

In my essay on **Parshat Vayikra**, I argued that the great, primary antecedent for a *chatat* — a sin offering — is the first extended episode involving sin in the history of humanity: Adam and Eve's decision to eat from the Tree of Knowledge of Good and Evil, followed almost immediately by Cain's killing of his brother Abel. I argued that the first chapter in that episode — consuming the forbidden fruit — prepared the way for the second chapter, Cain's killing of Abel. The latter was in some way a natural

---

1 By way of context, the Talmud, in Tractate Zevachim (101b), clarifies that there were actually three different *chatat* offerings brought that day the *Mishkan* was consecrated. One of these was a *chatat* brought as part of the Torah-ordained *musaf* offerings for Rosh Chodesh (the onset of the new month). The offering was not unique to the day of consecration per se; it was brought simply because the consecration ceremony coincided with the new month. The Talmud calls these standard *chatat* offerings *kodshei dorot*, namely, offerings that go on for generations. The other two *chatat* offerings, though, were indeed unique; they were designed specifically for the day of consecration, and have no analogue among any standard *chatat* offerings brought later in history. In the Talmud's terminology, they were *kodshei sha'ah*, offerings relevant only to this particular moment in time. The Talmud goes on to assert that the two latter types of *chatat* brought that day, the *kodshei sha'ah*, were indeed eaten properly by the sons of Aaron, and only the one Rosh Chodesh offering was improperly burnt. The significance of this distinction is something we will return to, at least briefly, a bit later.

culmination of the former, and the composite of the two becomes the spiritual ground out of which the idea of the *chatat* eventually emerges.[2]

To attempt to understand the dispute here, in **Parshat Shemini**, regarding the particular *chatat* offering that attended the consecration of the *Mishkan*, let's revisit that forbidden-fruit episode where, I suggested, the story of the *chatat* really begins.

God had given a world of paradise to Adam and Eve. There were all these wonderful trees, described by the text as נֶחְמָד לְמַרְאֶה וְטוֹב לְמַאֲכָל — "delightful to behold and delicious to eat" — but we humans more or less disregarded them. Instead of eating from *those* trees, the ones that had been gifted to us, we directed our interest toward the one tree we couldn't have, the Tree of Knowledge of Good and Evil.

Eating from that one tree was a violation of boundaries. And inasmuch as that's so, the forbidden fruit is a kind of touchstone for all the other things the Torah eventually places off-limits. When we honor these restrictions and do not violate them, on some level, we show that we have some respect toward the Gift Giver in the sky that we call God. We understand that we are guests in the great, expansive garden He has bestowed upon us — this wonderful domain that we call our world.

And now let's examine the converse. What happens when you transgress one of these commands? When you've done this, even if you haven't actually acted with malice, even if you were just a little too careless and you transgressed inadvertently — you've brought a certain kind of

---

2 As was noted in a footnote in the **Parshat Vayikra** essay, a *chatat* is offered only for inadvertent (שוגג) transgressions. This may *seem* to throw a wrench into my argument for a couple of reasons. Firstly, why would someone who transgresses intentionally not also engage in the same restitution process? In response to this difficulty, I would argue that when we *intend* (מזיד) to transgress a command of the Torah, when our lack of respect comes with malice aforethought — in that case, an offering is not appropriate, and can't offer atonement. The lack of respect is too blatant. But when our transgression is inadvertent, a product of carelessness more than anything else, that's when the Torah mandates that we offer a *chatat*.

Secondly, it seems odd that the story of mankind's sin in the Garden of Eden and or its continuation with Cain's slaying of Abel would serve as a touchstone for the *chatat*, when, seemingly, those acts were anything but inadvertent. In part II of the Vayikra essay, I try to tackle this challenge. If you haven't read that essay, I encourage you to take a look.

imbalance into your relationship with God. There were these two domains in this great world of ours — that which God has gifted to us, and that which God has reserved for Himself, as it were — and you improperly crossed over into God's domain, and consumed something you weren't supposed to have from there.[3]

With a *chatat* you are engaging in a curious, symbolic act of reciprocity: You consumed something that was out of bounds, something that was, in effect, in God's world — and now…you are allowing the inverse to happen. You are taking something that's rightfully in *your* domain, and offering it to God so that He may "consume" it. Now, obviously, God has no body or mouth to eat or consume anything,[4] but the Kohanim act as agents in this regard. God gives the Kohanim this meat from the *chatat* offering and says, in effect: *Consume this on my behalf, to help restore the balance between Me and the one who took improperly from My world.*

The *Olah* as the Inverse of a *Chatat*

So if that's what a *chatat* is, what is an *olah*? As I suggested back in **Parshat Vayikra**, when one offers an *olah*, one is adopting a very different stance. A quick look at one of the stories that are touchstones for the *olah*, the episode we know as the *Akeidah*, will demonstrate why.

In the *Akeidah*, Abraham was ready to give back his child, Isaac. God didn't take him, in the end, but Abraham's willingness to give that child to God expressed the feeling, or even the conviction, that in the Presence of God, I must abandon all pretense of having any domain that is *mine* in this world at all.

Abraham seems to recognize that even children, in whom we play an active role as co-creators, are a gift bestowed upon us by our Creator. And when the Giver of that gift asks for it to be returned, there can be

---

3 As mentioned in the essay on Vayikra, this notion of improperly crossing domains gives a new wrinkle of nuance to one of the synonyms for the word sin in Hebrew, namely עבירה, which can literally mean "crossing." This also, I would suggest, is the conceptual root of the English verb "transgress." The Latin root *trans* suggests the idea of crossing, too — for indeed, every transgression is in some way a kind of trespass, a violation of another's domain.

4 Interestingly, the phrase traditionally used to refer to burning offerings upon the altar is אכילת מזבח — "eating of the altar." (See Zevachim 13b.)

no holding back. At the end of the day, there is *no* domain at all in this world that is mine.

Awe and Surrender

Thus, if the cardinal virtue that animates the *chatat* is respecting another's domain, the virtue that animates the *olah* is awe. This, after all, is what the angel tells Abraham at the conclusion of the *Akeidah*:

Genesis 22:12

עַתָּה יָדַעְתִּי כִּי יְרֵא אֱלֹקִים אַתָּה	Now I know that you are in awe of God.

According to the text, awe of the Divine was the quality Abraham expressed atop that mountain. The sense of awe implies surrender and loss of self: Nothing is mine. Even the thing that appears to be *most* mine isn't really mine: *I surrender to You, the Master of all, any notion of having a domain of my own.*

The *Olah* and Aaron's Silence

So now let's come back to our story. In our little trip down memory lane to **Parshat Vayikra**, as we revisited this tension between the *chatat* and the *olah* — do any of these ideas resonate in **Parshat Shemini**, in this strange episode we've been examining involving Moses and his dispute with Aaron and his remaining sons?

I think they do.

Remember the story right before this odd dispute? Aaron's two elder sons had suddenly, shockingly, died. And what had Aaron's response been to this sudden tragedy? When the nation's greatest celebration, the consecration of the Tabernacle itself, turned into a personal horror for him — what had been his reaction? The text (Lev. 10:3) tells us that Moses tried to console him — הוּא אֲשֶׁר דִּבֶּר יְקֹוָה לֵאמֹר בִּקְרֹבַי אֶקָּדֵשׁ — "This is what Hashem spoke of, saying, 'I will show myself holy to those who come near me'" — but Aaron's response to that consolation, at the end of this very same verse, is terse and enigmatic:

וַיִּדֹּם אַהֲרֹן And Aaron was silent. Leviticus 10:3

How should we interpret that silence? It is hard to know. It is hard to know whether Aaron's silence was meant as a response to Moses' words of consolation, or whether it was instead a response to… God. The most basic, primal reality of the moment was that God had just taken his children from him. What if Aaron's silence was a response to *that*?

If so, his silence might indicate numbness. But it also might signify something else. There is a saying that the Sages of the Talmud have: Silence is tantamount to admission.[5] In that silence, Aaron expressed, perhaps, a stoic admission of a hard truth, the hardest of truths anyone could ever imagine admitting to. He could have chosen to see the death of his children at this climactic moment of national celebration as a cruel outrage to be protested against: *There can be no accepting this travesty!* Or, to move just a bit further down Elizabeth Kubler Ross' stages of grief, he could have bargained in disbelief with God over it: "How could You do this, God; how could You have taken them? *They were just trying to come close to You!*" But Aaron was instead silent. And silence is a kind of admission.

Aaron's silence, I would argue, is a kind of trembling acceptance. In it, perhaps Aaron touched the energy of the *Akeidah*, the energy of awe. It would have been an acceptance of the notion that, when you strip everything else away, there really are no domains. There is no "my domain" and "God's domain." My children weren't really mine; they were God's. All there really is… is one domain. And it is that of the Divine.

When a *Chatat* Is Treated as an *Olah*

We are now, I think, in a position to better understand this obscure little dispute between Moses and Elazar and Itamar, the remaining sons of Aaron. Just after the deaths of Nadav and Avihu, a *chatat* is offered in the newly consecrated *Mishkan*. It is offered on behalf of the entire community, but it isn't offered properly:

5 See *Bava Metzia* 6a.

Leviticus 10:16–17

וְאֵת שְׂעִיר הַחַטָּאת דָּרֹשׁ דָּרַשׁ מֹשֶׁה וְהִנֵּה שֹׂרָף וַיִּקְצֹף עַל אֶלְעָזָר וְעַל אִיתָמָר בְּנֵי אַהֲרֹן הַנּוֹתָרִם לֵאמֹר: מַדּוּעַ לֹא אֲכַלְתֶּם אֶת הַחַטָּאת בִּמְקוֹם הַקֹּדֶשׁ כִּי קֹדֶשׁ קָדָשִׁים הִוא וְאֹתָהּ נָתַן לָכֶם לָשֵׂאת אֶת עֲוֹן הָעֵדָה לְכַפֵּר עֲלֵיהֶם לִפְנֵי יְקוָה:	Moses inquired about the goat of the *chatat*, and it had already been burned! He was angry with Elazar and Itamar, Aaron's remaining sons, and said, "Why did you not eat the *chatat* in the sacred area? For it is most holy, and [the Almighty] has given it to you to bear the guilt of the community, and to achieve atonement for them before God."

In Moses' critique, as given to us by the text, we find some peculiar words. Moses doesn't just ask Elazar and Itamar why they improperly burnt the *chatat* instead of eating it. He adds: "For it is most holy… and to you it was given to achieve atonement." What was he saying here? He seems to not simply be referring to sacrificial law as a *fait accompli*. Instead, he seems to be providing a kind of rationale for the law, a *reason*[6] why the *chatat* had to be eaten. What was he saying?

Moses' words seem to be making a point to Elazar and Itamar about the underlying way a *chatat* works. A *chatat*, when it is first consecrated, becomes *kodesh kedoshim*, literally, *holy of holies*. This signifies that the *chatat* — which originally belonged to humans — has been taken in by the divine estate, so to speak. When the Kohanim eat the *chatat*, in turn, the divine estate consumes what it had taken in.[7] In a sense, all this is a mirror image of the first sin: When humans took the forbidden fruit, they reached for it and brought it into their domain — and then they *ate* it, consumed something that belonged to the Divine. When the Kohanim eat the *chatat*, they take something that belonged to humans and consume it on behalf of the Divine, closing the circle and restoring the boundary that had been violated.

In this story, though, the sons of Aaron had *not* eaten the *chatat*. And the question is: Why?

---

6 In fact, the Sages understand that part of the atonement entails the Kohanim eating the sacrifice (see Pesachim 59b).

7 In talmudic nomenclature, this is called *mishulchan gavoah ka zachu* — they receive their portion from the divine table (Menachot 6a); see also Num. 18:9.

Why, indeed. We talked earlier about the tension between the *olah* and the *chatat*. Bearing that in mind, let's realize that these particular Kohanim, Elazar and Itamar, had just personally lived through something that expressed...the complete *opposite* energy of a *chatat*. They had just been made viscerally aware of the fact that ... there is, at the deepest level, only one domain: that of the Divine. Indeed, in the context of this episode, the text calls Elazar and Itamar the בָּנָיו הַנּוֹתָרִים — "the children [of Aaron] who were left behind" (Lev. 10:16). The stark allusion to the deaths of their siblings reminds the reader that Elazar and Itamar, along with their father, had just surrendered *everything* — that which was *most* theirs. They had just watched God take their brothers from them. Indeed, they had witnessed their father's silence and acceptance of this, and perhaps they shared in that visceral silence, too.

And so Elazar and Itamar, "the remaining sons of Aaron," ended up treating this offering, this *chatat, not* as a *chatat,* but as an *olah*. They allowed it to be entirely consumed, just as if it were an *olah*. Their view of domains, heavenly and earthly, at that moment of supreme grief did not allow for the subtle parsing of the *chatat,* the notion that there was a human domain and a godly one. No. At that moment, that notion seemed like a laughable fiction. There was just one domain now. *The chatat was, in effect, an olah.*

The Kohen as Priest, The Kohen as Human Being

Yes, Elazar and Itamar were Kohanim. But they were also human beings. As humans, as private, individual citizens, what had they just lived through? Utter loss, utter surrender, the sense of no boundaries whatsoever. Their father's silence, if it could speak, might scream: "*Boundaries?!* The very word sounds like an outrage. *There are no boundaries.* I can take nothing for myself. Everything has been taken from me. All I can do is to stand still and surrender."

That's the energy of an *olah*. It represents, authentically, what they had just gone through. And this, perhaps, explains Aaron's response to Moses about the burned *chatat*. For although Aaron was silent, earlier, after Moses tried to console him, now, in response to the burned *chatat,* he speaks up to Moses, defending the actions of his children, Elazar and Itamar:

Leviticus 10:19	הֵן הַיּוֹם הִקְרִיבוּ אֶת חַטָּאתָם וְאֶת עֹלָתָם לִפְנֵי יְקֹוָה וַתִּקְרֶאנָה אֹתִי כָּאֵלֶּה וְאָכַלְתִּי חַטָּאת הַיּוֹם הַיִּיטַב בְּעֵינֵי יְקֹוָה	See, this day they brought their sin offering and their burnt offering before the Lord, and such things have befallen me! Had I eaten the sin offering today, would the Lord really have approved?

Such things have befallen me! Would God really have approved had I eaten the sin offering? In those words, it is almost as if Aaron is saying: "I feel I have no boundary of my own. How could I assert boundaries, even on behalf of God, when ... on the deepest of levels, I have been made to understand that there are no boundaries, that, in my anguish, I can truly lay claim to nothing?"

Leviticus 10:20	וַיִּשְׁמַע מֹשֶׁה וַיִּיטַב בְּעֵינָיו:	And when Moses heard this, he approved.

Ultimately, Moses accepts Aaron's argument. And in this acceptance we learn something about the two hats every Kohen wears. Yes, a Kohen represents the divine estate on the one hand, but he is also a human being. Sometimes those spiritual energies collide. This is one instance in which they did.[8]

---

8 I'm not suggesting here that personal or emotional considerations won the day in violation of halachah and its dictates. On the contrary, I would argue that personal considerations — in this case, the extreme grief felt by Aaron and his sons over the death of their kin — helped shape the halachic character of the situation. To see how this might be so, let me frame the argument I'm making in this essay in more formal halachic terms, using the framework given to us in Tractate Zevachim for the debate between Aaron and Moses.

I briefly introduced that framework above (see above, footnote 1). Essentially, the Talmud (Zevachim 101b) suggests that there were actually three different *chatat* offerings brought on the day the *Mishkan* was consecrated. Two were unique, designed specifically for the consecration of the *Mishkan*, and one was a standard *chatat*, brought as part of the *musaf* offerings for the new month (Rosh Chodesh),

When you're a High Priest, that almost always eclipses your role as a private individual. But not always. For one, brief moment, Aaron the human, in his own struggle with God, eclipsed Aaron the High Priest — and in Moses' acceptance of that, we learn ... that it was okay.

---

which happened to coincide with the *Mishkan*'s consecration. The Talmud suggests that Aaron's sons *did* eat the meat of the two former types of *chatat* brought that day, refusing only the meat of the one Rosh Chodesh offering they "improperly" burnt (see also Rashi on Lev. 10:16). Finally, at least one opinion in the Talmud attributes the refusal of Aaron's sons to eat that meat to the intense state of mourning the children of Aaron were experiencing, in the immediate aftermath of the death of their kin (this state of mourning is technically known as *aninut*).

Why, we might ask, did they refuse the meat of the Rosh Chodesh *chatat*, while eating the meat of the other two *chata'ot*? If they were experiencing *aninut*, and that was reason enough to refuse the meat of one *chatat*, why did it not lead them to *also* refrain from eating the meat of the others?

The Talmud offers an explanation. As Rashi (Lev. 10:16) explains, the former two *chata'ot* were utterly unique (*kodshei sha'ah*), and the other was a standard *chatat* (*kodshei dorot*). The logic for that distinction, I would suggest, can be seen in light of the argument I advanced in this essay. When it came to *kodshei sha'ah*, the unique *chatat* offerings mandated by the *Mishkan*'s consecration, these — on account of their extraordinary nature — were not seen by Aaron's children through the lens of an ordinary *chatat*. They did not view them as conveying the same message about God's domain and rectifying a transgression that we learn from the earliest of transgressions, or at least they felt that they would not represent that paradigm in a lasting way. As such, they accepted Moses' direction to eat their meat without objection — for since these were completely new offerings, without any real analog to any others both retrospectively and prospectively, the consumption of their meat didn't seem to violate the terms or spirit of their *aninut*.

On the other hand, when it came to the *chatat* for Rosh Chodesh — since it was a standard *chatat* — consumption of its meat would be inconsistent with their *aninut*, the searing grief they were experiencing over the loss of their brothers (see Zevachim, ibid.). Or, to frame the argument of the Talmud in the terms of this essay: The children of Aaron viewed *aninut* as consistent only with the "non-boundary-defined" world of the *olah*, not the "boundary-defined" world of the *chatat*.

All told, although their status as Kohanim might dictate that they partake of the meat of this offering, their state of *aninut* dictated otherwise. In effect, one might say, this created a conflict between their personal status and their status as Kohanim, agents of the divine estate. That conflict, in at least this one instance, was decided in favor of the former status, rather than the latter.

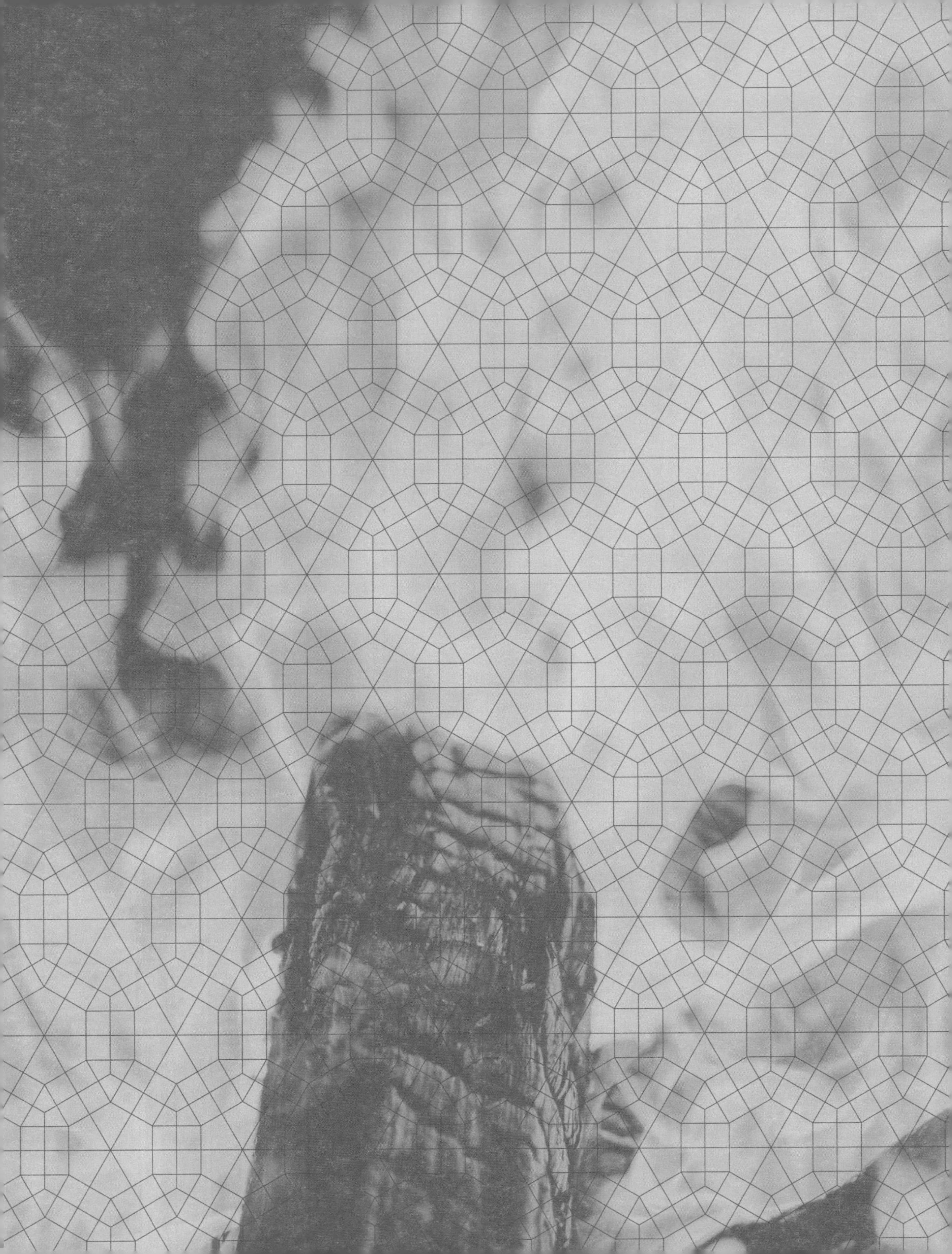

The Bizarre Purification Ritual of the *Metzora*

וְשִׁלַּח אֶת־הַצִּפֹּר הַחַיָּה
עַל־פְּנֵי הַשָּׂדֶה׃

And he shall send the live bird
free into the open country.

LEVITICUS 14:7

TAZRIA-METZORA

The Bizarre Purification Ritual of the *Metzora*

TZARA'AT: THE TORAH DEVOTES much space to describing this affliction, the states of impurity associated with it, and the ways in which one emerges from that impurity. But what is *tzara'at*, why does the Torah devote so much space to it, and how should we wrap our minds around its myriad laws? That, to paraphrase Winston Churchill, is a riddle wrapped in a mystery, inside an enigma.

The most basic aspect of that mystery concerns something as simple as identity: What is *tzara'at*, really? Clearly, it is a malady of some sort. But it can take many forms. It can show up as a whitish discoloration of the skin. It can also afflict the hair or the beard, causing a discoloration of the hairs upon the skin. It can even affect a house. Some translations render *tzara'at* as leprosy, but scant evidence supports that translation. Rabbi Samson Raphael Hirsch, for one, makes a convincing case that, biologically, *tzara'at* isn't actually leprosy.[1] Somehow, *tzara'at* — which doesn't obviously conform to any disease known to Western medicine — appears to be a kind of spiritual malady that manifests itself in physical form. A midrash associates *tzara'at* with the speaking *lashon hara*, gossip or slander about others.[2] Other sources associate *tzara'at* with a general stature of haughtiness, seeing it as some sort of consequence for a lack of humility.[3]

Perhaps the most peculiar aspect of *tzara'at*, though, concerns how the *metzora*, the person afflicted with this malady, can leave it behind. According to the Torah, one who contracts *tzara'at* becomes *tamei*, ritually

---

1 See Samson Raphael Hirsch, commentary on Lev. 13:59.

2 Tanchuma Metzora 1.

3 See Arachin 16a.

impure, and can become *tahor*, pure, again only by undergoing an elaborate ritual procedure, detailed in Leviticus chapter 14. (We will occasionally call this procedure by its Hebrew name, *taharat hametzora*.) That procedure is what I'd like to talk about here. It seems arcane at best, and at worst bizarre. As part of it, the Kohen takes two birds. One of them is killed. There's a piece of cedarwood, a scarlet thread, and a hyssop plant. These objects, along with the live bird, get dipped in the blood of the bird that's killed. The live bird then flies away. It all seems so strange. Should we just shake our collective heads in wonderment, shrug our shoulders, and move on? Or do we have a chance of making sense of any of this?

What Does the Purification Process of the *Metzora* Rhyme With?

An important clue, I think, comes from the strange mix of elements that comprise the purification process. For if we read carefully, we can detect an uncanny echo here. You've ... heard aspects of these laws before. Indeed, they recall another procedure ordained by the Torah, one that appears all the way back in the book of Exodus.

Let me show you what I mean.

We can start with a striking part of the *metzora*'s purification procedure: The role played by two birds taken by a Kohen. I talked a bit about these two birds above, but here's a somewhat more detailed look at what happens with them: One bird is left alive and is cast out into a field, and another, according to the text, is to be killed. The blood of the latter bird is meant to drip into a pool of clear water in an earthenware vessel, presumably reddening the appearance of that water so that it, too, appears bloody. Then the Kohen is told to take a piece of cedarwood, the live bird, a scarlet thread, and hyssop leaves — and dip them all into the water with the blood of the dead bird mixed into it.[4] Finally, at the end of the purification process, the *metzora* is permitted to come back into the camp, but they must still wait outside their home for seven whole days (see Lev. 14:4–8).[5]

Ask yourself, now: Does any of this sound at least vaguely familiar?

---

4 See Ibn Ezra on Lev. 14:6; see also Rashi.

5 See Keritot 8b for an analysis and qualifications of this requirement.

If the answer is no, here's a little hint for you: Think "wood, hyssop bush, and blood." When else, earlier in the Torah, back in the book of Exodus, do we encounter a procedure that incorporates these elements?

If you're still drawing a blank, note the fact that *taharat hametzora,* the *metzora*'s purification process, involves a bird that escapes death while another similar being (i.e., another bird) dies. When in the book of Exodus, did we have a process associated with ... certain beings who escape death, while other similar beings die? Well, guess what? It just so happens to be the very same procedure that involved wood, a hyssop bush, and blood.

So ... what is that earlier procedure, so laden with these echoes?

Welcome to...the Passover Offering

It is the procedure through which Israel left its centuries-long bondage and struck out on its own, as a free people.

Just before the climactic tenth plague strikes Egypt, God calls to Moses and tells him what Israel must do to secure immunity from the effects of the coming devastation. Intriguingly, this is the only plague from which Israel did *not* receive automatic immunity. When the Nile turns to blood, when frogs or other amphibians wreak havoc on Egypt, when all this comes about — only Egyptians are affected and not the Israelites. That's just the way it is. But not when it comes to the tenth plague. In preparation for the Smiting of the Firstborn, Israel is asked to *do* something in order to procure immunity from what is about to come. They are bidden to undertake an elaborate procedure — a procedure that bears an uncanny similarity to what we will encounter in the book of Leviticus, in the purification of the *metzora.*

Here is what Moses tells the people in advance of the tenth plague:

Exodus 12:21–23

וַיִּקְרָא מֹשֶׁה לְכָל זִקְנֵי יִשְׂרָאֵל
וַיֹּאמֶר אֲלֵהֶם מִשְׁכוּ וּקְחוּ
לָכֶם צֹאן לְמִשְׁפְּחֹתֵיכֶם
וְשַׁחֲטוּ הַפָּסַח: וּלְקַחְתֶּם אֲגֻדַּת
אֵזוֹב וּטְבַלְתֶּם בַּדָּם אֲשֶׁר
בַּסַּף וְהִגַּעְתֶּם אֶל הַמַּשְׁקוֹף
וְאֶל שְׁתֵּי הַמְּזוּזֹת

Moses summoned all the elders of Israel and said to them, "Go, pick out lambs for your families, and slaughter the Passover offering. Take a bunch of hyssop, dip it in the blood that is in the basin, and apply some of the blood that is in the basin to the lintel and to the two

מִן הַדָּם אֲשֶׁר בַּסַּף וְאַתֶּם לֹא תֵצְאוּ אִישׁ מִפֶּתַח בֵּיתוֹ עַד בֹּקֶר: וְעָבַר יְקוָה לִנְגֹּף אֶת־מִצְרַיִם וְרָאָה אֶת הַדָּם עַל־הַמַּשְׁקוֹף וְעַל שְׁתֵּי הַמְּזוּזֹת וּפָסַח יְקוָה עַל הַפֶּתַח וְלֹא יִתֵּן הַמַּשְׁחִית לָבֹא אֶל־בָּתֵּיכֶם לִנְגֹּף:	doorposts. None of you shall go outside the door of his house until morning. For when God goes through to smite the Egyptians, He will see the blood on the lintel and the two doorposts, and God will pass over the door and not let the Destroyer enter and smite your home.

The above verses detail the offering of the Paschal Lamb, or *Korban Pesach*, as it is known in Hebrew. In the procedure, one hears a foreshadow of so much of what the *metzora* must do: Doorposts, presumably made from wood, that get painted in blood seem to foreshadow the *metzora*'s piece of cedarwood that gets dipped in blood. The hyssop that is dipped in blood in the *Korban Pesach* mirrors the hyssop dipped in blood as part of *taharat hametzora*. Even the two birds of the *metzora*, one of which lives while the other dies, seem to find a surprising antecedent in the *Korban Pesach*, for here, two other similar beings go to different fates: Israel, called a firstborn nation by God (Ex. 4:22), *survives* the plague, while all the firstborn of Egypt perish during the plague.

The similarity between the two deepens further when we consider what happens immediately *after* the tenth plague. Not only does Israel survive, she is set free — or, as the verse puts it, *sent* free — into the wilderness:

Exodus 12:33

וַתֶּחֱזַק מִצְרַיִם עַל הָעָם לְמַהֵר **לְשַׁלְּחָם** מִן הָאָרֶץ כִּי אָמְרוּ כֻּלָּנוּ מֵתִים:	The Egyptians were urgent with the people, to **send them out** of the land in haste, for they said, "We are all dead men."

Now fast-forward to the *metzora*'s purification, and consider what happens to the live bird:

Leviticus 14:7

וְשִׁלַּח אֶת הַצִּפֹּר הַחַיָּה עַל פְּנֵי הַשָּׂדֶה:	And he shall **send** the live bird free into the open country.

Israel is sent out into the wilderness, into the open country, and likewise that live bird is released and sent "into the open country."

The truth is, though, that the Exodus wasn't complete after the tenth plague. Pharaoh's armies still pursued Israel, and a final showdown took place at the Sea of Reeds. And, wouldn't you know it, the parallels between *taharat hametzora* and Israel's Exodus experience appear to extend themselves to include that final event as well, the moment Israel finally said goodbye to Egypt for the last time. For consider what happened when the mighty Egyptian army was wiped out in the flowing waters of a sea:

וַיּוֹשַׁע יְקוָה בַּיּוֹם הַהוּא אֶת יִשְׂרָאֵל מִיַּד מִצְרָיִם וַיַּרְא יִשְׂרָאֵל אֶת מִצְרַיִם מֵת עַל שְׂפַת הַיָּם׃	Thus God delivered Israel that day from the Egyptians; Israel saw the Egyptians dead on the shore of the sea.	Exodus 14:30

When that took place; when Israel turned around and saw Egypt one last time, what did they see? They no longer saw taskmasters or soldiers; they no longer saw a threat. They saw… *blood in the water.* They saw the harmless remains of the Egyptian army, nothing but corpses thrashed by the sea, lapped at by the waves of a flowing ocean.

Fast-forward now to the book of Leviticus, and consider what is to be done with the dead bird, while the live one flies free:

וְצִוָּה הַכֹּהֵן וְשָׁחַט אֶת הַצִּפּוֹר הָאֶחָת אֶל כְּלִי חֶרֶשׂ עַל מַיִם חַיִּים׃	The priest shall order one of the birds slaughtered over fresh water in an earthen vessel.	Leviticus 14:5

The blood of the dead bird is made to seep into a pool of water. The blood-infused waters seem to recall the blood-infused waters of the sea, at the moment of Egypt's final defeat.

All in all, the procedure of *taharat hametzora* seems to reflect two linked events: Israel's experience during the tenth plague, and their experience during the Splitting of the Sea. Together, these seem to comprise the climactic moments when Israel is set free.

"One More *Nega* Shall I Bring upon Egypt"

If there's any doubt left in your mind as to whether the procedure of *taharat hametzora* is meant, in some way, to recall Israel's experience as they left Egypt, here's one last piece of evidence to help sway your skeptical mind. It is an easily overlooked word the Torah uses to describe *tzara'at*. That word is the Hebrew term *nega*:

Leviticus 13:9

נֶגַע צָרַעַת כִּי תִהְיֶה בְּאָדָם וְהוּבָא אֶל הַכֹּהֵן׃	The ***nega*** of *tzara'at*, when it shall afflict a person — he shall be brought before the priest.

When the Torah talks about *tzara'at*, over and over again, it refers to it as a *nega*. What is a *nega*? In English, we might translate it as a blight, or an affliction. But we might also translate it as … a *plague*.

The Torah's characterization of *tzara'at* as a *nega* is especially intriguing since, in the entire Five Books of Moses, that exact Hebrew term appears in only one other context.[6] And guess where *that* is, O fair reader?

Your intuition serves you well. It is in the Exodus story. The term *nega* is what the Torah uses to characterize that tenth and final plague visited upon Pharaoh: the killing of all Egypt's firstborn; the plague from which Israel achieved immunity, through the offering of the *Korban Pesach*:

Exodus 11:1

וַיֹּאמֶר יְקוָה אֶל מֹשֶׁה עוֹד נֶגַע אֶחָד אָבִיא עַל פַּרְעֹה וְעַל מִצְרַיִם	And the Lord said to Moses, "I will bring one more ***nega*** upon Pharaoh and upon Egypt."

6 Variations of the word appear elsewhere, as in the story of Abraham and Avimelech (see Gen. 20:6). I'm speaking here only of the precise noun, *nega*, that is used as a descriptor for *tzara'at*.

Déjà Vu All over Again

All told, it seems as if the events of the tenth plague and Israel's subsequent flight from Egypt are being reenacted, in some symbolic way, in the purification procedure for the *metzora.* Let's tally up the similarities:

THE *METZORA* ACHIEVES PURITY	ISRAEL ACHIEVES FREEDOM
A person is afflicted by a *nega.*	Egypt is afflicted by a *nega.*
A hyssop and a piece of wood are dipped in blood.	A hyssop is dipped in blood; blood is painted on wood.
One bird lives. The other bird dies.	One "firstborn" nation lives. The firstborn of the other nation dies.
The living bird is sent out, into an open field.	The living, firstborn nation is sent out into an open wilderness.
As the live bird flies free, the dead bird's blood seeps into flowing waters.	As Israel goes free into the wilderness, the corpses of the Egyptians thrashed by the waves wash up on the shore of the sea. Presumably, their blood seeped into the waters of the Sea of Reeds.

The correspondences between the purification procedure of the *metzora* and the process by which Israel achieved its freedom from Egypt are numerous and striking.[7] They don't seem to be the product of mere

7 One more especially mysterious parallel might connect the two as well. Consider the seven-day waiting period of the *metzora,* when he must sit outside his house. Intriguingly, the Pesach offering signals the onset of a seven-day waiting period, too, one which likewise keeps something out of the house. Indeed, the verse states this: שִׁבְעַת יָמִים שְׂאֹר לֹא יִמָּצֵא בְּבָתֵּיכֶם כִּי כָּל אֹכֵל מַחְמֶצֶת וְנִכְרְתָה הַנֶּפֶשׁ הַהִוא מֵעֲדַת

coincidence. And, indeed, we were not the first to see them. Ibn Ezra notes some of these correspondences briefly in his commentary to Leviticus.[8] But it is one thing to identify a correspondence and quite another thing to understand what that correspondence might *mean*; what the Torah might wish us to understand, now that we've perceived the clever echoes lurking in its text. The question we now need to consider is the great question: Why? *Why* does the Torah pattern the purification process of the *metzora* in a way that evokes the process by which Israel left Egypt?

To begin to understand this, I think we need to compile just a bit more evidence. In the interest of doing that, let's take a moment to consider some other aspects of the *tzara'at* precepts.

The *Metzora* and the Dead

Beyond the linkage we've seen between *taharat hametzora* and the Pesach offering, there seems to be a disquieting link between *tzara'at* and another phenomenon, namely, death.

For example: As mentioned briefly above, the *metzora* is considered *tamei*, impure; but not just impure in a standard kind of way. He or she becomes an *av hatumah,* a primary source of impurity, similar in almost all ways to the *tumah* evinced by a corpse.[9] Indeed, Aaron, brother of Miriam, speaks of her this way when he appeals to Moses on her behalf after she contracts *tzara'at*:

יִשְׂרָאֵל בַּגֵּר וּבְאֶזְרַח הָאָרֶץ — No leaven **shall be found in your houses for seven days**. For whoever eats what is leavened, that person shall be cut off from the community of Israel, whether he is a stranger or a citizen of the country (Ex. 12:39).

8 See Ibn Ezra on Lev. 14:4; see also Ramban there.

9 One ramification of this heightened level of *tumah* is: If a corpse is in a tent, it renders *tamei* (impure) other items in the tent, even those which aren't actually touching the corpse. There's only one other source of ritual impurity this profound, and it is a *metzora* (see Rambam, *Hilchot Tumat Tzara'at* 10:11–12). Interestingly, the Mishna that lists these primary sources of *tumah* mentions the impurity of the *metzora* right after that of a corpse (see Keilim 1:1).

אַל נָא תְהִי כַּמֵּת Let her not be as someone who has died. Numbers 12:12

The physical appearance of *tzara'at* likewise suggests as much: The Torah describes *tzara'at* in terms of a whitening of the skin; when Moses' hand temporarily becomes afflicted with *tzara'at*, it is described as appearing "white as snow" (Ex. 4:6). The notion of having skin appear so unnaturally pale evokes the deathly pallor of a corpse.

Now, it might be that the connection between *tzara'at* and death is superficial; it is just a matter of appearances, just a matter of *tumah*. Or, it might be that something more significant is afoot, that, for example, when Aaron appeals for Miriam to "not be as someone who has died," he is alluding to something almost obvious to him: a basic and fundamental similarity between the *metzora* and the dead. But what is the nature of this similarity? How should we understand it?

I'd like to suggest that in some mysterious but essential way, the *metzora* is not just similar to the dead, he or she is *actually* dead — at least from a certain perspective. Now, I realize that this proposition sounds preposterous: Death is a rather final state of being, and it doesn't seem to lend itself to differing perspectives. Any given person is either dead or alive, and this *metzora*... well, they may be ill, but they most certainly still have a pulse, and in that case, they would seem to be very much alive. In what sense, then, might the Torah consider the *metzora* dead?

The *Metzora*, the Mourner, and the *Menudeh*

A hint comes in a fascinating discussion the talmudic Sages have about the *metzora*. In Tractate Moed Katan, the Talmud talks about how someone should conduct him or herself while afflicted with *tzara'at*,[10] and, throughout that discussion, the Sages consistently compare three kinds of people to one another:

1. the *metzora* — someone afflicted with *tzara'at*;
2. the mourner — somebody mourning the loss of a loved one;

10 See Moed Katan 14b–16a.

3. and a *menudeh* — someone who is excommunicated from the community.

Over and over again, the Talmud poses queries concerning these three individuals. Can an excommunicated person wear shoes? Having determined an answer, it then goes on to ask: What about a *metzora*? And what about a mourner? The *menudeh*, that excommunicated person — can he wear *tefillin*? What about a *metzora*? And... how about greeting the person? We know, the Talmud goes on to say, that you're not supposed to greet a mourner, but what about greeting a *metzora*; what about greeting a *menudeh*?

You get the idea. Over and over, the Sages seem to compare these three different kinds of people. Broadly speaking, the Talmud seems to treat these three as if they are in the same general sandbox, as it were. We need to ask ourselves: What justifies that assumption? What might connect them all?

Well, let's see.

To see a commonality between the *metzora* and a *menudeh*, somebody who is excommunicated, certainly makes quite a lot of sense. In a very clear, straightforward way, the Torah declares that the *metzora* must situate himself outside the camp:

Leviticus 13:46

כָּל יְמֵי אֲשֶׁר הַנֶּגַע בּוֹ יִטְמָא טָמֵא הוּא בָּדָד יֵשֵׁב מִחוּץ לַמַּחֲנֶה מוֹשָׁבוֹ:	All the days in which the plague is in him he shall be *tamei*. He is *tamei*. He shall dwell alone. Outside of the camp shall be his dwelling.

So that makes sense. But why is the *metzora* somehow in the same boat as a mourner?

You might be tempted to respond: That's easy; a *metzora* is like a mourner because, as we saw above, he shares certain commonalities with a dead person. But that explanation, on a moment's reflection, falls short. Because being like the dead doesn't make you a mourner. Mourners themselves are very much alive; they just *mourn* the dead. So why treat the *metzora* as if they are in the same sandbox as a mourner?

The answer to that question holds the key, I believe, to unraveling many of the puzzles we've begun to consider over the last few pages.

Who Is the *Metzora* Mourning?

I once had a close relationship with a person who was dying. As he neared death, he told me something that stuck with me for years: "When someone dies", he said, "all his relatives and friends mourn him. But you know who ought to be the real mourner?"

"Who?" I asked.

"The person who died," he replied. "You see, the mourner's only losing *one* person they love. But the person who is dying — he or she is losing *everyone* dear to them."

Ponder that thought for a moment. What if that's true? What if, by rights, the dead should mourn, but they can't because they aren't alive to do so. Well, what if someone experienced a kind of death that still left him, biologically, very much alive? Should *that* person mourn himself?

I want to suggest to you that this is exactly what is going on with the *metzora*. The *metzora* is a kind of dead person. There is an aspect of him that is dead — but paradoxically, he is very much alive, at least in a biological sense. As such, he is treated by the Sages like a mourner. Who is he mourning? He is mourning himself. Which is to say: He is mourning being cut off from his friends, his family, his community, his loss of connection to anyone and everyone.

Indeed, beyond the mere biology of death, to die means to lose connection with everyone on this earth that you love. *That's* the real sorrow of death. Death is radical separateness, and mourning is the way we who are left in this world express our response to that separateness. This is why it is of no comfort at all for a mourner in a *shiva* house to hear that his or her beloved is "in a better place" now. The words run cold because they are beside the point. *Sure, maybe they're in a better place, but I am not with them, and that's what I really care about right now.* Mourning is a function of separation.

If so, maybe the *metzora*, all alone and outside the camp, mourns for himself. For he, too, is radically separated. In a way, he is even *more* separated than the dead are. For when one dies, one at least may achieve a certain kind of connection with other loved ones who have previously passed into the Next World and are waiting for him[11] there. But the *metzora* does not even have this kind of communion with others. He is neither here nor there, not yet a resident of the Next World, but not fully a part of this one anymore. He is as alone as one can imagine.

A Closer Look at Partial Death

This aloneness may partially explain why the *metzora,* still very much alive, is treated by the Torah as being dead somehow. But I think we have not yet arrived at a full explanation of the nature of the *metzora*'s experience — an understanding of *why,* exactly, he is experiencing a kind of death, even as he remains biologically alive. I want to suggest that this dichotomy is no illusion or mere metaphor. There may actually be a sense in which the *metzora* is fully alive and another sense in which he's actually died.

Earlier, we talked about how the purification procedure for the *metzora* seems to mimic the procedure of the *Korban Pesach,* the Pesach offering. Let's return now to that first ever *Korban Pesach* because I think the Pesach offering, of all things, helps us understand this dichotomy.

The Birth of Community

What happened the night we slaughtered that very first, original Pesach offering?

The people of Israel gathered in their homes with their families and, grouped together that way, they carried out the prescribed ceremony for the Pesach offering: They slaughtered the sheep, they brushed its blood on their doorposts, and they dined on the meat of the offering. And after the offering was consumed, and they actually walked through those bloody doorways — they left Egypt behind them for the last time. And at that moment, something new was created.

It was a nation.

---

11 Consider the phrase the Torah often uses to describe the moment of death: **יֵאָסֵף** אַהֲרֹן **אֶל עַמָּיו** כִּי לֹא יָבֹא אֶל הָאָרֶץ אֲשֶׁר נָתַתִּי לִבְנֵי יִשְׂרָאֵל — Let Aaron **be gathered in to his people**, for he will not come into the land that I have given to the Children of Israel (Num. 20:24). The Torah uses similar language to characterize the deaths of Abraham, Isaac, and Jacob, as well as the deaths of others, too. (See Gen. 25:8, 35:29, and 49:33.)

Until then, there had been no nation. Israel had descended to Egypt as a family. In Egypt, that family grew in size, and as it did, new sub-families were created. But now, on the very night Israel would exit Egypt, something happened: A larger element of community was created, one that transcended mere families. They were born anew as a nation.

This, indeed, explains something curious about the Pesach offering. Generally speaking, the Torah distinguishes between offerings brought by individuals (*korbanot shel yachid*) and communal offerings (*korbanot shel tzibur*). But the Pesach offering seems to be a hybrid of these. It has qualities of an individual offering (i.e., it is brought by individuals, banding together as families), but it also has qualities of a communal offering (e.g., it is brought even when the fourteenth of Nisan falls on a Sabbath[12]). One explanation for this unique, hybrid status is: The Pesach offering is not an individual offering, nor a communal offering. It is, instead, a bridge. It is *the offering by which the community of Israel was created.* The Pesach offering transformed us from being a loosely related bunch of people into an integrated nation.

Blood on the Door

When Israel offered its first Pesach offering, I want to suggest, we were born as a people. This, in turn, explains some additional unique facets of the *Korban Pesach*. For example: How were the people supposed to roast the sheep they ate that night?

כִּי אִם צְלִי אֵשׁ רֹאשׁוֹ עַל כְּרָעָיו וְעַל קִרְבּוֹ:	Roasted with fire; with its head over its knees, [bunched up] over its stomach.	Exodus 12:9

What remarkable attention to detail! Why does the Torah go out of its way…not just to tell you that the animal needed to be roasted, but precisely *how* it was to be roasted: With its head bunched up over its knees. Take a moment to ponder that. Does that particular position of the animal remind you of anything, by any chance?

It's the fetal position, the position of an embryo in its mother's womb.

---

12 See Pesachim 66b and Yoma 51a.

So, all night long, everyone needed to stay shut up in their houses:

Exodus 12:22	לֹא תֵצְאוּ אִישׁ מִפֶּתַח בֵּיתוֹ עַד בֹּקֶר׃	None of you shall go outside the door of his house until morning.

But then, in the morning, everyone would suddenly rush out — *bechipazon*, "in haste." And they would rush through a doorway.

A bloody doorway.[13]

The analogy to birth seems unmistakable. All night long, in the dark, we waited behind these closed doors. And in the morning, we rushed through a doorway covered in blood. We were *born*. Before that night, what were we? We were just a bunch of aggregated families. But that night, as we went through that door, a new entity came into being, a single entity: the nation of Israel.[14]

---

13 The doorway was covered in blood. The two doorposts and the lintel (Ex. 12:7); according to the text, even the threshold, on the ground, had blood on it (Ex. 12:7 and 12:22). [The plain meaning of בַּדָּם אֲשֶׁר־בַּסַּף is "the blood on the threshold." See, however, Rashi, who translates *saf* in this case as "basin."]

14 The *Korban Pesach* was offered as the tenth plague struck Egypt, the smiting of Egypt's firstborn. As if in anticipation of this moment, just before the first of the plagues hit Egypt, God had warned Pharaoh that he must not hold Israel back from serving Him. Why? Because… *beni bechori Yisrael* — "Israel is My firstborn child" (Ex. 4:22). That is an interesting designation, because we find no prior time in the Torah when Israel had been given such a moniker. One might well ask: When did Israel become a firstborn nation to God? When did it achieve this status? The answer might well be: In the future… at the future moment God is now warning Pharaoh of: the night of the tenth plague, which is also the night of Israel's national birth. It is as if God declared to Pharaoh back then that He would kill all firstborn that night except those newly minted as His own. For more on the idea of Israel as a "Firstborn Nation," see my earlier book, *The Exodus You Almost Passed Over* (Aleph Beta Press, 2016).

How We Count Time

Indeed, just before the Almighty informs Moses about the ritual of the Pesach offering, He digresses... and speaks to Moses about a seemingly out of place calendrical note:

God spoke to Moses and Aaron in the land of Egypt, saying: "This month shall be to you the beginning of months. It shall be the first month of the year to you."	וַיֹּאמֶר יְקֹוָק אֶל מֹשֶׁה וְאֶל אַהֲרֹן בְּאֶרֶץ מִצְרַיִם לֵאמֹר: הַחֹדֶשׁ הַזֶּה לָכֶם רֹאשׁ חֳדָשִׁים רִאשׁוֹן הוּא לָכֶם לְחָדְשֵׁי הַשָּׁנָה:

Exodus 12:1–2

Why was it so urgent to tell Moses this, right here and right now? The Exodus is about to reach its denouement. Pharaoh has sworn that the next time Moses sees him, he shall die. God has promised one more, climactic plague. Tension is in the air. God has some important things to tell Israel — most particularly, the laws of the Pesach offering, which they must bring if they are to gain immunity from the coming cataclysm. Is now the time we need to hear talk about future calendars, how we all should number our months?

But this law about numbering months isn't a digression; it is the whole point. It is a kind of topic sentence for the laws of the Pesach offering that follow. This month will be the month we use to start counting our years because... this is time-zero for us; *this is our birthday.* We count time from here because this is when we, as a people, came into existence. Our nation was born through the Exodus, and the ceremony that formalized that birth was the Pesach offering.

What Part of the *Metzora* Died?

Let's return now to the purification ceremony for the *metzora*, that ritual that so closely mirrors the procedure of the Pesach offering. I suggested to you earlier that the *metzora*, while biologically alive, is dead in some way. But in *what* way? Having understood something of the meaning of the *Korban Pesach*, we are now in a position to proffer a theory.

Consider this: You and I; members of Israel, or for that matter, members of any community — who are we, really? Are we individuals? Are we cogs in some large communal wheel? Maybe all of us ... are really two beings at the same time: An individual self, and a communal self. Both are real. Both coexist within us, seamlessly. At least when we are in good health. But sometimes, one of these can whither.

To wrap your mind around the idea of an individual self and a communal self, indulge me in a little thought experiment.

Imagine a conversation between someone and, say, a liver cell in your body. One fine day, someone approaches that liver cell and asks him: "Could you identify yourself, please?" The liver cell perks up and responds cheerfully: "Sure, you know, I'm a cell. A very fine one, too; I've got everything I need. I've got my cell membrane, I have got my nucleus, I have got my messenger RNA, my DNA. I have got my lysosomes, mitochondria, ribosomes. You name it, I got it. I have everything I need to survive in this environment I find myself in."

Has our friend, the liver cell, told you the truth about himself?

Well, to some extent, yes. For at one level, he is, indeed, a very independent cell. A truly remarkable and intricate set of cellular machinery supports the life that pulses within him. But, seen from another perspective, Mr. Liver Cell hasn't really told you the whole truth. He hasn't *really* nailed his identity unless he also identifies himself as part of something larger, as part of... a liver. He is, after all, a *liver* cell. In other words, there is a *communal* side to this cell, too. That communal side of the cell expresses itself in meaningful ways. The cell is designed, for example, to interact with the cells around it. It takes direction from the brain. It responds to metabolic activity around it. More than anything else, its destiny, its meaning in life, lies in something larger than its own little self: it is meant to contribute to the functioning of a liver.

And that liver — it, too, experiences a similar dichotomy. On the one hand, it has its own identity as an organ. But it is *also* part of something larger. It is part of a human being — in this case, *you*.

And so it is with you, or with any other individual human being: On the one hand, a person has an individual identity. He or she can be very independent. But that individual is also a part of something larger. They are part of a family; they are part of a community, and this, too, is part of their identity. The story of one's life cannot be told, in its entirety, with reference only to their individual self. One's life's story is bound up as well in their larger self, in the role they play in their families, in their communities, and in the world at large.

A Mini–Pesach Offering

What, then, shall we make of the *metzora,* this individual who is biologically alive but is in some other way dead; this person who must stay outside the camp; this person who mourns a part of himself that has withered away? Perhaps his individual self is very much alive. He lives; he breathes, he can walk and talk. He is independent. But there is another part of him — the *communal* part of his identity, we might say — that has atrophied. The communal part of the *metzora* is at death's door.

In connection with this, it is interesting to note what the Sages saw as causes of *tzara'at.* As mentioned at the beginning of this essay, rabbinic texts suggest that, in days of old, *tzara'at* could be triggered by *lashon hara* (slander) and haughtiness. Perhaps not coincidentally, these failings have an antisocial element to them. Not only do transgressions such as slander weaken our bonds with those around us, they betray a basic illusion about our sense of self. They beckon us to see ourselves in a false light — as *only* individuals. What belief system compels me to slander someone else? I slander others when I fall prey to the illusion that you and I live in a zero-sum, dog-eat-dog world, that the rational thing, therefore, is to put you down to push myself up. Sadly, when I view the world that way, I may not realize that I am attacking, in subtle ways, my very sense of self. The communal part of me, shunted aside and ignored, starts to languish and shrink away.

If the *metzora* really is an individual whose communal self is at death's door, perhaps the healing of the *metzora* is the story not just of their physical rehabilitation, but their spiritual one as well: Slowly, the *metzora* is building back his or her communal self. As a capstone to this process, after the *metzora* is physically healed, the Torah ordains that he or she is to partake in a private version, of sorts, of the Pesach offering. Why? Because this, after all, is the process by which all of us, once nothing more than mere individuals, entered the community of Israel. It is how each and every one of us finally became something more than individuals.

The Children of Israel started off in our little family houses, slaughtered a Pesach offering, and suddenly found ourselves integral parts of a nation, united by communal purpose and destiny. And now, here is the *metzora* — a single individual who has somehow become estranged from that community. After his long ordeal, to finally find his way back in, he offers a variation of the Pesach offering — and in so doing, reclaims his stake in the community whose embrace is still there for him, whose destiny and vision still beckons to him, and to which he, happily, may now contribute anew.

ACHAREI MOT

How Yom Kippur's Backstory Illuminates Its Purpose

וְאַל יָבֹא בְכָל עֵת אֶל
הַקֹּדֶשׁ מִבֵּית לַפָּרֹכֶת
אֶל פְּנֵי הַכַּפֹּרֶת אֲשֶׁר עַל
הָאָרֹן וְלֹא יָמוּת כִּי בֶּעָנָן
אֵרָאֶה עַל הַכַּפֹּרֶת׃

He [Aaron] is not to come at will into the Holy Chamber behind the curtain, in front of the cover that is upon the Ark, so he will not die; for I appear in a cloud over the cover.

LEVITICUS 16:2

How Yom Kippur's Backstory Illuminates Its Purpose

Is Yom Kippur Magic?

BACK WHEN I WAS young, I remember being taught that Yom Kippur has an almost magical quality about it. The phrase I remember hearing was: עַצְמוֹ שֶׁל יוֹם הַכִּפּוּרִים מְכַפֵּר — the essence of the day grants atonement. The idea, at least as my young self-understood it, was that sure, you are supposed to repent, ask forgiveness, say you're sorry to your friends and acquaintances for ways you might have offended them during the previous year. But still, at its core, there was something about the day *itself* that granted absolution from our various sins. And that always seemed ... well, almost fantastical to me. How would that even work? Did God "magically" grant the day this miraculous quality? It seemed ... far-fetched.

But lo and behold, later in life, I found that it's not just something my teachers made up. No less an authority than Rambam codifies this idea in his *Mishneh Torah*.[1] It is actually a normative part of our tradition that Yom Kippur has some sort of inherent quality to it that leads to atonement. So, is it *really* magic? Or is there some kind of rationale for the quality this day possesses? Is there a way to wrap our minds around it?

Bear that question in mind for a moment, and let me introduce you to one more thing about the day that always puzzled me.

A Curious Day of Awe

One of the things we say about Yom Kippur is that it is a day of "awe." Now certainly, the haunting melodies one hears in synagogue on Yom Kippur seem to reinforce that notion. But still, it is not entirely clear *why*

1 See Rambam, *Hilchot Teshuvah* 1:3.

the day should have this quality. After all, the overriding theme of Yom Kippur seems to be forgiveness of sins. Why would *that* be associated with awe, of all things? Awe is a very particular feeling, a sense of incredible smallness in the face of something overwhelmingly great.[2] Seemingly, we should be happy to be forgiven, not awestruck. One might perhaps suggest that we are concerned — apprehensive, maybe — that maybe our sins are too great for God to overlook, and perhaps that we won't be entirely forgiven. But would that really be enough to make Yom Kippur a day of awe? It might make it a day of apprehension. A day of feeling very nervous. But awe? Not really.

I think some answers to these questions can be found if we go back to the Torah's own introduction to Yom Kippur. That introduction appears right at the opening of **Parshat Acharei Mot**. Let's dive in and take a look.

If You Had to Introduce Yom Kippur...

Parshat Acharei Mot outlines the service in the *Mishkan* that the Kohen Gadol, the High Priest, would undertake every year on Yom Kippur. But before we even look at any of those details, let's spend a moment considering the Torah's preamble to this service. It is rather surprising.

To see just how surprising it is, don't even read it yet. Instead, imagine there was no preamble and it was up to you to create one, that the Almighty was consulting with you about how to introduce the reader to the Yom Kippur service. You've got a sentence or two to work with. What would you write?

I don't know about you, but I might try something like this:

> *And God said to Moses: Tell everyone, that once a year, there will be a wonderful day — a day when I, the Almighty, purify you and forgive you of all your sins.*

With that introduction neatly in place, you could easily go from there. You could tack on a date for this most wonderful of days, and jump right in and discuss the service of the day.

All in all, that would seem like a pretty simple way of introducing Yom Kippur. It is direct and clear, even a tad inspiring.

---

2 See our discussion of awe earlier, in the essays on **Parshat Vayikra** and **Parshat Shemini** in this volume.

But that's not how the Torah introduces the day. Not by a long shot.

Yom Kippur's Topsy-Turvy Introduction

Here is what the Torah, in **Parshat Acharei Mot**, *actually* gives us by way of introduction:

וַיְדַבֵּר יְקוָה אֶל מֹשֶׁה אַחֲרֵי מוֹת שְׁנֵי בְּנֵי אַהֲרֹן בְּקָרְבָתָם לִפְנֵי יְקוָה וַיָּמֻתוּ: וַיֹּאמֶר יְקוָה אֶל מֹשֶׁה דַּבֵּר אֶל אַהֲרֹן אָחִיךָ וְאַל יָבֹא בְכָל עֵת אֶל הַקֹּדֶשׁ מִבֵּית לַפָּרֹכֶת אֶל פְּנֵי הַכַּפֹּרֶת אֲשֶׁר עַל הָאָרֹן וְלֹא יָמוּת כִּי בֶּעָנָן אֵרָאֶה עַל הַכַּפֹּרֶת: בְּזֹאת יָבֹא אַהֲרֹן אֶל הַקֹּדֶשׁ	God spoke to Moses after the death of the two sons of Aaron who died when they drew close before God. And God said to Moses: Tell your brother Aaron that he is not to come at will into the Holy Chamber behind the curtain, in front of the cover that is upon the Ark, so he will not die; for I appear in a cloud over the cover. [Instead], this is how Aaron shall enter the Holy Chamber.	Leviticus 16:1–3

These verses tell us about danger. There is something inherently risky about Aaron coming into the most holy part of the Tabernacle, the place separated from the rest of the Tabernacle by a curtain, the place in which the only piece of furniture is an Ark overlaid with a golden cover. It is a place where the Presence of God makes itself manifest in a cloud hovering over that cover. Coming into that place, the Holy of Holies, is dangerous business. And if it is done the wrong way, the one who enters will die — even if that person is the High Priest himself. That is the preamble to the Yom Kippur service the Torah gives us. From there, the verses then go on to provide a detailed account of the service of the day — the procedure, in effect, by which Aaron, the High Priest, can successfully enter that place (Lev. 16:3–12).

And strangely enough, as we read through the lengthy descriptions of the service...we actually have no idea *when* any of it is supposed to happen. Eventually, the reader arrives at the end of the list of procedures, and then, almost as an afterthought, the Torah tells us about the "when" for all of the above:

Leviticus 16:29–30

וְהָיְתָה לָכֶם לְחֻקַּת עוֹלָם בַּחֹדֶשׁ הַשְּׁבִיעִי בֶּעָשׂוֹר לַחֹדֶשׁ תְּעַנּוּ אֶת נַפְשֹׁתֵיכֶם וְכָל מְלָאכָה לֹא תַעֲשׂוּ הָאֶזְרָח וְהַגֵּר הַגָּר בְּתוֹכְכֶם: כִּי בַיּוֹם הַזֶּה יְכַפֵּר עֲלֵיכֶם לְטַהֵר אֶתְכֶם מִכֹּל חַטֹּאתֵיכֶם לִפְנֵי יְקוָה תִּטְהָרוּ:	And this shall be to you a law for all time: In the seventh month, on the tenth day of the month, you shall afflict yourself; you shall do no manner of work, neither the citizen nor the alien who resides among you. For on this day [God] will forgive you, to purify you; of all your sins, you shall be purified before God.

That last sentence (which, mind you, comes some thirty verses into the Torah's description of the service) — *that* would seem to be the topic sentence for the whole, extended paragraph. But for some reason, it doesn't come at the beginning of the paragraph. It comes at the very end.

Bottom line: The way the Torah introduces Yom Kippur seems topsy-turvy. First, we get some important words of advice: *Don't come into the Holy of Holies* ***this*** *way; instead, come into the Holy of Holies this other way.* Then we hear about a long list of things to do. And finally: *Do this on the tenth day of the seventh month. And by the way, did we forget to mention what will happen when you do all this? You get forgiven for all your sins. You get purified before God.*

But isn't forgiveness the *whole point* of Yom Kippur? Why does the Torah bury the lede, to borrow a line from journalism? Why be so cagey about what Yom Kippur is really about?

Unless maybe ... Yom Kippur isn't *really* about what we think it's about.

The Failed Experiment

It sounds almost ridiculous to suggest this — but what if Yom Kippur *isn't* primarily about forgiveness of sins after all? To be sure, that's *part* of the day, but maybe it is actually a secondary by-product of something else that's even more primary. Maybe forgiveness really *is* a footnote to the main theme of Yom Kippur.

But what, then, would the main theme of the day be?

The words of the text in **Parshat Acharei Mot** actually tell us the answer to this. Let's go back to the Torah's brief introduction to the Yom

Kippur service. We looked at it before, but let's read the words a bit more slowly this time. They may well have some secrets to reveal to us.

וַיְדַבֵּר יְקוָה אֶל מֹשֶׁה אַחֲרֵי מוֹת שְׁנֵי בְּנֵי אַהֲרֹן בְּקָרְבָתָם לִפְנֵי יְקוָה וַיָּמֻתוּ:	God spoke to Moses after the death of the two sons of Aaron, who died when they drew close before God.	Leviticus 16:1

In earlier chapters of Leviticus, we learned about how, during the consecration ceremony for the *Mishkan*, Nadav and Avihu — two sons of Aaron — had died. They had taken burning incense, placed it on fire pans, and brought that into the Holy of Holies, only to meet their deaths when fire shot out from that consecrated space and engulfed them (Lev. 10:1). In beginning its discussion of the Yom Kippur service with a reference to those deaths of Nadav and Avihu, the Torah seems to be saying that those unfortunate deaths are the backdrop against which the Yom Kippur service needs to be understood.[3] But why?

A clue would seem to come from the verse itself:

בְּקָרְבָתָם לִפְנֵי יְקוָה וַיָּמֻתוּ	Who died when they drew close before God.	Leviticus 16:1

The Torah does more here than simply remind us of the deaths of Nadav and Avihu; it also suggests something about *why* Nadav and Avihu did what they did — that is, *why* they took incense into the Holy of Holies, just as the *Mishkan* was being consecrated. They were seeking, in the words of

3 My appreciation to Beth Lesch, one of the scholars at Aleph Beta, for alerting me to the primacy of the Nadav and Avihu event as the context for Yom Kippur. Interested readers are invited to watch her video on the topic at alephbeta.org, entitled *The Untold "Backstory" of Nadav and Avihu,* in which she probes the nature of the Nadav and Avihu story, and how the Sinai Revelation story serves as a precursor to it. Many of the conclusions there dovetail with this essay.

the text, to "draw close before God."[4] I would like to suggest that Nadav and Avihu were trying a radical experiment. They were trying to achieve an *ultimate* kind of closeness to God. A kind of closeness that had only been achieved once before in human history. And their attempt — their failed attempt — to do this provides the necessary background to understand what Yom Kippur is all about.

When was that first time in human history where that radical closeness was successfully achieved? I'm glad you asked. The Torah reminds us of it as we continue to read the words of the introduction:

Leviticus 16:2

כִּי בֶּעָנָן אֵרָאֶה עַל הַכַּפֹּרֶת:	For I appear in a cloud over the [Ark's] cover.

Let's put two and two together. What, exactly, was in that Holy Ark, the one underneath that divine cloud? The answer, of course, is: *The two tablets upon which were inscribed the Ten Commandments.* So ask yourself: When have I heard about all this before? When *else* was there a divine cloud hovering over these very same tablets?

The answer is … when those tablets were first given:

---

4 For indeed, when, several chapters earlier, the Torah initially related their story to us, we were only told *what* they did, not *why* they did it: וַיִּקְחוּ בְנֵי אַהֲרֹן נָדָב וַאֲבִיהוּא אִישׁ מַחְתָּתוֹ וַיִּתְּנוּ בָהֵן אֵשׁ וַיָּשִׂימוּ עָלֶיהָ קְטֹרֶת וַיַּקְרִבוּ לִפְנֵי יְקוָה אֵשׁ זָרָה אֲשֶׁר לֹא צִוָּה אֹתָם — "Now Aaron's sons, Nadav and Avihu, each took his fire pan, put fire in it, and laid incense on it; and they offered before God an alien fire, which He had not commanded them" (Lev. 10:1). Here though, several chapters later, in the opening of **Parshat Acharei Mot**, we come across a phrase that distinctly recalls the language of this earlier verse. And even as it recalls that language, it also *alters* it: **בְּקָרְבָתָם** לִפְנֵי יְקוָה — "[Nadav and Avihu] died when **they drew close** before God" (Lev. 16:1). When the Torah first recounts what these sons of Aaron did, it tells us that they took incense and **וַיַּקְרִבוּ** לִפְנֵי יְקוָה — "**they offered it** before God." Now, we hear almost the same thing, but the form of the verb *kof-resh-bet* is reconjugated, so that it reads: **בְּקָרְבָתָם** לִפְנֵי יְקוָה — "**when they drew close** before God." Put the two together and you suddenly have a story: They offered incense before God … because they were trying to bring *themselves* close before God. In other words, the incense was just a tool; what they were really doing was seeking a close encounter with the Divine.

וַיֹּאמֶר יְקוָה אֶל מֹשֶׁה עֲלֵה אֵלַי הָהָרָה וֶהְיֵה שָׁם **וְאֶתְּנָה לְךָ אֶת לֻחֹת הָאֶבֶן** וְהַתּוֹרָה וְהַמִּצְוָה אֲשֶׁר כָּתַבְתִּי	God said to Moses, "Come up to Me on the mountain and wait there, **and I will give you the stone tablets** with the teachings and commandments which I have inscribed.	Exodus 24:12
וַיַּעַל מֹשֶׁה אֶל הָהָר וַיְכַס **הֶעָנָן** אֶת הָהָר. וַיִּשְׁכֹּן כְּבוֹד יְקוָה עַל הַר סִינַי	And Moses ascended the mountain, and **the [divine] cloud** covered the mountain. And the glory of God rested on Mt. Sinai.	Exodus 24:15–16

God's cloud once hovered over the tablets at Sinai. There, the setting for God's revelation in the world was a mountain, an impressive artifact of nature, made wholly and completely (like everything else in nature) by God. And once the *Mishkan* was consecrated and became operative, the Sinai experience would be recreated in a different setting. The same divine cloud would hover over those same tablets in a man-made space, in a building we call the *Mishkan*.[5]

The consecration of the *Mishkan* therefore signaled an opportunity. Just as Moses managed to have an other worldly, close encounter with God at Sinai, perhaps humankind could achieve something similar in the *Mishkan*. Could the closeness of Sinai somehow be recreated in this man-made building?

The children of Aaron, perhaps, were trying to do just that. The *Mishkan* had just been consecrated. It had just become operative. And at that very moment, Nadav and Avihu acted. They tried to approach its inner sanctum, the place where God's cloud hovered over those tablets.

---

5 Indeed, *Mishkan* literally means the "dwelling place," or "the resting place" — the place God comes to call "home." And dwelling or resting is precisely what the cloud was doing atop Mt. Sinai. Indeed, the very word *Mishkan* is nothing but a noun form of the verb used at Sinai to describe what the cloud was doing: וַיְכַס הֶעָנָן אֶת הָהָר. **וַיִּשְׁכֹּן כְּבוֹד** יְקוָה עַל הַר סִינַי — "The [divine] cloud covered the mountain. And the glory of God **came to rest** on Mt. Sinai" (Ex. 24:15–16). See my essay on **Parshat Terumah**: "Finding Shelter in a World Not Your Own," in *Exodus: A Parsha Companion* (Maggid Books, 2020) for more on this idea.

But they did so in a way that God didn't command, and they died in the process. Their experiment failed.

Why Nadav and Avihu?

Why, we might ask, were Nadav and Avihu, of all people, the ones who sought that close encounter in the *Mishkan*? Why were they, in particular, drawn to suddenly make an approach to the Divine? Perhaps the answer is: Because they had an inkling of how special the experience would be. After all, they had come so close, once before....

Ask this: What *else* do we know about Nadav and Avihu? It turns out that we hear of Nadav and Avihu, acting together, only one other time before this in the Torah. When? You might have guessed it: At the *original* Sinai experience. Indeed, right at the very moment Moses was called by God to ascend the mountain, enter the divine cloud, and receive those tablets — *that's* where we hear about Nadav and Avihu:

Exodus 24:1–2

וְאֶל מֹשֶׁה אָמַר עֲלֵה אֶל יְקוָה אַתָּה וְאַהֲרֹן **נָדָב וַאֲבִיהוּא** וְשִׁבְעִים מִזִּקְנֵי יִשְׂרָאֵל וְהִשְׁתַּחֲוִיתֶם מֵרָחֹק: וְנִגַּשׁ מֹשֶׁה לְבַדּוֹ אֶל יְקוָה וְהֵם לֹא יִגָּשׁוּ

Then [God] said to Moses, "Come up to the Divine, with Aaron, **Nadav and Avihu,** and seventy elders of Israel, and bow low from afar. Moses alone shall come near the Lord; but the others shall not come near."

Nadav and Avihu were among the precious few chosen to ascend Mt. Sinai. *But only partway.* At some point, they were instructed to take leave of Moses and to allow him to complete the journey to the divine cloud alone.

What might it have been like to be Nadav and Avihu at that moment? What would it have been like to go partway up the mountain and then to bid Moses farewell, as he made the last leg of his journey to the mystery of the Divine? Indeed, even though Nadav and Avihu didn't fully ascend Mt. Sinai, they still beheld an astonishing glimpse of the divine mystery:

Exodus 24: 9–10

וַיַּעַל מֹשֶׁה וְאַהֲרֹן נָדָב וַאֲבִיהוּא וְשִׁבְעִים מִזִּקְנֵי

When Moses, Aaron and Nadav and Avihu and the seventy elders of Israel

יִשְׂרָאֵל: וַיִּרְאוּ אֵת אֱלֹקֵי יִשְׂרָאֵל וְתַחַת רַגְלָיו כְּמַעֲשֵׂה לִבְנַת הַסַּפִּיר וּכְעֶצֶם הַשָּׁמַיִם לָטֹהַר:	[began to] go up [the mountain], they glanced [a vision] of the God of Israel; and beneath Him was something like sapphire brickwork, like the very essence of the heavens in its purity.

Nadav and Avihu couldn't enter the cloud as Moses did. But still, they got a taste of what a close encounter with the Master of the Universe might be like. They had an epiphany in the foothills of Sinai, as it were. So it doesn't seem coincidental that later, on the day the *Mishkan* was consecrated, it is Nadav and Avihu, of all people, who seek to enter the inner sanctum of the *Mishkan*... to fully realize the encounter that so tantalized them, the encounter they had once been denied. After all, the cloud of the Divine Presence that had rested at Sinai... was now *here*, resting right above the Ark. They were so close, yet so far. They were drawn to the cloud. The attempt to make contact was so compelling, it just *had* to be undertaken, come what may.

Is the *Mishkan* a Tease?

Their experience, of course, ended in failure. Without being commanded, they unilaterally brought incense into the inner sanctum of the Tabernacle, and they perished. But what they were motivated by was a real and genuine spiritual yearning. If God, our Parent in Heaven, the being who is beyond space and time, is going to somehow, paradoxically, enter the confines of our little time- and space-bound world — well, once He's in the neighborhood, we humans certainly would like a chance to spend some time with Him. We *crave* the chance to spend some time with Him.

That craving is both wonderful *and* dangerous. Mortals, composed as we are of mere flesh and blood, can't normally withstand an encounter with the Master of the Universe and live through the intensity of that experience. Indeed, the story of Nadav and Avihu is the story of what happens when we indulge that craving without any guardrails.[6] And so, it might

6 The careful reader will note that the first time Nadav and Avihu beheld a vision of God, when they stopped short partway up the mountain, the brothers feasted:

seem like the *Mishkan* is a tease. Here is God finally dwelling among us, but we can't go the last mile. We can't actually make contact.

But along comes the Almighty, in **Parshat Acharei Mot**, with some surprising news: A close encounter is indeed possible, after all.

One day a year, God indulges our craving. One day a year, God allows us to recreate Sinai, to do successfully what Nadav and Avihu tried to do unsuccessfully. To achieve this, God gives us directives to follow, a way to make the quest for contact with the Divine both safe and possible. And we enact those directives on a Day of Awe:

Leviticus 16:2–3

וְאַל יָבֹא בְכָל עֵת אֶל הַקֹּדֶשׁ...כִּי בֶּעָנָן אֵרָאֶה עַל הַכַּפֹּרֶת: בְּזֹאת יָבֹא אַהֲרֹן אֶל הַקֹּדֶשׁ	Do not come at will into the Holy Chamber...for I appear in a cloud over the cover. [Instead], this is how Aaron shall enter the Holy Chamber.

A day of awe, indeed. On that one awesome day, we — like Moses — fast. We don't allow bread, water, or food of any kind to cross our lips, just as Moses went without food for the entirety of his stay atop the mountain.

וַיֶּחֱזוּ אֶת הָאֱלֹקִים וַיֹּאכְלוּ וַיִּשְׁתּוּ — "They beheld [a vision] of God and they ate and drank" (Ex. 24:11).

It was an understandable reaction: How could one see what they saw and not feel compelled to celebrate? And yet, when Moses climbs the rest of the mountain alone and enters the divine cloud, he stays there for forty days and forty nights. And tellingly, we learn something about those days and nights in which he was alone with God on the mountaintop: אַרְבָּעִים יוֹם וְאַרְבָּעִים לַיְלָה לֶחֶם לֹא אָכַלְתִּי וּמַיִם לֹא שָׁתִיתִי — "For forty days and forty nights, bread I did not eat, and water I did not drink" (Deut. 9:18).

If feasting is an understandable reaction to getting closer to the Divine, it is not what one does when one actually *encounters* the Divine. Intriguingly, some Sages suggest one reason for Nadav and Avihu's death in the *Mishkan* is that they approached the Holy of Holies after imbibing wine (Rashi on Lev. 10:2). In their epiphany at Sinai, their vision from only partway up the mountain, they both ate and drank. But actual communion with God cannot be met with the pure joy and abandon suggested by feasting and drinking. It demands guardrails. The forty-day fast of Moses is a reminder of the kind of near-transcendence such an experience would demand of a human.

And then, just like what happened at the mountain, a single representative of humanity makes an otherworldly journey, a journey into a slice of space and time here in our world that God calls His own. It happens in the Holy of Holies. And it happens on Yom Kippur.[7]

A Tale of Two Clouds

Once a year, a cloud that comes from God — the cloud that rests on top of the Ark in the Holy of Holies — merges with another cloud, a cloud that comes from humans:

---

7 Another link between Nadav and Avihu's epiphany at Sinai and the Yom Kippur experience lies in the nature of the vision the brothers beheld in their first epiphany. The text tells us that in their mysterious vision, they saw a kind of "heavenly brickwork" that appeared **כְּעֶצֶם** הַשָּׁמַיִם **לָטֹהַר** — "like **the very essence** of the heavens in its **purity**" (Ex. 24:10). Later, when the Day of Atonement is described in **Parshat Emor**, it is possible that we hear an echo of those haunting words. For there, we find that the word **עֶצֶם**, "**the very essence**," repeatedly appears: אַךְ בֶּעָשׂוֹר לַחֹדֶשׁ הַשְּׁבִיעִי הַזֶּה יוֹם הַכִּפֻּרִים הוּא...וְכָל מְלָאכָה לֹא תַעֲשׂוּ **בְּעֶצֶם** הַיּוֹם הַזֶּה כִּי יוֹם כִּפֻּרִים הוּא לְכַפֵּר עֲלֵיכֶם לִפְנֵי יְקוָה אֱלֹקיכֶם: כִּי כָל הַנֶּפֶשׁ אֲשֶׁר לֹא תְעֻנֶּה **בְּעֶצֶם** הַיּוֹם הַזֶּה וְנִכְרְתָה מֵעַמֶּיהָ: וְכָל הַנֶּפֶשׁ אֲשֶׁר תַּעֲשֶׂה כָּל מְלָאכָה **בְּעֶצֶם** הַיּוֹם הַזֶּה וְהַאֲבַדְתִּי אֶת הַנֶּפֶשׁ הַהִוא מִקֶּרֶב עַמָּהּ — Mark, the tenth day of this seventh month is Yom Kippur.... You shall do no work throughout **the very essence** of that day. For it is a Day of Atonement, on which atonement is made on your behalf before the Lord your God. Indeed, any person who does not afflict himself throughout **the very essence** of that very day shall be cut off from his kin; and whoever does any work throughout the **very essence** of that day, I will cause that person to perish from among his people. (Lev. 23:27–30)

It might be a coincidence. But at the close of **Parshat Acharei Mot**'s description of Yom Kippur, we hear another echo of Sinai: כִּי בַיּוֹם הַזֶּה יְכַפֵּר עֲלֵיכֶם **לְטַהֵר** אֶתְכֶם מִכֹּל חַטֹּאתֵיכֶם לִפְנֵי יְקוָה **תִּטְהָרוּ** — For on this day [God] will forgive you, to **purify** you of all your sins; you shall **be purified** before God. (Lev. 23:29–30)

In each of these descriptions of the Day of Atonement, the day when Nadav and Avihu's failed experiment is successfully recreated, the reader seems to hear the faint echoes of Nadav and Avihu's very first epiphany at Sinai, the event that seems to become the touchstone for Yom Kippur.

Leviticus 16:13

וְנָתַן אֶת הַקְּטֹרֶת עַל הָאֵשׁ
לִפְנֵי יְקוָה וְכִסָּה עֲנַן הַקְּטֹרֶת
אֶת הַכַּפֹּרֶת אֲשֶׁר עַל הָעֵדוּת
וְלֹא יָמוּת:

He shall put the incense on the fire before God, so that the cloud from the incense envelops the cover that is over [the Ark of] the Covenant — and he will not die.

"And he will not die," the text interposes — as if to say: You might have thought this High Priest who dares to enter the *Mishkan*'s inner sanctum would die! Something astonishing is happening here. **Parshat Acharei Mot** is telling us that the High Priest is recreating something akin to the Nadav and Avihu moment. He is taking burning incense, like Nadav and Avihu once did, and he is passing into the Holy of Holies, like they did. And then the cloud that rises from his incense — this man-made cloud, as it were — envelops the covering of the Ark, and it merges with the divine cloud atop the Ark.

It is a moment of contact. An emanation of the Divine and an emanation of humanity...these clouds, they merge. And yet...he, the High Priest, does not die!

And here's the really amazing thing: Not only does God allow this connection, He actually shows us how to go about creating it. Perform this service, the Torah tells us, and at its climax...you'll have that Nadav and Avihu moment. I'll indulge your craving for closeness with the Divine. Once a year, we can get *this* close, and you can live to tell the tale.[8]

This, then, is why Yom Kippur is a day of awe: It is the day we make contact. To directly encounter your Creator, the One who is the source of all life, the Master of the Universe. It is certainly enough to give you butterflies in your stomach. It's an overwhelming opportunity.

---

8 The Vilna Gaon asserts that the service outlined in **Parshat Acharei Mot** is demanded on Yom Kippur, but it can in fact be followed on other days, too. Any time the Kohen Gadol seeks to enter the Holy of Holies, he may follow this procedure and thereby avoid the certain death that would come to him if he would attempt divine communion without guardrails (*Chochmat Adam, Sha'ar HaSimchah, Hanhagat Chevra Kadisha Veha'evel*; see also Vayikra Rabbah 21:7).

Forgiveness as By-Product

So the impetus for the Yom Kippur service is our craving to make contact with the Divine. And we want this closeness because...we want it, not for any other ulterior motive: Divine connection is an end in and of itself, pure and simple. Nevertheless, it is still true that divine contact *does* have a by-product. And that by-product, **Parshat Acharei Mot** tells us, just happens to be forgiveness:

כִּי בַיּוֹם הַזֶּה יְכַפֵּר עֲלֵיכֶם לְטַהֵר אֶתְכֶם מִכֹּל חַטֹּאתֵיכֶם לִפְנֵי יְקֹוָה תִּטְהָרוּ׃	For on this day [God] will forgive you, to purify you; of all your sins, you shall be purified before God.	Leviticus 16:30

Why is forgiveness a byproduct of Divine closeness? Hidden in the words of the text is an explanation. It has to do with the language the Torah employs for forgiveness. Look at the word the verse uses for this. Not in English, but in Hebrew: יְכַפֵּר

Its root, you'll notice, are the three letters *kaf-peh-resh*. And, intriguingly enough, although here, at the end of the Torah's description of the Yom Kippur service, the text seems to clearly use the root to mean forgiveness or atonement, the Torah has also, until this point, used the very same root to mean something very different:

Leviticus
1:1–3, 13–15

א וַיְדַבֵּר יְקוָה אֶל מֹשֶׁה אַחֲרֵי
מוֹת שְׁנֵי בְּנֵי אַהֲרֹן בְּקָרְבָתָם
לִפְנֵי יְקוָה וַיָּמֻתוּ: **ב** וַיֹּאמֶר
יְקוָה אֶל מֹשֶׁה דַּבֵּר אֶל אַהֲרֹן
אָחִיךָ וְאַל־יָבֹא בְכָל עֵת אֶל
הַקֹּדֶשׁ מִבֵּית לַפָּרֹכֶת אֶל־
פְּנֵי **הַכַּפֹּרֶת** אֲשֶׁר עַל הָאָרֹן
וְלֹא יָמוּת כִּי בֶּעָנָן אֵרָאֶה עַל
הַכַּפֹּרֶת: **ג** בְּזֹאת יָבֹא אַהֲרֹן אֶל
הַקֹּדֶשׁ בְּפַר בֶּן בָּקָר לְחַטָּאת
וְאַיִל לְעֹלָה...

1 God spoke to Moses after the death
of the two sons of Aaron who died
when they drew close before God.
2 God said to Moses: Tell your
brother Aaron that he is not to come
at will into the Holy Chamber behind
the curtain, in front of the **cover that
is upon the Ark**, so he will not die;
for I appear in the cloud over **the
[Ark's] cover**. **3** This is how Aaron
shall enter the Holy Chamber: with a
bull of the herd for a sin offering and a
ram for a burnt offering...

יג וְנָתַן אֶת הַקְּטֹרֶת עַל הָאֵשׁ
לִפְנֵי יְקוָה וְכִסָּה עֲנַן הַקְּטֹרֶת
אֶת **הַכַּפֹּרֶת** אֲשֶׁר עַל הָעֵדוּת
וְלֹא יָמוּת: **יד** וְלָקַח מִדַּם הַפָּר
וְהִזָּה בְאֶצְבָּעוֹ עַל־פְּנֵי **הַכַּפֹּרֶת**
קֵדְמָה וְלִפְנֵי **הַכַּפֹּרֶת** יַזֶּה שֶׁבַע
פְּעָמִים מִן הַדָּם בְּאֶצְבָּעוֹ:
טו וְשָׁחַט אֶת שְׂעִיר הַחַטָּאת
אֲשֶׁר לָעָם וְהֵבִיא אֶת דָּמוֹ
אֶל מִבֵּית לַפָּרֹכֶת וְעָשָׂה אֶת
דָּמוֹ כַּאֲשֶׁר עָשָׂה לְדַם הַפָּר
וְהִזָּה אֹתוֹ עַל **הַכַּפֹּרֶת** וְלִפְנֵי
הַכַּפֹּרֶת:

13 He shall put the incense on the fire
before God, so that the cloud from
the incense envelops the **cover that
is over the Ark** of the Covenant, so
that he will not die. **14** He shall take
some of the blood of the bull and
sprinkle it with his finger over the
Ark's cover on the east side; and
in front of the **Ark's cover** he shall
sprinkle some of the blood with his
finger seven times. **15** He shall then
slaughter the people's goat of sin
offering, bring its blood behind the
curtain, and do with its blood as he
has done with the blood of the bull:
he shall sprinkle it over the **Ark's
cover** and in front of the **Ark's cover.**

As you can see, the *kaf-peh-resh* root gets used over and over again throughout the Yom Kippur service to create the word *kaporet,* the label the Torah gives to the cover that was placed on top of the Ark of the Covenant. So why, then, would the Torah do this? Why use the same root, over and over, to mean both "cover" and "atone," iteratively, in the same chapter?

Seemingly, the text wants to create a link in the mind of a reader between these two concepts... *cover* and *atone, cover* and *atone, cover* and *atone.* Why? Maybe because the text is trying to tell you something about these two things: That, on some level, they are almost one and the same idea. In other words, the text may be telling us that the essence of forgiveness — how atonement actually *works* — is bound up in the idea of covering.

Atonement and Envelopment

How might that be so? I think it has something to do with the paradigmatic event which the Yom Kippur service is designed to recreate: Moses' encounter with God's cloud at Sinai. There, the idea of covering — or envelopment — was actually front and center:

וַיְכַס הֶעָנָן אֶת הָהָר	The [divine] cloud enveloped the mountain.	Exodus 24:16

Likewise, on the Day of Atonement, when we recreate this experience, the idea of covering or envelopment is back. When the High Priest offers his cloud of incense in the Holy of Holies...

וְכִסָּה עֲנַן הַקְּטֹרֶת אֶת הַכַּפֹּרֶת אֲשֶׁר עַל הָעֵדוּת	The cloud from the incense envelops the cover that is over [the Ark of] the Covenant.	Leviticus 16:13

I'd like to suggest to you that, on some level, the reason Yom Kippur is a day of "atonement" is because it is a day on which humankind makes contact with God. We become covered, or enveloped, by an emanation of the Divine, and this has the effect of leaving us pure. Indeed, if we see envelopment as an alternative translation for *kaf, peh, resh*, what if we read the very last verse of the Yom Kippur service (the verse that ostensibly talks about atonement) this way:

Leviticus 16:30

כִּי בַיּוֹם הַזֶּה **יְכַפֵּר** עֲלֵיכֶם
לְטַהֵר אֶתְכֶם מִכֹּל חַטֹּאתֵיכֶם
לִפְנֵי יְקֹוָה תִּטְהָרוּ׃

For on this day [God] **will envelop you,** to purify you; of all your sins, you shall be purified before God.

In other words, what is special about Yom Kippur is that it is the day on which God envelops us. We make contact with the Divine; our cloud merges with His. And what is the *effect* of this? We become purified. In a famous mishnah, Rabbi Akiva said it this way:

Yoma 8:9

אָמַר רַבִּי עֲקִיבָא, אַשְׁרֵיכֶם
יִשְׂרָאֵל, לִפְנֵי מִי אַתֶּם מִטַּהֲרִין,
וּמִי מְטַהֵר אֶתְכֶם, אֲבִיכֶם
שֶׁבַּשָּׁמַיִם, שֶׁנֶּאֱמַר ... (ירמיה
יז), מִקְוֵה יִשְׂרָאֵל יקוה, מַה
מִּקְוֶה מְטַהֵר אֶת הַטְּמֵאִים, אַף
הַקָּדוֹשׁ בָּרוּךְ הוּא מְטַהֵר אֶת
יִשְׂרָאֵל:

Rabbi Akiva said: Fortunate are you, O Israel! Before whom do you become pure? And who is it that purifies you? Your Father in Heaven, as it says:…"A mikveh of Israel is God" (Jer. 17:1). Just as a mikveh purifies the unclean, so too does the Holy One, blessed be He, purify Israel.

In Rabbi Akiva's words, our Parent in Heaven washes over us, takes us in. It is almost like a moment of rebirth. We go back from where we came and reemerge. Usually, that journey is not one that a child can survive and live. Just as no child can retreat back into the womb and survive, no human can become one again with God and survive. And yet somehow, Yom Kippur allows that to happen. And inasmuch as, once a year, God created a path for at least a single representative of humanity, the Kohen Gadol in the Holy of Holies, to make this perilous journey and emerge whole on the other side — that encounter with our Source has a by-product: We become purified. We are washed clean. Our close encounter with the Divine leaves us pure.[9]

Once a year, an immense opportunity awaits us. God waits to envelop us. Alas, we no longer have the service in the Tabernacle prescribed by

---

9 For more on the idea of mikveh in this vein, see the animated video entitled *Why Does the Mikveh Make Me Pure?* authored by Beth Lesch, at alephbeta.org.

Parshat Acharei Mot. But as I mentioned earlier, the Sages tell us that "the essence of the day" envelops us, too. Rambam, for one, suggests that the notion of encounter with the Divine is somehow built into Yom Kippur.[10] Indeed, an echo of **Parshat Acharei Mot**'s breathless moment of closeness with the Divine still awaits us, every year. And if, in advance of that, we can see our way to making a clean break with our sins and committing to a fresh new path in life, we too can emerge from that mysterious encounter unsullied, pure as a newborn child.

10 Rambam, *Hilchot Teshuvah*, 1:3.

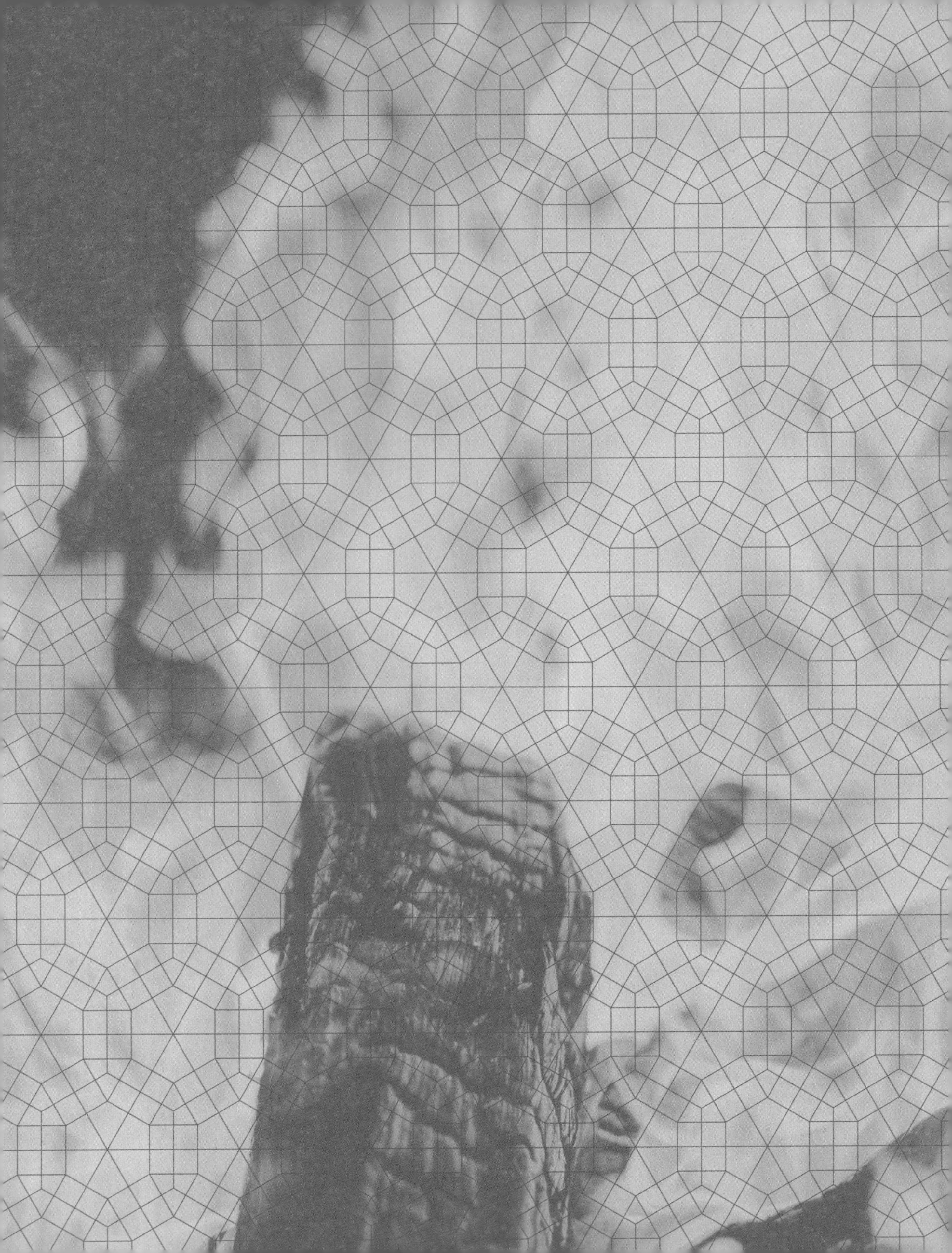

KEDOSHIM

When Bad Things Happen Between Good People

וְאָהַבְתָּ לְרֵעֲךָ כָּמוֹךָ Love your neighbor as yourself.

LEVITICUS 19:18

When Bad Things Happen Between Good People

PARSHAT KEDOSHIM CONTAINS ONE of the most famous phrases in the entire Torah:

וְאָהַבְתָּ לְרֵעֲךָ כָּמוֹךָ	Love your neighbor as yourself.	Leviticus 19:18

In the years since Rabbi Akiva suggested that these three words expressed a foundational principle of the Torah,[1] they've gone viral, as it were. "Love your neighbor as yourself" has become something of a catchphrase in everything from ancient works of Jewish ethics and philosophy to popular culture in the here and now. We hear the phrase intoned in sermons; we see it on our kids' color war banners; we find it invoked in political debate. Mothers and fathers use it to teach their children how to share on the playground. It permeates society, religious and secular alike.

But there's something... ever so slightly odd about the phrase. In Hebrew, it begins with a *vav*, which means the phrase actually reads: "*And* love your neighbor as yourself." Inquiring minds might want to know: What is that pesky "and" doing there? It seems utterly superfluous, so much so that most of the time, the "and" — at least in English — usually gets dropped. After all, when's the last time you saw a kid's color war banner trumpeting: "*And* love your neighbor as yourself"?

Well, if the "and" seems superfluous to *us*, evidently, it didn't seem superfluous to the Torah. And the reason, I'd suggest, is that "love your neighbor as yourself" is connected to that which precedes it. It appears as part of a larger verse, which in turn is part of a larger paragraph. In other words, "love your neighbor as yourself" is more than a three-word slogan

1 See *Bereishit Rabba* 24:7; Rashi on Lev. 19:18.

(in the Hebrew). To see the full import of the phrase, we have to see the "and"; meaning, we have to pull back the zoom lens and look at the larger context. When we do, a strikingly powerful idea will stand revealed, one whose potential to transform our lives is considerably greater than the disembodied three words that happen to form its climax.

Toy Story

Here is the larger context for that "love your neighbor as yourself" phrase:

Leviticus 19:17–18

לֹא תִשְׂנָא אֶת אָחִיךָ בִּלְבָבֶךָ
הוֹכֵחַ תּוֹכִיחַ אֶת עֲמִיתֶךָ וְלֹא
תִשָּׂא עָלָיו חֵטְא: לֹא תִקֹּם
וְלֹא תִטֹּר אֶת בְּנֵי עַמֶּךָ וְאָהַבְתָּ
לְרֵעֲךָ כָּמוֹךָ אֲנִי יְקֹוָה:

Do not hate your brother in your heart; reprove your fellow; do not, on his account, bear a sin. Do not take revenge or nurse a grudge against your countrymen. Love your neighbor as yourself; I am God.

Those two verses contain a small army of ideas, coming one after another rather relentlessly. To see the larger meaning of the verses, I'd like to play a little game with you. We might call it: *Take It Apart and Put It Back Together Again.*

This little game may seem simple, but it makes for an especially useful tool when reading the Torah's text. Like the best things you learned in kindergarten, once you learn how to use the tool well, it can be surprisingly salient.

To play *Take It Apart and Put It Back Together Again* just channel your inner child and harness your innate curiosity. What happens when you give a curious child a toy? First, they might play with it. But once the kid tires of that, he or she will invariably start to take the toy apart. In disassembling it, the child begins to understand what makes the toy go, what mechanism makes it do what it does. But truthfully, the child doesn't really complete his or her process of discovery until he stops taking the thing apart and tries to put it all back together again. To be sure, it is not always possible to reassemble poor Humpty-Dumpty. But if the child succeeds, they *really* come to understand that toy. They discern how the parts combine to create a working, marvelous whole.

So here is my challenge: Can we do the same with these verses? Can we take them apart and see their various components — and then, having seen the parts, can we successfully reconstruct the whole?

Heart Hatred

Let's begin by simply enumerating the ideas that appear here in **Parshat Kedoshim** (Lev. 19:17–18), as the lead-up to "love your neighbor as yourself." We will take a quick glance at each, and, as we do, we will try to notice anything odd, intriguing, or curious about the way the Torah expresses each idea.

The first idea in our list of phrases is this:

לֹא תִשְׂנָא אֶת אָחִיךָ בִּלְבָבֶךָ	Do not hate your brother in your heart.	Leviticus 19:17

At first blush, the Torah seems to be decrying hatred as a bad thing. We might solemnly nod our heads in agreement, until we notice ... some extra words in the phrase: *Wait a minute, what, exactly, does "in your heart" add to the picture?* By telling us not to hate our brother *in our hearts,* the text seems to narrow the scope of its admonition. Is the Torah suggesting that not *all* types of hatred are to be shunned, that only hatred "in your heart" should be avoided? Strange; hatred seems like such a negative emotion. Moreover, what, exactly, would that mean? What's the difference between just hating someone and hating them "in your heart"?

These are good questions. But for now, let's just make a mental note of these questions and move on. Once we put the toy back together, as it were, we will likely be in a better position to understand the curiosities of each individual part.

The Rest of the Sequence

The next ideas in the Torah's sequence are:

- הוֹכֵחַ תּוֹכִיחַ אֶת עֲמִיתֶךָ — "reprove your fellow." If you see someone doing something wrong, tell them about it.
- וְלֹא תִשָּׂא עָלָיו חֵטְא — "and do not, on his account, bear a sin." This phrase requires some parsing. If we translate the phrase carefully, tak-

ing note of the word עָלָיו, the Torah is not simply saying "do not bear a sin upon yourself," a more garden-variety phrase, but "do not on *his account* bear a sin." It sounds almost as if someone *else* might be doing something wrong, but *you*, somehow, could end up bearing the weight of that sin. Strange; how could that be? We'll have to try and figure out what this might be all about.

- לֹא תִקֹּם — "do not take revenge." Seems pretty straightforward.
- וְלֹא תִטֹּר — "and do not nurse a grudge." The word תִטֹּר here is interesting. It literally means to "guard" or "protect," as if one who bears a grudge against another is in some sense protecting that grudge. The English phrase "nurse a grudge" conveys something of this sense. One is not just bearing a grudge; he or she is safeguarding it — as if it were something precious that one wanted to gently nurture. The language of protection here is something we will want to come back to and explore further.
- וְאָהַבְתָּ לְרֵעֲךָ כָּמוֹךָ — "and love your fellow as yourself." [2]

---

2 Standing back and looking at this group of ideas, it seems that something else stands out about them, too. All these phrases regulate our interactions with other people. But what *kind* of other people? In other words: Who, exactly, is it that you aren't supposed to hate in your heart? Who should you reprove? Who is it that you shouldn't bear a grudge against? And who is it that you should love as yourself? Curiously, there is not a single answer to these questions; there are four of them. The Torah employs no less than four different descriptors for the people with whom we are interacting throughout these verses. Rendered somewhat literally, we might translate them as follows:

- "Do not hate your brother in your heart."
- "Reprove your kinsman."
- "Don't nurse a grudge against your countrymen."
- "Love your fellow as yourself." (One might, perhaps, translate this as "love your friend as yourself," but רֵעַ in this context probably means "fellow," as it does, for example, in Exodus 2:13, when Moses sees two Hebrews fighting and he accosts the aggressor with: "Why do you strike your רֵעַ — i.e., your fellow?")

What, exactly, are we to make of these changes? It is hard to tell, but it seems as if a kind of shift is taking place, as we move from phrase to phrase. The descriptors seem to move outward in concentric circles. The person closest to you is your brother; then your other relation, or your kinsman; then, your countryman; then, seemingly, just anyone — your fellow human being. It is as if, as we move from

Okay, so much for separating out the component parts. What about putting it all back together? Do these ideas truly just stand alone, or do they interact with one another to create a larger whole? If the latter, it is almost as if the Torah is relying on the reader to supply the implied transitions between the ideas. One might think of the ideas in the verses as if they were bones in a skeleton — and the question now becomes: What are the ligaments here? How do these bones connect with one another? Let's see if we can intuit what some of those connectors, or implied transition words, might be.

Putting the Toy Back Together Again

A good place to start would be the first two ideas we listed above: "Don't hate your brother in your heart," followed immediately by "reprove your kinsman." What, if anything, might be the missing transition word between those phrases?

I'd suggest it might be: The word *instead*. "Don't hate your brother in your heart. *Instead*… reprove him."

In this way of reading the verse, the Torah is actually offering a remarkable answer to the question: Is it okay to hate someone? The answer, as it turns out, is...yes. Surprisingly enough, hatred, per se, isn't off the table. What's off the table is hating someone… *in your heart*.

Fair warning: The basic ideas I'm expressing here about how these phrases are linked are not really my own; they were, for the most part, advanced hundreds of years ago by Ramban.[3] So here, in essence, is how

---

idea to idea, we learn something about how to extend our sense of connection outward. We are able to take those closest to ourselves, and those a little further out, and a little further out, still — and figure out how to "love them as ourselves": Find ways to connect, in solidarity with them all, much as we connect with our own sense of self (see Rabbi Shimon Shkopf, introduction to *Sha'arei Yosher*; cf. *Ohr HaChaim* on Lev. 19:17–18).

3 While the essence of the ideas in this essay come from Ramban (Lev. 19:17–18), I am building on those ideas somewhat, drawing them out to what I see as their natural conclusion. For reference, here are Ramban's words:

והנכון בעיני כי "הוכח תוכיח" כמו והוכיח אברהם את אבימלך (בראשית כא כה) ויאמר הכתוב אל תשנא את אחיך בלבבך בעשותו לך שלא כרצונך אבל תוכיחנו מדוע ככה עשית עמדי ולא תשא עליו חטא לכסות שנאתו בלבך ולא תגיד לו כי בהוכיחך

Ramban reads these first two phrases: Things sometimes go wrong between people. Things make you annoyed, and when they go badly enough, the natural human response is antipathy, hatred. But what are you supposed to *do* with that feeling? How one answers *that* question, actually, is where human relationships are made or broken. The Torah's answer to it, in effect, is: Don't forbid yourself from hating them. It is too dramatic a step, and may be humanly impossible. Forbid yourself from hating them ... *in your heart.*[4]

In other words, the feeling of hatred, in and of itself, is not the problem; the problem is smiling when you feel hatred. Keeping hatred in your heart; burying it deep inside, while you pretend that everything is fine — *that's* the problem.

Well, then, what should one do *instead* of hating someone in your heart? The Torah's answer to that is:

Leviticus 19:17	הוֹכֵחַ תּוֹכִיחַ אֶת עֲמִיתֶךָ וְלֹא תִשָּׂא עָלָיו חֵטְא׃	Reprove your kinsman; do not, on his account, bear a sin.

הוֹכֵחַ can literally mean to show or make clear. *Show your cards,* the Torah seems to be saying. Hatred likes to be secretive, to bury itself. Don't give in to that impulse. Be upfront. Find a way to tell your friend about your concerns.

And if you successfully do that? Well, that brings us to the next phrase in the verse: "And you will not, on his account, bear a sin." In other words:

אותו יתנצל לך או ישוב ויתודה על חטאו ותכפר לו ואחרי כן יזהיר שלא תנקום ממנו ולא תטור בלבבך מה שעשה לך כי יתכן שלא ישנא אותו אבל יזכור החטא בלבו ולפיכך יזהירנו שימחה פשע אחיו וחטאתו מלבו ואחרי כן יצוה שיאהב לו כמוהו.

4 See also Rambam, *Hilchot De'ot* 6:5, where he expresses these ideas quite forcefully:

וְלֹא הִזְהִירָה תּוֹרָה אֶלָּא עַל שִׂנְאָה שֶׁבַּלֵּב. אֲבָל הַמַּכֶּה אֶת חֲבֵרוֹ וְהַמְחָרְפוֹ אַף עַל פִּי שֶׁאֵינוֹ רַשַּׁאי אֵינוֹ עוֹבֵר מִשּׁוּם לֹא תִשְׂנָא.

"The Torah didn't forbid anything except hatred that remains buried in one's heart. But one who, for example, strikes his fellow and curses him — even though he is not allowed to do any of this, he does not transgress a Torah prohibition labeled 'do not hate' [for indeed, there is no such prohibition at all...]."

Imagine someone else has wronged you. That's their problem, really; it is *their* sin, not yours. But, if you fail in your response to the situation — if you end up hating the one who wronged you "in your heart" — well then, paradoxically, the tables will be turned and you'll end up being the one in the wrong. Try, then, to avoid that fate. Don't be the one to bear another's sin. Find a way to show your cards.

Rashi (Lev. 19:17) adds another wrinkle to these words. He suggests the phrase "And you will not, on his account, bear a sin" is intended as a warning: Show your cards to the other… but be careful as to how you do this. Don't do it in a way that causes *you* to be the wrongdoer. In other words, don't confront them about your concerns publicly, and embarrass them in front of others. Or, don't be gleefully confrontational, trying to back your opponent into a corner. Be constructive, not hurtful. Figure out how they can best hear what you want to tell them. If you do that, you've done right by them. You've shown your cards properly.

Let's continue, and examine the next words the verses lay out before us. These words speak of revenge — and of grudges that get nursed, almost as if they were something precious....

When Resentment Displaces Affection

לֹא תִקֹּם וְלֹא תִטֹּר אֶת בְּנֵי עַמֶּךָ	Do not take revenge or nurse a grudge against your countrymen.	Leviticus 19:18

Here, we learn of the poisonous consequences of *not* following the Torah's advice about what to do with feelings of anger or hatred. We learn of what it really means to "bear sin." Imagine that someone really offends you, and you end up hating them, deep in your heart — but all the while you smile, and never let the other know that they upset you. What sin, exactly, comes about when you take this approach?

Well, on the surface, things are swell. You certainly look happy enough. If you're a good enough actor, you can walk around seeming rather pleasant. Moreover, your pleasant exterior might even help you to rationalize why it's okay — nay, even virtuous — to keep your anger to yourself: *Why should I rock the boat and bring up how hurt I felt? I can handle it. I can still smile when I see them in the hallway. I'm perfectly fine. Yes, my job here is to be perfectly nice.* But *is* everything fine? The verses' sobering judgment is: *It's not.*

Why? Because secret hatred never really stays secret. The only question is: How, exactly, will it come out? What form will it take? And that's what the text tells us about:

Leviticus 19:18

לֹא תִקֹּם וְלֹא תִטֹּר	Do not take revenge or nurse a grudge.

What's the difference between taking revenge against someone and bearing a grudge against them? Rashi (Lev. 19:18) considers this question, and interprets the two as mirror images of one another. He gives two examples to illustrate the point. Here they are, with only a bit of poetic license: "I asked you to lend me an ax and you didn't lend me an ax. So tomorrow, when you ask for my wheelbarrow, I'm not lending the wheelbarrow to you." That's revenge. It is pretty straightforward. But the truth is, you don't have to actually withhold that wheelbarrow in order to act maliciously. In other words, your response to the wheelbarrow request can *seem* sweeter but be no less poisonous: Say you *do* lend the wheelbarrow when tomorrow comes — but with a snide reminder: "Sure you can borrow my wheelbarrow! I'm not like some people who don't lend axes." That's bearing a grudge.

People can easily rationalize their grudges. I stoically walk around smiling, telling myself I can handle my anger, that when he wants to borrow something *of course* I'll lend it to him. But it's with bitterness. Whether you say it or not, your eyes and your heart say it: *"I'm not like some people who don't lend axes. I'm not like you."*

Bearing a grudge is in some ways even more insidious than taking revenge. I mentioned before that the Hebrew expression לֹא תִטֹּר has an interesting connotation. It means to "protect," even to "nurture." Indeed, when things are going well between you and me, I protect and nurture ... my *relationship* with you. I speak kindly and respectfully to you. I give you the benefit of the doubt. I may buy you a little gift here and there. But when things go wrong between us, something twisted happens. I continue to protect and nurture, but instead of nurturing affection, I nurture ... resentment. I nurse a grudge.

Indeed, resentment, smoldering beneath a facade of polite smiles, has a way of tricking its bearer. Without my ever really noticing it, the affection in our relationship starts to dwindle, and resentment steps into the void. I end up nursing that grudge, carefully coddling it. For in some tragic way, it is all that I have left of our relationship. It is all that is keeping us connected.

And so, the Torah tells us: *Don't seek revenge; don't nurse a grudge.* You *can't* bury hatred inside, without anyone else being the wiser. It just doesn't work. Repressed hatred can't, really, be contained. It *always* comes out — either overtly, in an explosion of revenge, or covertly, in the form of the grudge that lurks behind your smile. One way or another it will come out.

A Path to Love

Finally, the Torah brings us to the culmination of our journey:

וְאָהַבְתָּ לְרֵעֲךָ כָּמוֹךָ And love your neighbor as yourself. Leviticus 19:18

Consider the mighty implications of that final *vav*, that little "*and*" before "love your neighbor as yourself." It connects this last phrase to all those that came before it, as if to say, *There was a journey here! It took all of the above to get to love!* Indeed, those famous words, "love your neighbor as yourself," aren't meant to stand by themselves, as if they were some disembodied slogan. The Torah isn't making an exclamatory declaration of blind fact: *Here is what everybody has to do: Love everybody!* No. The Torah is giving you… a *path* to love.

It is a realistic path, meant for real people. Because sometimes bad things happen between good people. The Torah is giving you a path to love in the face of those bad things.

The path starts with the possibility of hatred. You want to hate the one who just offended you? Fine! But at all costs, don't hate them in your heart. Almost as if to inoculate the aggrieved party against the seduction of hatred, the Torah *allows* hatred — under certain circumstances. *Of course you can hate, no problem, hate away! Just do one thing first: Show your cards.* If you feel aggrieved, then lay out, carefully and constructively, in the best way you can, what it is that's bothering you, and talk about it with the person you think offended you.

Stop and consider what a powerful check on hatred that really is. If I'm *allowed* to hate — but first I have to make my case to you about what went wrong and how I feel about it — well, what, exactly, are the possibilities?

Let's imagine: What might happen next?

One possibility is: I might start to realize I don't really have a case to make. The requirement to actually verbalize to the person who supposedly offended me, how I see the situation — might, in itself, be enough to wake me up to the possibility that I haven't necessarily sized up the situation accurately, that there is another side to this story, one that I hadn't fully considered. That's one way of draining the energy out of my feeling of righteous outrage.

Alternatively, let's say I *do* make my case sensitively and carefully. Then what might happen? Ramban (as I mentioned before, this theory really comes from him) plays out the possibilities:

One possibility: Maybe we reconcile. I've shown them what's on my mind. That gives them a chance, possibly, to explain: "My goodness; I think you really misunderstood me. Here's what I was really trying to say...."

Or let's say there was no misunderstanding. Once I make my case; once I let another know that I was hurt by something they said or did... that gives the other a chance to apologize. They can reply: "You know, that really wasn't very sensitive of me. I'm sorry I said it; I feel bad about it."

And finally, of course, there's one more possibility: If, at the end of the day, you show your cards to the one who offended you — "Here's why I was hurt by what you did" — and they agree that there was no misunderstanding, that they really *did* want to hurt you; and they are unwilling, even now, to show any remorse for that — well, if that's the case, then, sure, go ahead and hate them. But at least you gave it the ol' college try. At least you showed your cards. You didn't bury your hatred while you smiled on the outside. You didn't allow the tables to be turned so that you bore the weight of wrongdoing in your relationship with them.

In asking us all to put our cards on the table when we find ourselves offended, the Torah is asking us to take a bold chance. We are being asked not to give up on a relationship with a brother, a kinsman, a countryman, or even a fellow human being.[5] The Torah is laying out for us a pathway to friendship; a pathway to love. A pathway that, intriguingly enough, began with the possibility of hatred.

The Birth of Friendship

Isn't it interesting that the Torah begins this sequence of verses by considering the possibility of hatred, and ends it by advancing the possibility of love? By doing this, the text is suggesting, I think, something sobering and truthful about friendship: It isn't the case that friends are those we never get into fights with. More than that, it isn't even true that friends are all people we started out liking. Maybe your relationship with someone got off on the wrong foot. Maybe they annoyed you or seem to have slighted you. That doesn't mean they can't become, or can't stay, your friend. Indeed, where your relationship with them ends up depends less on what first happened between you that you don't like, and more on what you choose, now, to do about that.

Yes, what you do now, *after* someone annoys you — that is the crucial thing. If you follow the Torah's path, as laid out in these verses, you stand the best possible chance of transforming that person from a potential enemy into an actual friend.

From *Ra* to *Rei'a*

This basic truth may perhaps be hinted at in a double entendre that lurks in the phrase "love your neighbor as yourself." The word for "neighbor" there, in Hebrew, is רע — a word that sometimes means "friend" (see, for example, Prov. 27:10). And yet these very same letters — רע — in Hebrew, admit of yet another meaning, too: When vowelized differently, the same letters mean "evil," "bad," or "wrong' — terms we associate with those who are the last people we might wish to befriend.

The double entendre might, perhaps, be revealing. For in the overall arc of these two verses, we might say, the Torah is suggesting how we might transform one kind of רע into another. Things can go wrong between us and our brothers, our kinsmen, our countrymen, our fellow human beings. That's the way life goes. Any of these people you once felt close to,

---

5 See above, n. 2.

at some point, may seem to wrong you. But when that happens, the important thing to remember is: *This doesn't have to be the end of the road for you and them.* There's a way to transform, for the good, a moment of wrongdoing. If we succeed in showing our cards, in speaking sensitively to the one we are angry at and inviting a genuine response; and if we can then listen to that response with real openness and curiosity — if we can do all that, we stand a chance of salvaging the relationship. We can banish vengeance and the nursing of grudges. And in so doing, we can lay fertile ground for friendship to make a comeback.

A Postscript

TRUTH TO TELL, I had originally intended to end this essay on **Parshat Kedoshim** right where you and I just left it, with the words above. But in the weeks after I wrote this, I was chatting about these ideas with a lively group of students, and something emerged from that discussion I want to share with you. Hence, this postscript.

It all began when one of the students, Avi Shinnar, noticed something rather intriguing: An apparent correlation between the ideas we'd been talking about in **Parshat Kedoshim** and a story that happened way back in the book of Genesis. Somehow, all the ideas we had been talking about in **Parshat Kedoshim** — *don't hate your brother in your heart; reprove him; don't take revenge or bear a grudge; love your neighbor as yourself* — seemed to come to life in that earlier story. There they expressed themselves not as a series of laws, but as an actual human drama.

A closer look at the texts revealed a number of linguistic correspondences between the two passages as well. It seemed like the more you looked, the more you saw. I found myself wondering: Are we, the readers of the Torah, meant to see these two texts as connected somehow? Could this earlier story in Genesis be some kind of precursor, or template, for the laws we've been looking at in **Parshat Kedoshim**?

It would be really something if that were true. *But was it true?* In these pages, I'd like to at least show you some of the resonances we saw, and begin to explore with you what, if anything, it might all mean.

All in the Family

So what story was it, back in Genesis, that seemed to resonate with these verses in **Parshat Kedoshim**? I'm glad you asked. The story Avi was talking about was the conflict between Cain and Abel.

Why even think that the story of Cain and Abel has anything to do with these verses in **Parshat Kedoshim**? Well, if you think about Cain and Abel, the first thing that comes to mind is . . . hatred between brothers — and, lo and behold, in **Parshat Kedoshim**, the Torah just happens to admonish us not to secretly hate one's *brother*, of all people:

Leviticus 19:17	לֹא תִשְׂנָא אֶת אָחִיךָ בִּלְבָבֶךָ	Do not hate your brother in your heart.

Do those words perhaps allude to a moment in time, way back at the dawn of human history, when the terrible scourge of secret hatred got its start in human history — specifically between *brothers*? Maybe. But one could, of course, object: That's not really how you and I are used to seeing the Cain and Abel story, is it? After all, while Cain might have hated Abel — he *did* end up killing him, remember — it doesn't, at first blush, seem like he hated him *secretly*. He did after all strike his brother dead. What's "secret" about all that?

But if we look at the story a little more carefully — review its steps in slow motion, as it were — we will actually find an element of secret hatred there after all. Moreover, once we see this, we will notice something else, too: Murder *wasn't* a foregone conclusion in the Cain and Abel confrontation. The text actually seems to go out of its way to suggest how and why another possible ending *should have* — and very nearly almost *did* — come about.

So let's go back to the Cain and Abel story and refresh our memory about how this conflict between brothers played itself out.

Cain Is Angry. But at Whom?

The outline of the story itself is familiar to us: Cain and Abel both bring offerings to God. While God turns toward Abel's offering with favor, the Almighty is, for some reason, displeased with Cain's. At this, Cain responds with fury:

Genesis 4:5	וַיִּחַר לְקַיִן מְאֹד וַיִּפְּלוּ פָּנָיו	And Cain was very angry and his face fell.

That Cain is motivated by anger at this moment is explicit in the text. But it is not entirely clear toward whom, exactly, that anger is directed. Two possible targets suggest themselves. On the one hand, Cain might be angry at his brother: *What was Abel doing outshining me before God?* Alternatively, it might be the Almighty Himself that Cain is angry at: *Why, God, did You not accept my offering?*

Evidently, Cain decided it is Abel that he is angry at, for he strikes him and ends up killing him. But one wonders why. All Abel did was bring an offering, just as his brother did. He had no way of knowing, or controlling, how God would respond. It was God, after all, who made the choice that disappointed Cain. It may well be that this first story of human conflict is, in actuality, a story of displaced anger. Cain might have been angry at the Almighty — but convinced himself he was angry at Abel instead. Abel, after all, is certainly the easier target. You can't see God. You can't touch Him. You can't hit Him with a rock.

What Did He Say?

Another thing that bears notice about Cain's attack against Abel is that it is preceded by a conversation. Or at least, the beginnings of one. For just before Cain strikes Abel, he seems to invite his brother into the fields for a little chat:

וַיֹּאמֶר קַיִן אֶל הֶבֶל אָחִיו	And Cain said to Abel, his brother.	Genesis 4:8

It is a strange kind of phrase, this "and Cain said to Abel, his brother." You would expect the next words to be...what Cain actually says to Abel. But we never hear about that.[6] It's almost like he said ... nothing. Instead, the verse gives us this brute fact:

וַיָּקָם קַיִן אֶל הֶבֶל אָחִיו וַיַּהַרְגֵהוּ	And Cain got up against his brother, Abel, and killed him.	Genesis 4:8

---

6 Here, I am looking directly at the words of the Torah. We do not see that Cain said anything. However, midrashim abound offering different versions of what this conversation was about. See, for example, *Bereishit Rabba* 22:7 *Midrash Tanchuma Bereishit* 9:2.

The sense of the text is that there was a kind of interrupted conversation here. Cain was *about* to say something to Abel, but then, at the last minute, he didn't.[7] And in the void left by his silence, Cain's actions preempted his words: He got up and killed his brother.

All in all, the text implies that Cain *almost* did what the verses in Leviticus suggest you *should* do in a situation like this: *Don't hate your brother in your heart. Tell him what the issue is; show your cards to him.* But instead, Cain turned his back on that course of action at the last moment. He attacked Abel instead of talking to him. What might have happened had Cain actually followed through on that conversation with his brother? Perhaps words might have led to reconciliation. But in their absence, smoldering anger erupted into violence instead.

"Getting Up" to Kill

What kind of violence? We don't really know exactly how Cain killed Abel. The Torah only tells us that Cain did, in fact, kill him. But the careful reader will notice that the text tells us just a smidgen more than this. Look once more at the verse that describes Cain's attack; do you notice anything extraneous about it?

Genesis 4:8

וַיֹּאמֶר קַיִן אֶל הֶבֶל אָחִיו וַיְהִי בִּהְיוֹתָם בַּשָּׂדֶה **וַיָּקָם** קַיִן אֶל הֶבֶל אָחִיו וַיַּהַרְגֵהוּ׃

And Cain said to Abel, his brother — and when they were in the field together, Cain **got up** toward his brother, Abel, and killed him.

---

7 Remember, the verse doesn't say *vayedaber Kayin el Hevel,* that Cain "spoke" to Abel. Instead, it says *vayomer Kayin el Hevel,* that Cain "said" to Abel — and that's what makes the phrase puzzling. Think about it from the standpoint of basic grammar: If x *spoke* to y, I don't need to know what x *said* for that to be a complete thought. But if x *said* to y…well, for that to be a complete thought, I need to know what x said. The Torah seems to break its own rules of grammar by telling us that Cain "said" to Abel… but then *not* telling us what Cain said. The explanation I put forth here — that the Torah is intentionally creating the sense of an interrupted conversation here — was suggested to me years ago by a teacher of mine, Rabbi Yosef Leibowitz.

What more information, really, am I given by the text with this little addition about Cain "getting up toward his brother"? Let's say the text had omitted it, and all we heard was that, when Cain was in the field with Abel, he killed him. Would we *really* know any less about what happened? Why, then, did the text bother to tell us that Cain "got up" toward his brother?

It seems just a little thing, and had there been nothing else unusual about that phrase, וַיָּקָם קַיִן — "*and Cain got up* toward his brother," perhaps we would just shrug our shoulders and move on. But there *is* something else unusual about it. It turns out that this phrase has an echo: A word composed of these very same letters, in the very same order, appears once more in this very same story of Cain and Abel.

It happens just a few lines later. After Cain kills Abel, God tells him that the earth will be cursed on his account, and that he will be a wanderer, never able to settle down. Cain hears this and tells God that he fears that anyone who finds him will kill him. The Almighty responds to him with this reassurance:

לָכֵן כָּל הֹרֵג קַיִן שִׁבְעָתַיִם **יֻקָּם**	Therefore, anyone who kills Cain will meet with sevenfold **vengeance**.	Genesis 4:15

There it is — the same three letters, in the same order: יקם, *yukam*. But this time, the letters are vowelized so as to mean something else: *vengeance.*[8] God tells Cain that should anyone kill him for his actions, Cain's death will be severely avenged.

Could this resonance with the earlier יקם be mere coincidence? Possibly. But if we widen our field of view a little bit, we will notice that it isn't just the one word יקם that connects Genesis 4:8 to Genesis 4:15. More elements of the two verses also echo one another:

---

8 *Vayakom*, from the root *kof-yod-mem*, means "and he got up." The same letters, vowelized as *yukam*, come from an entirely different root, *nun-kof-mem*, and mean "he will be avenged."

GENESIS 4:15	GENESIS 4:8
לָכֵן כָּל הֹרֵג קַיִן שִׁבְעָתַיִם יֻקָּם	וַיָּקָם קַיִן אֶל הֶבֶל אָחִיו וַיַּהַרְגֵהוּ
Therefore, anyone who **kills Cain** will meet with sevenfold **vengeance**.	And he **got up, Cain** did, against his brother, Abel, and **killed him**.

Somehow, what is happening in the later verse seems to have had its antecedent in the earlier verse. When God spoke to Cain about his death being "avenged" (יקם) should anyone kill him, it sounds like the template for that, somehow, was… Cain "getting up" (יקם) and killing his brother. Almost as if the former use of the term יקם didn't *just* mean "getting up," but is meant to suggest overtones of vengeance as well.

In other words, in adding these seemingly superfluous words, that Cain "got up toward" his brother and killed him, the text is telling us not so much *how* Cain attacked Abel but *why* he did so. We are hearing something important about Cain's motive. *Why* did he strike his brother? The answer is: It had to do with vengeance. So much so that later, when God promises vengeance for Cain's killer, God appears to refer back to Cain's own act — as if to say, "Cain, you should know something about killing in vengeance. Isn't that, after all, what you once did?"

But if the Torah is, in fact, hinting to us that when Cain "got up" and killed Abel, what pushed him to act was a desire for revenge, we could be excused for asking: *Revenge for what?* What, after all, did Abel really do to Cain that might warrant vengeance? Sure, I can understand why Cain might *resent* Abel. Cain might say that Abel copied his idea of bringing an offering to God, and then one-upped him by bringing a more pleasing offering. But still, at the end of the day, *vengeance* seems a little out of place here. After all, it was God, not Abel, who turned away from Cain's offering. That was God's choice, not Abel's. All of which brings us back to the question I raised earlier: *Who, really, is Cain angry at here?* It would seem like the more appropriate target of his anger is his Father in Heaven. *God, why accept his offering and not mine? I'm Your creature, too. Do You love him more than You love me?*

The Antidote to Misplaced Vengeance

Let's add all this up, then. The text suggests that Cain's actions were fueled by a desire for revenge, and yet this desire for revenge seems oddly misplaced. Cain's anger might have been more logically directed against God. And that, it seems to me, injects a note of tragedy into the story. It makes Abel's death seem senseless. It's as if Cain worked himself up against the wrong target, blindly vowing vengeance against someone who never, seemingly, acted with malice in the first place. Which, it seems to me, brings us right back to the Torah's commands in **Parshat Kedoshim**:

GENESIS 4:8 **CAIN AND ABEL**	**LEVITICUS 19:18** **DON'T EXACT VENGEANCE**
וַיְהִי בִּהְיוֹתָם בַּשָּׂדֶה **וַיָּקָם** קַיִן אֶל הֶבֶל אָחִיו וַיַּהַרְגֵהוּ׃ Cain **got up [in revenge]** against his brother, Abel, and killed him.	לֹא **תִקֹּם** וְלֹא תִטֹּר אֶת בְּנֵי עַמֶּךָ וְאָהַבְתָּ לְרֵעֲךָ כָּמוֹךָ אֲנִי יְקוָה׃ Do not **take revenge** or nurse a grudge against your countrymen. Love your neighbor as yourself.

We suggested earlier that the whole point, really, of the Torah's demand that we reprove those we think we hate — *show your cards, rather than hate in your heart* — was to prevent a tragedy of this very sort from occurring. In requiring us to talk to those we think offended us, to show our cards to them and tell them why we are upset, the Torah is in effect creating a powerful check on unnecessary or even unwarranted anger. If I'm not allowed to pretend we are buddies when I really hate you; if I have to actually talk with you about why I am upset, rather than harbor anger in my heart — all sorts of possibilities emerge: You can apologize or explain. Or… in trying to think over what I'm going to say when I confront you and have our little talk, I might well come to realize that my grounds for hating you are illusory. I may come to understand that you are not the one I'm really angry at. One way or another, the Torah's imperative to "show my cards" defuses the all-too-human, adrenaline-fueled, rush to revenge.

If, indeed, the case of Cain somehow prefigures these laws in **Parshat Kedoshim**, it may well be that those very laws are intended, by the Torah, to point us toward fixing what went wrong in that first, primal story, so that we don't make the same mistakes Cain did. The unfinished conversation between Cain and Abel is perhaps meant to make us ponder: If Cain had actually followed through on talking to Abel, would he still have been convinced that he needed to take vengeance against him? Or, once his cards were truly on the table, perhaps it would have become clear to Cain that, embarrassingly enough, the one you *think* you want to kill is not, actually, the one who hurt you after all.

A Burden of Shifting and Unimaginable Proportions

If Cain ever comes to realize this truth, it comes too late. After killing his brother by his own hand, with the benefit of hindsight, Cain feels utterly unable to bear the burden of his impetuous act:

Genesis: 4:13

וַיֹּאמֶר קַיִן אֶל יְקוָה גָּדוֹל עֲוֹנִי מִנְּשֹׂא	And Cain said to God: My sin is greater than I can bear.

Remarkably, this phrase, too — "my sin is greater than I can bear" — finds an echo in the precepts we've been looking at in **Parshat Kedoshim**:

GENESIS 4:13 CAIN AND ABEL	LEVITICUS 19:17 THE LAWS IN PARSHAT KEDOSHIM
וַיֹּאמֶר קַיִן אֶל יְקוָה גָּדוֹל עֲוֹנִי **מִנְּשׂוֹא:** And Cain said to God: My sin is greater than I can **bear**.	הוֹכֵחַ תּוֹכִיחַ אֶת עֲמִיתֶךָ וְלֹא **תִשָּׂא** עָלָיו חֵטְא: Reprove your fellow (show your cards), and do not **bear** his sin upon you.

Parshat Kedoshim warns us that when we fail to explain why we feel hurt, and instead allow our anger at our supposed nemesis to fester in secret — in these situations, the moral burden of the situation can quickly and surprisingly shift. It might *seem* as if the guilty party is the one who offended you. But if you keep your hatred locked in your own heart and don't reveal to the other why you think they've hurt you, you might find *yourself* bearing the moral burden of the conflict instead of your supposed nemesis. That shift will invariably feel surprising, given that, in the beginning, thoughts of vengeance are usually motivated by righteous indignation. The indignant one always thinks they are in the right, but they may well be wrong about that, if they fail to closely examine their assumptions. Indeed, they are *certainly* wrong about it, if they fail to speak up, make their case for real, and give the other a chance to explain or apologize.

The bottom line is this: By *not* having that difficult conversation with your nemesis, you are laying the groundwork for the conflict between you two to spiral out of control, in cycles of needless and avoidable vengeance and counter-vengeance. And when those spirals escalate to an ultimate point, as they did with Cain, the newfound burden of wrongdoing can seem unbearable, indeed:

גָּדוֹל עֲוֹנִי מִנְּשֹׂא׃	And Cain said to God: My sin is greater than I can bear.	Genesis: 4:13

A Cautionary Tale

Viewed through the prism of **Parshat Kedoshim**, the story of Cain and Abel stands revealed as a cautionary tale. It demonstrates exactly what *not* to do when you find yourself suddenly stirred by righteous anger and thoughts of vengeance. *Don't* let the temptation of secret hatred lay its insidious trap. *Don't* keep anger sequestered in your heart, safely away from the light of day. *Don't* short-circuit your attempt to speak to the one who you think hurt you. Showing your cards to your adversary might seem hard to do. *But do it anyway.* For if you can muster the courage, strength, and sensitivity to talk, constructively, about what's on your mind, you may find, to your surprise, that your brother has not earned your vengeance, after all. Moreover, you might just find that the brother you were tempted to hate — forever, secretly — is someone who, going forward, you can actually count as a friend. For indeed, recall how those precepts in **Parshat Kedoshim** end. Not with hate, but with love:

Leviticus 19:18

וְאָהַבְתָּ לְרֵעֲךָ כָּמוֹךָ	And love your neighbor as yourself.

The Central Tenet of the Torah

If we are right about the Cain and Abel story being a kind of antecedent for the series of laws we've been looking at in **Parshat Kedoshim**, and if we are right that the reader of the Cain and Abel narrative is meant to perceive how excruciatingly close the story came to a radically different, and much happier, ending — we might gain a somewhat new perspective on those famous, immortal words of Rabbi Akiva about **Parshat Kedoshim**'s dictum that one should "love your neighbor as yourself":

Sifra, Kedoshim, 4:12

אָמַר רַבִּי עֲקִיבָא זֶה כְּלָל גָּדוֹל בַּתּוֹרָה	Rabbi Akiva says: This is the central tenet of the Torah.

Where did Rabbi Akiva get that contention from? What made him so deeply convinced that this, of all things, was the most basic principle in the Torah? It may well be that Rabbi Akiva had an obvious source for that conviction of his. What story did the Torah choose to tell as it began to recount human history for its readers? Mankind leaves paradise and then — a primal conflict between brothers ensues. And what was that conflict meant to illustrate?

It illustrates how a single conversation between brothers — or the lack of one — can be a kind of knife's edge on which the destiny of brothers can turn. Had Cain been able to muster the courage and sensitivity to constructively broach, with his brother, his feelings of anger and intense disappointment — had he taken *that* path, instead of the path of silence, followed by vengeance, the tale of Cain and Abel would have stood for time immemorial as a living example of how a relationship could come back from the brink. Their drama would have embodied **Parshat**

Kedoshim's insistence that hatred *can* be surmounted, that the impetus to revenge *can* be conquered, and that brotherly love *can* be renewed even when their relationship has been marred by rage.

Alas, this first story of human conflict ended differently. But even so, Rabbi Akiva would argue, its primacy as the first story of the Torah is not diminished. It stands eternally, in the Torah, as a living testament of what *not* to do when the possibility of secret hatred beckons to us. And that is what the precepts we've been studying in **Parshat Kedoshim** codify. They are the most basic tenets of the Torah, emerging from the most basic story that human history begins with: The impetus to hate secretly *must* be conquered. Anger and disappointment *must* see the light of day. And if we learn those very hard lessons, our closest relationships, even when beset by crisis, can live to see another day.

THE CAIN AND ABEL NARRATIVE AND PARSHAT KEDOSHIM'S PASSAGES ABOUT SECRET HATRED AND REVENGE

CAIN RELATES TO ABEL	
GENESIS 4:3–15 **CAIN AND ABEL**	**LEVITICUS 19:17–18** **SECRET HATRED AND REVENGE**
וַיְהִי מִקֵּץ יָמִים וַיָּבֵא קַיִן מִפְּרִי הָאֲדָמָה מִנְחָה לַיקוָה: וְהֶבֶל הֵבִיא גַם הוּא מִבְּכֹרוֹת צֹאנוֹ וּמֵחֶלְבֵהֶן וַיִּשַׁע יְקוָה אֶל הֶבֶל וְאֶל מִנְחָתוֹ: וְאֶל־קַיִן וְאֶל מִנְחָתוֹ לֹא שָׁעָה[9] וַיִּחַר לְקַיִן מְאֹד וַיִּפְּלוּ פָּנָיו: וַיֹּאמֶר יְקוָה אֶל קָיִן לָמָּה חָרָה לָךְ וְלָמָּה נָפְלוּ פָנֶיךָ: הֲלוֹא אִם תֵּיטִיב שְׂאֵת וְאִם לֹא תֵיטִיב לַפֶּתַח חַטָּאת רֹבֵץ וְאֵלֶיךָ תְּשׁוּקָתוֹ וְאַתָּה תִּמְשָׁל בּוֹ: וַיֹּאמֶר קַיִן אֶל הֶבֶל	לֹא תִשְׂנָא אֶת אָחִיךָ בִּלְבָבֶךָ הוֹכֵחַ תּוֹכִיחַ אֶת עֲמִיתֶךָ וְלֹא תִשָּׂא עָלָיו חֵטְא: לֹא תִקֹּם וְלֹא תִטֹּר אֶת בְּנֵי עַמֶּךָ וְאָהַבְתָּ לְרֵעֲךָ כָּמוֹךָ אֲנִי יְקוָה:

9 Karen Goldberger points out: Here it is God not "liking" Cain — but God doesn't keep that to Himself: He reproves Cain, showing His cards; thereby, God models to Cain what the latter should do with *his* anger toward his brother.

אָחִיו וַיְהִי בִּהְיוֹתָם בַּשָּׂדֶה וַיָּקָם קַיִן אֶל הֶבֶל אָחִיו וַיַּהַרְגֵהוּ: וַיֹּאמֶר יְקוָה אֶל קַיִן אֵי הֶבֶל אָחִיךָ וַיֹּאמֶר לֹא יָדַעְתִּי הֲשֹׁמֵר אָחִי אָנֹכִי: וַיֹּאמֶר מֶה עָשִׂיתָ קוֹל דְּמֵי אָחִיךָ צֹעֲקִים אֵלַי מִן הָאֲדָמָה: וְעַתָּה אָרוּר אָתָּה מִן הָאֲדָמָה אֲשֶׁר פָּצְתָה אֶת פִּיהָ לָקַחַת אֶת דְּמֵי אָחִיךָ מִיָּדֶךָ: כִּי תַעֲבֹד אֶת הָאֲדָמָה לֹא תֹסֵף תֵּת כֹּחָהּ לָךְ נָע וָנָד תִּהְיֶה בָאָרֶץ: וַיֹּאמֶר קַיִן אֶל יְקוָה גָּדוֹל עֲוֹנִי מִנְּשֹׂא: הֵן גֵּרַשְׁתָּ אֹתִי הַיּוֹם מֵעַל פְּנֵי הָאֲדָמָה וּמִפָּנֶיךָ אֶסָּתֵר וְהָיִיתִי נָע וָנָד בָּאָרֶץ וְהָיָה כָל מֹצְאִי יַהַרְגֵנִי: וַיֹּאמֶר לוֹ יְקוָה לָכֵן כָּל הֹרֵג קַיִן שִׁבְעָתַיִם יֻקָּם וַיָּשֶׂם יְקוָה לְקַיִן אוֹת לְבִלְתִּי הַכּוֹת אֹתוֹ כָּל מֹצְאוֹ:	
In the course of time, Cain brought an offering to the Lord from the fruit of the soil; and Abel, for his part, brought the choicest of the firstlings of his flock. The Lord paid heed to Abel and his offering, but to Cain and his offering He paid no heed. **Cain was much distressed** and his face fell. And the Lord said to Cain, "Why are you distressed, And why is your face fallen? Surely, if you do right, there is uplift. But if you do not do right Sin crouches at the door; its urge is toward you, yet you can be its master." **Cain said to his brother Abel**...and when they were in the field, **Cain set** upon his brother Abel and killed him. The Lord said to Cain, "Where is your brother Abel?" And he said, "I do not know. **Am I my brother's keeper?**" Then He said, "What have you done? Hark, the voice of your brother's blood cries out to Me from the ground! Therefore, you shall be more cursed than	Do not hate your brother in your heart; reprove your fellow; do not, on his account, bear a sin. **Do not take revenge** or nurse a grudge against your countrymen. Love your neighbor as yourself; I am God (Lev. 19:17–18).

the ground, which opened its mouth to receive your brother's blood from your hand. If you till the soil, it shall no longer yield its strength to you. You shall become a ceaseless wanderer on earth." Cain said to the Lord, "**My punishment is too great to bear!** Since You have banished me this day from the soil, and I must avoid Your Presence and become a restless wanderer on earth — anyone who meets me may kill me!" The Lord said to him, "I promise, if anyone kills Cain, sevenfold **vengeance** shall be taken on him." And the Lord put a mark on Cain, lest anyone who met him should kill him (Gen. 4:3–15).	

CAIN RELATES TO ABEL	
CAIN AND ABEL	**SECRET HATRED AND REVENGE**
Cain becomes enraged.	"Don't hate your brother in your heart."
Cain invites Abel to a conversation...but it is short-circuited; he never says anything to him.	"Reprove your kinsman"; tell him your concerns.
Cain "gets up" toward his brother, seeking revenge against him.	"Don't take revenge."
Cain protests that he is not his brother's keeper.[10]	"Don't keep a grudge."
"My sin is greater than I can bear."	"Don't bear his sin upon yourself."

---

10 The connection here is based on the Hebrew root for "keep," (*shin-mem-reish*), which appears both in Cain's protest that he is not his brother's "keeper," and in **Parshat Kedoshim**'s insistence that one should not "keep," or nurse, a grudge. The correspondence between the two passages is particularly intriguing, I think. For there is something about Cain's dismissive stance — his sarcastic retort to God that he isn't responsible for the safety of his brother — that deeply resonates with the passive-aggressive stance toward rage that fuels a grudge. **Parshat Kedoshim** tells us we must not "guard" or "keep" a grudge — and one might think that Cain, *after* he killed his brother, has finally settled the score with him, and is no longer in a position to be keeping grudges. But in a way, it's not true: Although Cain has already killed Abel, he *still* acts with passive-aggressive spite toward him, tauntingly suggesting that he is not his brother's "guard" or "keeper."

Cain's protestations deceptively minimize his own guilt: He killed his brother, and yet he is pretending he didn't do more than fail to "guard" him. But even more insidiously, Cain is suggesting that he didn't act with malice, only with justified apathy. And that, really, is the essence of grudge bearing: the lie we tell, even to ourselves, about our own lack of *malevolent motivations: "I'm not like some people I know who don't lend axes. Sure, you can have my wheelbarrow!"*

EMOR

A Solar System in Time

אֵלֶּה מוֹעֲדֵי יְקוָה מִקְרָאֵי
קֹדֶשׁ אֲשֶׁר תִּקְרְאוּ אֹתָם
בְּמוֹעֲדָם׃

These are the *mo'adim* (holidays) of God, the sacred occasions, which you shall celebrate each at its appointed time.

LEVITICUS 23:4

EMOR: PART 1

A Solar System in Time

PARASHAT EMOR IS HOME to a brief and fairly businesslike description of the *mo'adim*, the major festivals described by the Torah — Pesach, Shavuot, Sukkot, and others. This listing, which occurs in Leviticus 23, doesn't give us that much more than the dates on which each holiday appears, a skeletal description of the day, and sometimes, a smattering of its applicable laws. Despite the brevity of the text about each of these festivals, though, I believe that, taken together, these descriptions combine to tell a rather grand story. To begin to show you some of that, let me invite you to join me in a little thought experiment.

A Very Good Place to Start

Come with me back in time, a good many centuries ago, to the moment when our ancestors were setting up the prayers for various festivals. Imagine you were one of those Sages. Your task, should you choose to accept it, is to nominate various selections of biblical texts as Torah readings, to be read aloud in the synagogue, on holidays such as Pesach, Sukkot, and Shavuot. The possibilities are endless, and it is all up to you.

Each of these festivals have multiple days, so there's more than one opportunity for a Torah reading. You figure that, for each festival, you can select sections from anywhere in the Torah that deal with that particular festival. Maybe the Splitting of the Sea for the last days of Pesach; maybe the Revelation of the Torah on Sinai for Shavuot. Those feel like easy ones. But then an idea strikes you. For at least one day of those festivals with multiple days, like Pesach and Sukkot, wouldn't it be nice to also have some sort of common Torah reading, to kind of send the message that these festivals are all part of something larger, that there's a broad commonality here?

It seems like a great idea. So you go about paging through the Torah with gusto, searching for a section of text that could work. And lo and behold, you notice that Leviticus chapter 23 seems like a great fit. This section of the Torah lists *all* the various holidays in chronological order and tells us a little bit about each one. What better text to read aloud in synagogue on holidays than this, the Torah's own description of its various festivals?

But now the question faces you: *Where*, exactly, should the reading begin? And a quick scan of the chapter convinces you that…verse 4 looks like a pretty logical place to start:

Leviticus 23:4

אֵלֶּה מוֹעֲדֵי יְקוָה מִקְרָאֵי קֹדֶשׁ
אֲשֶׁר תִּקְרְאוּ אֹתָם בְּמוֹעֲדָם:

These are the *mo'adim* (holidays) of God, the sacred occasions, which you shall celebrate each at its appointed time.

Indeed, verse 4 really does seem perfect. It has a nice, introductory ring to it: "These are the holidays of God, the sacred occasions." It sounds bold and declarative. And right after this introduction, the Torah dives right in, giving the reader a quick portrait of the first holiday in its yearly calendar, Pesach. It really *does* seem like the perfect place to begin.

But guess what? If we leave our thought experiment for a moment, and reenter real life — we find that the actual Sages whose job it was to decide these things — well, they agreed with us, but only partially. They *did* pick Leviticus 23 as a broad, overarching narrative to be read on various different days of the festivals.[1] But they didn't have us start at verse 4.

Where do they have us start? I'll tell you in a moment, but first, let's continue our thought experiment — and see if we can guess the logical starting place.

Let's go back to the drawing board, and see if we can find the perfect beginning verse for that multi-festival Torah reading. Let's see what comes a little earlier than this. Is there an obvious starting point that presents itself in the preceding verses?

---

1 This becomes the Torah reading for the second day of Pesach (outside of Israel) and the first and second (outside of Israel) days of Sukkot.

Try, Try Again

Sure enough, the verses just before this *do* tell us about another holiday. They tell us about the Sabbath:

וַיְדַבֵּר יְקֹוָה אֶל מֹשֶׁה לֵּאמֹר:
דַּבֵּר אֶל בְּנֵי יִשְׂרָאֵל וְאָמַרְתָּ
אֲלֵהֶם מוֹעֲדֵי יְקֹוָה אֲשֶׁר
תִּקְרְאוּ אֹתָם מִקְרָאֵי קֹדֶשׁ אֵלֶּה
הֵם מוֹעֲדָי: שֵׁשֶׁת יָמִים תֵּעָשֶׂה
מְלָאכָה וּבַיּוֹם הַשְּׁבִיעִי שַׁבַּת
שַׁבָּתוֹן מִקְרָא קֹדֶשׁ כָּל מְלָאכָה
לֹא תַעֲשׂוּ שַׁבָּת הִוא לַיקֹוָה
בְּכֹל מוֹשְׁבֹתֵיכֶם:

God spoke to Moses, saying: Speak to the Israelite people and say to them: These are My *mo'adim*, the appointed times of God, which you shall proclaim as sacred occasions. On six days work may be done, but on the seventh day there shall be a Sabbath of complete rest, a sacred occasion. You shall do no work; it shall be a Sabbath of God throughout your settlements.

Leviticus 23:1–3

So, maybe we could begin our reading on the holidays here. The Torah once again gives us that nice, introductory line: *These are My appointed times, the appointed times of God, which you shall proclaim as sacred occasions.* Sounds like a good enough starting line for a Torah reading. And the Sabbath, after all, *is* a holiday....

But let's face it, folks — there's a reason this wasn't your first choice for where to begin. Because while it is true that the Sabbath *is* a holiday, it isn't a holiday in the same way that, say, Pesach or Sukkot is. Those are *annual* festivals, and the Sabbath occurs *weekly*. So it seems a little odd to start our Torah reading for Pesach and Sukkot with a different kind of holiday altogether (a weekly one).

So is our "runner-up candidate" where the Torah reading for festivals actually starts?

No it's not. We just swung and missed again; strike two.

Strike Two

Where do we, in synagogues around the world, start the common Torah reading for Pesach and Sukkot? We do read chapter 23, but we start even a few verses before the spots we've contemplated, toward the end of chapter 22. We start with a topic that, frankly, seems to have nothing *at all* to do with *any* festival, yearly, weekly, or otherwise:

Leviticus 22: 27–28

שׁוֹר אוֹ כֶשֶׂב אוֹ עֵז כִּי יִוָּלֵד וְהָיָה שִׁבְעַת יָמִים תַּחַת אִמּוֹ וּמִיּוֹם הַשְּׁמִינִי וָהָלְאָה יֵרָצֶה לְקָרְבַּן אִשֶּׁה לַיקוָה: וְשׁוֹר אוֹ שֶׂה אֹתוֹ וְאֶת בְּנוֹ לֹא תִשְׁחֲטוּ בְּיוֹם אֶחָד:	When an ox or a sheep or a goat is born, it shall stay seven days with its mother, and from the eighth day on it shall be acceptable as an offering by fire to God. No animal from the herd or from the flock shall be slaughtered on one single day with its own child.

Yes, believe it or not, *that's* where we actually begin reading the Torah on holidays. And the obvious question is: *Why*? Why, in the world would we start *there*?

Date Patterns

A clue lies in a remarkable pattern lurking just underneath the surface of the text. The pattern encompasses the entirety of Leviticus chapter 23, and yes, even these last verses of Leviticus 22, which had seemed, at first glance, so disconnected from chapter 23. Once you see the clue, the last verses of 22 really *do* seem connected to the very different laws of festivals that follow it.

Glance through some of the calendrical listings in **Parashat Emor**, and you should be able to see what I'm talking about. The pattern has to do with the dates on which the various festivals are celebrated. And it has to do with the lengths of times the various holidays last. Scan through the first verses of the chapter — you can find them below — and as you do, ask yourself: *What stands out*? Are there any repeated elements in this text? Are there any numbers, or variations on numbers, that seem to show up over and over again?

Ready? Here we go:

ויקרא כ״ג: ב׳–ט״ז

ב דַּבֵּר אֶל־בְּנֵי יִשְׂרָאֵל וְאָמַרְתָּ אֲלֵהֶם מוֹעֲדֵי יְקֹוָה אֲשֶׁר תִּקְרְאוּ אֹתָם
מִקְרָאֵי קֹדֶשׁ אֵלֶּה הֵם מוֹעֲדָי: **ג** שֵׁשֶׁת יָמִים תֵּעָשֶׂה מְלָאכָה וּבַיּוֹם
הַשְּׁבִיעִי שַׁבַּת שַׁבָּתוֹן מִקְרָא קֹדֶשׁ כָּל מְלָאכָה לֹא תַעֲשׂוּ שַׁבָּת הִוא
לַיקֹוָה בְּכֹל מוֹשְׁבֹתֵיכֶם: **ד** אֵלֶּה מוֹעֲדֵי יְקֹוָה מִקְרָאֵי קֹדֶשׁ אֲשֶׁר תִּקְרְאוּ
אֹתָם בְּמוֹעֲדָם: **ה** בַּחֹדֶשׁ הָרִאשׁוֹן בְּאַרְבָּעָה עָשָׂר לַחֹדֶשׁ בֵּין הָעַרְבָּיִם
פֶּסַח לַיקֹוָה: **ו** וּבַחֲמִשָּׁה עָשָׂר יוֹם לַחֹדֶשׁ הַזֶּה חַג הַמַּצּוֹת לַיקֹוָה שִׁבְעַת
יָמִים מַצּוֹת תֹּאכֵלוּ: **ז** בַּיּוֹם הָרִאשׁוֹן מִקְרָא קֹדֶשׁ יִהְיֶה לָכֶם כָּל מְלֶאכֶת
עֲבֹדָה לֹא תַעֲשׂוּ: **ח** וְהִקְרַבְתֶּם אִשֶּׁה לַיקֹוָה שִׁבְעַת יָמִים בַּיּוֹם הַשְּׁבִיעִי
מִקְרָא קֹדֶשׁ כָּל מְלֶאכֶת עֲבֹדָה לֹא תַעֲשׂוּ: **ט** וַיְדַבֵּר יְקֹוָה אֶל מֹשֶׁה
לֵּאמֹר: **י** דַּבֵּר אֶל־בְּנֵי יִשְׂרָאֵל וְאָמַרְתָּ אֲלֵהֶם כִּי תָבֹאוּ אֶל הָאָרֶץ אֲשֶׁר
אֲנִי נֹתֵן לָכֶם וּקְצַרְתֶּם אֶת קְצִירָהּ וַהֲבֵאתֶם אֶת עֹמֶר רֵאשִׁית קְצִירְכֶם
אֶל הַכֹּהֵן: **יא** וְהֵנִיף אֶת הָעֹמֶר לִפְנֵי יְקֹוָה לִרְצֹנְכֶם מִמָּחֳרַת הַשַּׁבָּת
יְנִיפֶנּוּ הַכֹּהֵן: **יב** וַעֲשִׂיתֶם בְּיוֹם הֲנִיפְכֶם אֶת הָעֹמֶר כֶּבֶשׂ תָּמִים בֶּן שְׁנָתוֹ
לְעֹלָה לַיקֹוָה: **יג** וּמִנְחָתוֹ שְׁנֵי עֶשְׂרֹנִים סֹלֶת בְּלוּלָה בַשֶּׁמֶן אִשֶּׁה לַיקֹוָה
רֵיחַ נִיחֹחַ וְנִסְכֹּה יַיִן רְבִיעִת הַהִין: **יד** וְלֶחֶם וְקָלִי וְכַרְמֶל לֹא תֹאכְלוּ עַד
עֶצֶם הַיּוֹם הַזֶּה עַד הֲבִיאֲכֶם אֶת קָרְבַּן אֱלֹקֵיכֶם חֻקַּת עוֹלָם לְדֹרֹתֵיכֶם
בְּכֹל מֹשְׁבֹתֵיכֶם: **טו** וּסְפַרְתֶּם לָכֶם מִמָּחֳרַת הַשַּׁבָּת מִיּוֹם הֲבִיאֲכֶם אֶת
עֹמֶר הַתְּנוּפָה שֶׁבַע שַׁבָּתוֹת תְּמִימֹת תִּהְיֶינָה: **טז** עַד מִמָּחֳרַת הַשַּׁבָּת
הַשְּׁבִיעִת תִּסְפְּרוּ חֲמִשִּׁים יוֹם וְהִקְרַבְתֶּם מִנְחָה חֲדָשָׁה לַיקֹוָה:

LEVITICUS 23:2–16

2 Speak to the Israelite people and say to them: These are My *mo'adim*, the appointed times of God, which you shall proclaim as sacred occasions. **3** On six days work may be done, but on the seventh day there shall be a Sabbath of complete rest, a sacred occasion. You shall do no work; it shall be a Sabbath of God throughout your settlements. **4** These are the appointed times of God, the sacred occasions, which you shall celebrate each at its appointed time: **5** In the first month, on the fourteenth day of the month, at twilight, there shall be a Passover offering to God, **6** and on the fifteenth day of that month God's Feast of Unleavened Bread. You shall eat unleavened bread for seven days. **7** On the first day you shall celebrate a sacred occasion: you shall not work at your occupations. **8** Seven days you shall make offerings by fire to

God. The seventh day shall be a sacred occasion: you shall not work at your occupations. **9** God spoke to Moses, saying: **10** Speak to the Israelite people and say to them: When you enter the land that I am giving to you and you reap its harvest, you shall bring the first sheaf of your harvest to the priest. **11** He shall elevate the sheaf before God for acceptance in your behalf; the priest shall elevate it on the day after the Sabbath. **12** On the day that you elevate the sheaf, you shall offer as a burnt offering to God a lamb of the first year without blemish. **13** The meal offering with it shall be two-tenths of a measure of choice flour with oil mixed in, an offering by fire of pleasing odor to God; and the libation with it shall be of wine, a quarter of a hin. **14** Until that very day, until you have brought the offering of your God, you shall eat no bread or parched grain or fresh ears; it is a law for all time throughout the ages in all your settlements. **15** And from the day on which you bring the sheaf of elevation offering — the day after the Sabbath — you shall count off seven weeks. They must be complete: **16** you must count until the day after the seventh week — fifty days; then you shall bring an offering of new grain to God.

When you're done hunting for the pattern, turn the page. You'll find the same text reproduced again — but this time, it will include my own highlights, delineating the pattern, as I see it playing out. Come with me, and we can compare notes.

Okay, here's that same text again — this time with my highlights:

ויקרא כ״ג:ב׳–ט״ז

ב דַּבֵּר אֶל־בְּנֵי יִשְׂרָאֵל וְאָמַרְתָּ אֲלֵהֶם מוֹעֲדֵי יְקוָה אֲשֶׁר תִּקְרְאוּ אֹתָם
מִקְרָאֵי קֹדֶשׁ אֵלֶּה הֵם מוֹעֲדָי: **ג** שֵׁשֶׁת יָמִים תֵּעָשֶׂה מְלָאכָה וּבַיּוֹם **הַשְּׁבִיעִי**
שַׁבַּת שַׁבָּתוֹן מִקְרָא קֹדֶשׁ כָּל מְלָאכָה לֹא תַעֲשׂוּ **שַׁבָּת** הִוא לַיקוָה בְּכֹל
מוֹשְׁבֹתֵיכֶם: **ד** אֵלֶּה מוֹעֲדֵי יְקוָה מִקְרָאֵי קֹדֶשׁ אֲשֶׁר תִּקְרְאוּ אֹתָם בְּמוֹעֲדָם:
ה בַּחֹדֶשׁ **הָרִאשׁוֹן** **בְּאַרְבָּעָה עָשָׂר** לַחֹדֶשׁ בֵּין הָעַרְבָּיִם פֶּסַח לַיקוָה:
וּבַחֲמִשָּׁה עָשָׂר יוֹם לַחֹדֶשׁ הַזֶּה חַג הַמַּצּוֹת לַיקוה **שִׁבְעַת** יָמִים מַצּוֹת
תֹּאכֵלוּ: **ו** בַּיּוֹם **הָרִאשׁוֹן** מִקְרָא קֹדֶשׁ יִהְיֶה לָכֶם כָּל מְלֶאכֶת עֲבֹדָה לֹא
תַעֲשׂוּ: **ז** וְהִקְרַבְתֶּם אִשֶּׁה לַיקוָה **שִׁבְעַת** יָמִים בַּיּוֹם **הַשְּׁבִיעִי** מִקְרָא קֹדֶשׁ
כָּל מְלֶאכֶת עֲבֹדָה לֹא תַעֲשׂוּ: **ח** וַיְדַבֵּר יְקוָה אֶל מֹשֶׁה לֵּאמֹר: **ט** דַּבֵּר אֶל
בְּנֵי יִשְׂרָאֵל וְאָמַרְתָּ אֲלֵהֶם כִּי תָבֹאוּ אֶל הָאָרֶץ אֲשֶׁר אֲנִי נֹתֵן לָכֶם וּקְצַרְתֶּם
אֶת קְצִירָהּ וַהֲבֵאתֶם אֶת־עֹמֶר רֵאשִׁית קְצִירְכֶם אֶל הַכֹּהֵן: **י** וְהֵנִיף אֶת
הָעֹמֶר לִפְנֵי יְקוָה לִרְצֹנְכֶם **מִמָּחֳרַת** **הַשַּׁבָּת** יְנִיפֶנּוּ הַכֹּהֵן: **יא** וַעֲשִׂיתֶם בְּיוֹם
הֲנִיפְכֶם אֶת הָעֹמֶר כֶּבֶשׂ תָּמִים **בֶּן שְׁנָתוֹ** לְעֹלָה לַיקוָה: **יב** וּמִנְחָתוֹ שְׁנֵי
עֶשְׂרֹנִים סֹלֶת בְּלוּלָה בַשֶּׁמֶן אִשֶּׁה לַיקוָה רֵיחַ נִיחֹחַ וְנִסְכֹּה יַיִן רְבִיעִת הַהִין:
יג וְלֶחֶם וְקָלִי וְכַרְמֶל לֹא תֹאכְלוּ עַד עֶצֶם הַיּוֹם הַזֶּה עַד הֲבִיאֲכֶם אֶת קָרְבַּן
אֱלֹקֵיכֶם חֻקַּת עוֹלָם לְדֹרֹתֵיכֶם בְּכֹל מֹשְׁבֹתֵיכֶם: **טו** וּסְפַרְתֶּם לָכֶם **מִמָּחֳרַת**
הַשַּׁבָּת מִיּוֹם הֲבִיאֲכֶם אֶת עֹמֶר הַתְּנוּפָה **שֶׁבַע שַׁבָּתוֹת** תְּמִימֹת תִּהְיֶינָה:
טז עַד **מִמָּחֳרַת** **הַשַּׁבָּת הַשְּׁבִיעִת** תִּסְפְּרוּ **חֲמִשִּׁים יוֹם** וְהִקְרַבְתֶּם מִנְחָה
חֲדָשָׁה לַיקוָה :

Leviticus 23:2–16

2 Speak to the Israelite people and say to them: These are My *mo'adim*, the appointed times of God, which you shall proclaim as sacred occasions. **3** On six days work may be done, but on the **seventh** day there shall be a **Sabbath** of complete rest, a sacred occasion. You shall do no work; it shall be a **Sabbath** of God throughout your settlements. **4** These are the appointed times of God, the sacred occasions, which you shall celebrate each at its appointed time: **5** In the **first** month, on the **fourteenth** day of the month, at twilight, there shall be a Passover offering to God, **6** and on the **fifteenth** day of that month God's Feast of Unleavened Bread. You shall eat unleavened bread for **seven** days. **7** On the **first** day you shall celebrate a sacred occasion: you shall not work at your occupations. **8** **Seven** days you shall make offerings by

fire to God. The **seventh** day shall be a sacred occasion: you shall not
work at your occupations. **9** God spoke to Moses, saying: **10** Speak to
the Israelite people and say to them: When you enter the land that I am
giving to you and you reap its harvest, you shall bring the first sheaf of
your harvest to the priest. **11** He shall elevate the sheaf before God for
acceptance in your behalf; the priest shall elevate it on **the day after
the Sabbath**. **12** On the day that you elevate the sheaf, you shall offer
as a burnt offering to God a lamb of the **first** year without blemish.
13 The meal offering with it shall be two-tenths of a measure of choice
flour with oil mixed in, an offering by fire of pleasing odor to God;
and the libation with it shall be of wine, a quarter of a hin. **14** Until
that very day, until you have brought the offering of your God, you
shall eat no bread or parched grain or fresh ears; it is a law for all time
throughout the ages in all your settlements. **15** And from the day on
which you bring the sheaf of elevation offering — **the day after the
Sabbath** — you shall count off **seven weeks**. They must be complete:
16 you must count until the day after the **seventh week** — **fifty** days;
then you shall bring an offering of new grain to God.

RED	Seven (or a Multiple of Seven)
BLUE	One
PURPLE	A Combination of Sevens and One

The pattern boils down to two numbers — sevens and ones — repeating themselves, and combining in all sorts of permutations.

First, we hear of the Sabbath — a holiday, we are told, that occurs every **seventh** day. Immediately after that, we hear about Pesach. When does it occur? In the **first** month, toward twilight on the **fourteenth** (multiple of seven) of the month. And then, a **single** day after that, on the **fifteenth**[2]

2 Fifteen, inasmuch as it is 7+7+1, is a permutation of sevens and ones.

of the month, a festival begins: The festival of *matzot*.[3] How long does it last? **Seven** days. And of those, are any of them particularly special? Yes, as a matter of fact, some are: The **first** day is holy, and the **seventh** day is holy. And, the text tells us, on all **seven** days, special offerings are brought.

After this, the train of sevens and ones continues. Next, we hear of the Omer, a special offering that serves to permit the consumption of the new crop of wheat. When is it brought? Sevens and ones once more: We bring the Omer **one** day after the first day of Pesach, after which we are meant to count **seven** "Sabbaths," or, seven weeks. What happens when these **seven** weeks draw to their conclusion? Well, a **single** day after the **seventh** of these **seven weeks** — a new holiday arrives, a festival whose very name expresses the seven-focused counting which leads up to it: It is aptly named Shavuot, or "Weeks."

Indeed, the more you read Leviticus chapter 23, the more you find these sevens and ones. After Shavuot, for example, the Torah next introduces us to a festival we now know as Rosh HaShanah. It doesn't call it Rosh HaShanah, though. Instead, the text describes it as a day when we "remember the blast of the shofar" (*zichron teru'ah*), and calls it a Shabbaton, a "Sabbath-like" event. When does it occur? Sevens and ones again: In the **seventh** month, on the **first** of that month.

There's no doubt about it: These numbers disproportionately dominate the dates of the *mo'adim*.[4] It is almost as if, once we start talking about the Torah's festivals, we've suddenly been thrust into some newfangled "seven-centric" number system, in which the only numbers that exist are ones and sevens, or the various permutations that arise from them. The reader has to wonder: Why are these numbers repeated so often? What is the text trying to tell us about the nature of its festivals by virtue of these numbers?

---

3 Nowadays, we tend to use the term Passover to denote both what the text here calls "Pesach" and then "Chag HaMatzot," the holiday of matzot. The way the text describes things here in Leviticus, "Pesach" refers to a single day holiday on which the Pesach offering is brought. This occurs in the afternoon on the fourteenth of Nisan. By nightfall, however — the onset of the fifteenth of Nisan — a new, seven-day festival begins, known as the holiday of matzot.

4 There are some outliers, too. Yom Kippur, for example, occurs on the *tenth* day of the seventh month. But the overwhelming majority of these festivals find their way onto the calendar in some permutation or combination of a seven and (or) a one.

Whatever the answer to that question is, one thing stands out as especially intriguing: Remember that section of the Torah that immediately precedes the listing of festivals, the one that contains those laws about when an animal is fit to be brought as an offering? That section, too, contains the telltale sevens and ones:

Leviticus 22:27–28

שׁוֹר אוֹ כֶשֶׂב אוֹ עֵז כִּי יִוָּלֵד וְהָיָה **שִׁבְעַת** יָמִים תַּחַת אִמּוֹ וּמִיּוֹם **הַשְּׁמִינִי** וָהָלְאָה יֵרָצֶה לְקָרְבַּן אִשֶּׁה לַיקוָה : וְשׁוֹר אוֹ שֶׂה אֹתוֹ וְאֶת בְּנוֹ לֹא תִשְׁחֲטוּ בְּיוֹם **אֶחָד**:	When an ox or a sheep or a goat is born, it shall stay **seven** days with its mother, and from the **eighth**[5] day on it shall be acceptable as an offering by fire to God. No animal from the herd or from the flock shall be slaughtered on **one single** day with its own child.

That, I think, has something to do with why the Sages chose this section as the beginning point for the Torah portion we read on Pesach and Sukkot. Yes, these laws about animals fit to be brought as an offering seem to have nothing to do with the festivals. But these precepts *are* functions of sevens and ones, just like the festivals that immediately follow them. I believe these numbers are telling a story. They signify that, in some underlying way, these laws actually *are* thematically connected with the festivals that follow them.

What, then, is the meaning of this new "seven-centric" number system we have suddenly been thrust into, here in **Parashat Emor**? It can't simply be random that all these festivals and laws seem to build themselves around various permutations of sevens and one. What does it signify?

A Solar System in Time

Allow me to suggest a theory. It goes back to something we talked about a bit earlier.

Remember how we noticed that the Sabbath, inasmuch as it is a weekly event, not a yearly one, is the one holiday that seems a bit out of place in **Parashat Emor**'s listing of festivals? Well, maybe it is not so out of place,

---

5 Eight is of course a combination of sevens and ones: 1+7=8.

after all. Maybe the Sabbath comes at the beginning of all the *mo'adim* because...it is a topic sentence of sorts. In that "topic sentence" the Torah is highlighting the idea of the Sabbath, setting it up as the prototype — the construct — out of which all other festivals are built.

It would thus not be coincidental that, in the context of Leviticus 23, the Torah labels several of these *mo'adim* as being what it calls a Shabbaton.[6] Indeed, in some kind of way, each of these annual festivals are really "Sabbath-like events"; it is just that, instead of appearing in the cycle of a week, they appear in the cycle of a year.

We might imagine a conceptual model here. Imagine a solar system: stars, planets, that sort of thing. Now shift that imagery into the realm of... time. It is almost as if, in setting out these festivals, the Torah is delineating a kind of solar system of Sabbath-like events. In the solar system that you and I are used to thinking about, various planets all revolve around the sun, but they do so in different arcs. Some orbits are further out, some are closer in; some planets take longer to go around the sun, and some make their revolutions more quickly. In a similar way, one might imagine a solar system, of sorts, for the Sabbaths-like events we commemorate, each with its own "orbit" around the center.

At the core of this solar system is the most central, paradigmatic celebration of all: not a human holiday, but a divine one. In our little model, this holiday is akin to the sun; it is central and sheds light on all human festivals. It is the point around which they all revolve. I'm thinking here of God's original Sabbath, which the Almighty celebrated privately, alone in His numinous solitude.

Indeed, that first of all Sabbaths was God's very own. Notice that this celebration of the Sabbath by God doesn't involve any humans, nor do humans, at the time, even know about it. We, the readers of the text, many years after Creation, know about it. But at the time, God didn't command Adam and Eve to observe that Sabbath or even tell them that He was resting. For all we know, Adam and Eve were entirely unaware of the Sabbath's existence. That first Sabbath was God's, and God's alone. He was the Being to rest in it. No one else shared in its experience:

---

6 For example, I mentioned above that this word is used to describe Rosh HaShanah. Below, I suggest that "Shabbaton" might well mean a "Sabbath-like event," and offer this as a translation. In the next section of the essay, I will expand on this point, offering evidence for such a translation.

Genesis 2:3

וַיְבָרֶךְ אֱלֹקִים אֶת יוֹם הַשְּׁבִיעִי וַיְקַדֵּשׁ אֹתוֹ כִּי בוֹ שָׁבַת מִכָּל מְלַאכְתּוֹ אֲשֶׁר בָּרָא אֱלֹקִים לַעֲשׂוֹת:	And [God] rested on the seventh day… and God blessed the seventh day and sanctified it, because on it, He rested from all His creative labor.

We'll come back to the question of what, exactly, it means to say that "God rested," but for now, suffice it to say that this primal Sabbath, the day of Creation that God blessed and sanctified — serves as the prototype after which all the holidays we celebrate are modeled. The festivals that we humans celebrate, those delineated in Leviticus chapter 23 after the Sabbath — those festivals are almost like planets, each possessing its own connection, its own orbit around that initial linchpin of the system, the original, divine Sabbath.

The most proximate "planet" to the central "star" that is God's Sabbath is… a human holiday so similar to the Creator's own Sabbath it actually bears the same name. I'm referring here to the holiday named Sabbath' that the Torah asks us humans to celebrate each week, our own, recurring approximation of God's original Sabbath. This orbit is the most frequent of the festivals — it occurs weekly. But there are other Sabbath-like events, too; those with longer orbits, that occur within the arc of a year. Indeed, some Sabbath-like events have orbits that reach even beyond the year, having arcs measured in multiple years. I'm thinking here of Shemittah and Yovel, both of which the Torah describes as a Sabbath (and both of which appear in the Torah just a few verses after the Torah's description of the *mo'adim* here in Lev. 23). These represent additional orbits of seven and fifty years, respectively.

Indeed, this solar system model, in which the Sabbath is a touchstone for all the other *mo'adim*, may help us understand why the Torah actually introduces the *mo'adim* to us *twice* (using the virtually identical phrase "these are My *mo'adim*"). First the Torah introduces the weekly festival that is the prototype for the Torah's holidays. Then it introduces us to all the "planets" — all the iterations of the Sabbath that we meet over the course of the year:

INTRODUCTION OF THE PARADIGM	
דַּבֵּר אֶל־בְּנֵי יִשְׂרָאֵל וְאָמַרְתָּ אֲלֵהֶם **מוֹעֲדֵי יְקֹוָה אֲשֶׁר תִּקְרְאוּ אֹתָם מִקְרָאֵי קֹדֶשׁ אֵלֶּה הֵם מוֹעֲדָי׃** שֵׁשֶׁת יָמִים תֵּעָשֶׂה מְלָאכָה וּבַיּוֹם הַשְּׁבִיעִי שַׁבַּת שַׁבָּתוֹן מִקְרָא קֹדֶשׁ כָּל מְלָאכָה לֹא תַעֲשׂוּ שַׁבָּת הִוא לַיקֹוָה בְּכֹל מוֹשְׁבֹתֵיכֶם׃ (Lev. 22:2–3)	Speak to the Israelite people and say to them: **These are My *mo'adim*, the appointed times of God, which you shall proclaim as sacred occasions.** On six days work may be done, but on the seventh day there shall be a Sabbath of complete rest, a sacred occasion. You shall do no work; it shall be a Sabbath of God throughout your settlements.
INTRODUCTION OF THE FESTIVALS THAT FLOW FROM THE PARADIGM	
אֵלֶּה מוֹעֲדֵי יְקֹוָה מִקְרָאֵי קֹדֶשׁ אֲשֶׁר תִּקְרְאוּ אֹתָם בְּמוֹעֲדָם׃ בַּחֹדֶשׁ הָרִאשׁוֹן בְּאַרְבָּעָה עָשָׂר לַחֹדֶשׁ בֵּין הָעַרְבָּיִם פֶּסַח לַיקֹוָה׃ (Lev. 22:4–5)	**These are the *mo'adim* of God, the sacred occasions, which you shall celebrate each at its appointed time**: In the first month, on the fourteenth day of the month, at twilight, there shall be a Passover offering to God.

The Peculiarity of God's Primal Sabbath

Let's try to extend and refine this idea a little bit. What, exactly, would it mean to see other *mo'adim* as Sabbath-like events?

To understand that, we have to go back to the prototype — the central star that is the nexus of our system, as it were: God's original Sabbath. The more clearly we perceive the nature of this event, the more we will be able to understand everything that flows from it: Both the human Sabbath, and the other *mo'adim,* the Sabbath-like arcs that grace our year. So, let's journey together, for a moment, back to God's primal Sabbath.

A basic question faces us when we seek to understand this first of all future Sabbaths: Why would an all-powerful Creator need to rest after creating a universe? How hard, after all, would it have been for Him to do this? Did the Almighty really need a break after all that work to catch His breath?

I raised this question with you in our Exodus volume of these *Parsha Companions,*[7] and there, I suggested that this conundrum forces us to revisit what we mean when we talk about work and rest, at least in the context of the Sabbath. Going back to that primal Sabbath, what, exactly, was the nature of the "rest" that God engaged in on that first seventh day? It must have been the opposite, the natural counterpoint for, the "work" that He engaged in on the days of Creation leading up to the seventh. But the truth is, the notion of "work" with reference to God also presents us with befuddling possibilities. Work suggests exertion, an idea hardly compatible with an all-powerful being. What exactly was God's "work" all about?

God's Rest

A solution comes if we think of God's endeavors during Creation not as "work" but as *creative activity*. The Almighty was building a universe, bringing things into being and molding and shaping them, deliberately, to make an environment that suited His will. In English, we have various words for this kind of creative process, but the Torah has its own word for it: *melachah*. When God created the world in those six, primal days, He did so through the process of *melachah*, and when He "rested" on the seventh day, it is involvement in *melachah* that God refrained from:

Genesis 2:2	וַיְכַל אֱלֹקִים בַּיּוֹם הַשְּׁבִיעִי **מְלַאכְתּוֹ** אֲשֶׁר עָשָׂה וַיִּשְׁבֹּת בַּיּוֹם הַשְּׁבִיעִי מִכָּל **מְלַאכְתּוֹ** אֲשֶׁר עָשָׂה	On the seventh day God finished **His *melachah*** that He had been doing, and He ceased on the seventh day from all **His *melachah*** that He had done.

Resting from *melachah* is not the same as resting from labor. "Labor," or "work," suggests an activity that requires exertion and makes one

7 See my essay there, to **Parshat Vayakhel**.

weary — and naturally, then, the point of rest after work is to take a break so you can recoup your energy. But Sabbath rest is not the counterpart to labor; it's the counterpoint to *creativity*. Sabbath rest is about letting go of the impulse to create. It is about resisting the urge to keep fiddling with what you've made and instead, to just let it be.

The impulse to create is seductive. One is tempted to create and create and never rest. But this comes with hidden costs, and indeed, the price of creating without stopping is very great. Ever met an artist who, somehow, is never quite done with their painting, who just can't resist the temptation to keep on adding more and more brushstrokes? What happens to their precious painting? It eventually collapses under the surfeit of creativity lavished upon it. What about the parent who can never let go of their child, even as they walk them down to the *chuppah*? Every creator, at some point, needs to let go or risk destroying that which they tried so hard to build. At some point, it is time to stop shaping it, and it is time to establish a relationship with it instead.

Even an all-powerful creator needs to engage in *this* kind of rest. And that's the point of Sabbath: to engage in *this* kind of rest. On the negative side, the Sabbath forces a break from ad-nauseum creativity. And on the positive side, the Sabbath represents a chance to relish what we've made and simply "be" connected to it. For indeed, so long as a creator stays in the process of creating, they are "busy" and not at rest. It takes letting go and stopping to be able to finally "be present"; to finally relate to that which they've made.

The Ties That Bind

I believe now we are in a position to appreciate the common denominator that binds together the various aspects of the verses which comprise the Torah reading for the festivals: the idea of ceasing to act as creator, and instead allowing for the creator to engage with that which they've produced. It's this quality that unites the laws of the Sabbath, the *mo'adim* — and even those laws of the baby calf:

Leviticus 22:27–28

שׁוֹר אוֹ כֶשֶׂב אוֹ עֵז כִּי יִוָּלֵד
וְהָיָה שִׁבְעַת יָמִים תַּחַת אִמּוֹ
וּמִיּוֹם הַשְּׁמִינִי וָהָלְאָה יֵרָצֶה
לְקָרְבַּן אִשֶּׁה לַיקוה: וְשׁוֹר אוֹ
שֶׂה אֹתוֹ וְאֶת בְּנוֹ לֹא תִשְׁחֲטוּ
בְּיוֹם אֶחָד:

When an ox or a sheep or a goat is born, it shall stay seven days with its mother, and from the eighth day on it shall be acceptable as an offering by fire to God. No animal from the herd or from the flock shall be slaughtered on one single day with its own child.

For its first seven days of existence, a calf must be with its mother. Only after that are you free to offer it on the altar. Why? Because ... a Sabbath, of sorts, must be observed first, a kind of Sabbath for the mother of this calf.

Indeed, this first law, the one that precedes the *mo'adim*, seems to suggest that on some level, Sabbath-like events exist not just in the world of humans, but in the animal world — and humankind, for its part, is sometimes called upon to honor those Sabbaths, too. Consider the calf that has been born. For *you*, that animal might represent a potential offering; but for her, the animal who is its mother, this calf is her offspring, the product of her creative energies. *Let the mother "be" with the calf — let it experience a bit of independence from her, and let her relate to it; let there be this Sabbath, of sorts, for her — and only then is it acceptable for you to take the calf from her as an offering.*[8]

But if the laws of the calf reveal a Sabbath that humans must respect within the animal world, the laws of the *mo'adim* introduce us to different kinds of Sabbaths still. These festivals, occurring within their yearly cycle, bid us, in all sorts of other ways, to emulate God's original Sabbath.

To see more concretely what I mean by the festivals being "Sabbath-like-events" and how they reflect the light of the primordial Sabbath, let's

---

8 As a matter of biological fact, a calf achieves independence far more quickly than human offspring do. While in the first moments after birth the calf is bewildered and helpless, it is generally a quick learner and adapter to the world in which it finds itself. Most calves, for example, learn to walk within the first hour after birth. Hence, in the first seven days of a calf's life, the mother is indeed relating to an offspring who has achieved some meaningful form of independence, an important facet of a Sabbath-like experience.

examine one of those festivals: the seven-day holiday of Pesach. The Torah here calls it *Chag HaMatzot*, the Festival of Matzot — and this will become our first clue as to how this festival expresses a Sabbath-like character.

Pesach as a Kind of Sabbath

Admittedly, at first glance, Pesach seems to have almost nothing to do with the idea of the Sabbath. But maybe that first glance is overlooking something. Let's talk about that name: *Chag HaMatzot*, the Festival of Unleavened Bread. If you think about it, the notion of abstaining from leavened products ... might just have something to do with the Sabbath after all.

As if to nudge us in this conceptual direction, consider how the Torah, elsewhere, describes the prohibition against consuming *chametz* (leavened grain products):

שִׁבְעַת יָמִים מַצּוֹת תֹּאכֵלוּ אַךְ בַּיּוֹם הָרִאשׁוֹן **תַּשְׁבִּיתוּ** שְּׂאֹר מִבָּתֵּיכֶם כִּי כָּל אֹכֵל חָמֵץ וְנִכְרְתָה הַנֶּפֶשׁ הַהִוא מִיִּשְׂרָאֵל מִיּוֹם הָרִאשֹׁן עַד יוֹם הַשְּׁבִעִי׃	Seven days you shall eat unleavened bread; on the very first day **you shall remove** *chametz* from your homes, for whoever eats leavened bread from the first day to the seventh day, that person shall be cut off from Israel.	Exodus 12:15

Now, in English, the words "you shall remove" might seem unremarkable to you, but in Hebrew, those words actually scream: "Sabbath." The Hebrew term here is: *tashbitu*, which is really nothing more than "Sabbath" transformed into a verb and then issued forth as a command. Translated literally, the phrase doesn't really mean "you shall remove *chametz* from your homes," but "*you shall* **rest** *chametz from your homes!*" At some level, the festival of matzot seems to be about taking a rest from *chametz*.

Now, it seems like quite a stretch to see a link between avoiding *chametz* and the Sabbath ideas we sketched out above. After all, what creative rest is expressed by staying away from bagels or English muffins? But maybe the reason we don't immediately see the connection between the Sabbath and the Torah's *tashbitu* command to desist from leaven has to do with the times in which we live. Nowadays, most of us are fairly alienated from the real process of bread making. Ask a kid in twenty-first-century suburbia where bread comes from and they'll answer, "From the grocery store." But bread *doesn't* come from the store. It doesn't even come from flour and water. The process of bread making actually starts much earlier than this. It starts with ... a seed.

Let's start from the very beginning, and plot the actual steps we human beings go through when we make — or shall we say, when we *create* — bread.

The Hidden Creativity in Bread Making

Here is how a master baker, a fellow by the name of Peter Reinhart, characterized that process, in a talk I was fortunate enough to view.[9] The bread-making process begins, of course, when we plant wheat. *And what does this grain look like?* Wheat, in the fields, is vibrant and alive; think the lush "amber waves of grain" memorialized so vividly in "God Bless America." But then we do something to that wheat. We harvest it.

The word "harvest," though, is of course, a euphemism. It makes us feel a little better about what we are *really* doing. When we cut down the wheat, what we are really doing is...killing it.

But the wheat, because it is a plant, doesn't die the way an animal would. It doesn't expire in a single moment, by the slice of a knife. For wheat, even severed from the ground, can still remain alive so long as it is provided with water (think flowers in a vase). So when we harvest wheat, we make sure that doesn't happen. We deprive the newly cut wheat stalks of water. In ancient times, the stalks would be left out in the fields, exposed to the hot sun, until they slowly dry, go brittle, and die. And then, when the wheat is good and dead, we, the aspiring bread makers, start to take it apart. We separate the wheat kernels from the rest of the stalk, throwing away the latter and keeping the former.

---

9 See "The Art and Craft of Bread," a TED Talk by Peter Reinhart, July 2008, https://www.ted.com/talks/peter_reinhart_the_art_and_craft_of_bread?language=en (accessed January 2021). See also Peter Reinhart's talk at Google, July 2008, "Peter Reinhart's Whole Grain Breads," https://www.youtube.com/watch?v=BK5mC_SkIPI (accessed January 2021).

Death, Squared

Those precious wheat kernels, what are they, really? *They are seeds* — the mysterious key to the grain's ability to reproduce itself. Those seeds are the last, great hope of the wheat, even in death, for some kind of survival, some kind of legacy. And yet, those seeds — that's what we humans are after. We take those seeds and we pulverize them. We grind them into something we call flour.

First we kill the wheat. Then we destroy its ability to regrow itself. It is death to the wheat, squared.

So now we have flour. And what do we do with it? We take that crushed essence of wheat, and we mix it with...*water*. Yes, now — now that it is just a *little too late* for the wheat to stay alive — *now* is when we bring water back into the equation. With that flour mixed with water, we create dough, let it rest, and then....

And then something magical happens: *The dough begins to rise.*

How does that happen? Well, that's yeast at work.[10] But let's ask: How, exactly, does yeast cause dough to rise?

It turns out that the yeast is breathing. Yes, that's right — yeast is actually an organism, perched in the great taxonomy of life, precariously between the plant and animal worlds. The yeast slips out of dormancy, begins to eat the starches and sugars in the dough, and as it does, it exhales. It breathes out carbon dioxide, the same compound we humans exhale when we breathe, and it secretes alcohol — a process we label "fermentation."

In fermentation, the dough ceases to be a mere thing, and has now become... *alive.* Indeed, the very word "leaven" derives, etymologically, from the word "enliven": The dough, with the yeast flourishing inside it, is a substance that has been brought to life.

That brings us to the next stage of bread making. Now that the dough has been brought to life, what do we humans go and do? We put the dough in the oven. In this veritable furnace, the temperature quickly rises. The

---

10 We typically add yeast to the dough. But actually, even without humans adding yeast, the dough still rises. It turns out that yeast is naturally present on the husks of wheat (it's just a feature of how God set up the world), and if the newly formed dough is left to rest, that naturally occurring yeast will emerge out of dormancy, come to life, and will cause the dough to rise.

warming temperature, at first, goads the yeast into even more frenzied activity, causing the dough to expand even more quickly. But as the temperatures rises still further, the microorganisms we call yeast explode into the baking bread, giving the bread its wonderful flavor.

All in all, as we take the finished product out of the oven, it is newly dead once more. But that death has not been in vain. For now what is before us is something new: bread. And as we take a warm slice and consume its goodness, it comes inside us and gives *us* life, bringing the circle of life, death, and then life again, to completion.

Playing God

Stand back and consider what's happened here: We planted wheat, only to slowly kill it. Then, by adding water and making dough, we brought that dough to life, resuscitating it; only to kill it once more by throwing it into the oven. Every time we make a loaf of bread, it is like we are playing God. We foster life and then snuff it out, wielding the mysterious forces of life and death as tools to serve our own creative ends.

Indeed, when yeast exhales its breath into dough, filling it with the magic vitality of life — what does that process remind you of, from the earliest stories in the Torah? When *else* did someone breathe the breath of life into a warm, fertile, dough-like substance?

That's what happened, of course, when the Master of the Universe created *us*, this species of ours we call mankind. We were brought to life out of malleable, fertile earth:

Genesis 2:7

וַיִּיצֶר יְקוָה אֱלֹקִים אֶת הָאָדָם עָפָר מִן הָאֲדָמָה וַיִּפַּח בְּאַפָּיו נִשְׁמַת חַיִּים וַיְהִי הָאָדָם לְנֶפֶשׁ חַיָּה׃

God formed man from the dust of the earth, and breathed into his nostrils the breath of life — and man became a living being.

We mimic the process of our very own creation when we make bread.

We do so because God is not the only creator in this universe in which we find ourselves. *We* are creators, too. In recognition of this, God asked something of us: Rest each week on the Sabbath from *melachah*, the creative work that we engage in when we build and shape the world around us; and on *Chag HaMatzot*, the Festival of Unleavened Bread, it is rest from *chametz*, from a different kind of domination we exert over the plant world. In all the various realms of our creative, God-like endeavors, God asks us to learn the secret of rest; to be careful with creativity so that it does not become all-consuming. God asks us to learn how to stop, let go, and voluntarily relinquish the God-like powers of creativity to shape our world.

EMOR: PART 2

A Solar System in Time

IN PART 1 OF our essay on **Parshat Emor**, I began to advance a theory that the yearly festivals, the *mo'adim* described in Leviticus 23, were all, in some way or another, "Sabbath-like events." In line with this, I argued that abstaining from *chametz* on Pesach is Sabbath-like, in that it requires us to desist from "playing God" in our bread-making activities. But I want to pause a moment to consider a possible challenge that one might advance against this theory.

One might well argue that this theory is, at best, only *partially* true. For when we "rest" from consuming, or producing, *chametz* on the *Chag HaMatzot*, we are actually abstaining from only *one* of the two creative cycles of life and death that we wield every time we make bread:

	1ST LIFE-AND-DEATH CYCLE OF BREADMAKING	2ND LIFE-AND-DEATH CYCLE OF BREADMAKING
LIFE	We plant wheat...	We add water to the flour to make dough, bringing the bread to life, through yeast's organic activity.
DEATH	...but leave it in the fields to dry and die, and then crush its seeds to make flour.	We kill the newly enlivened dough when we bake it in the oven.

The reader will notice that the Sabbath experience of *Chag HaMatzot* represents a rest only from the second life-and-death cycle involved in bread making. So curious minds might therefore wonder: What about the *first* life-and-death aspect of bread making — where we plant the wheat and then harvest it? Is there a Sabbath for that, too? Indeed, we play God in a very real way when we bring wheat kernels to life, intentionally planting and cultivating them for our designs, only to kill the vibrant stalks when we harvest them as raw material for our bread. So... does the Torah ask us to observe some Sabbath-like event with reference to *this* aspect of bread making, too?

It turns out that such a "Sabbath'" may well exist.

Back to Leviticus 23

If we take another look at the Torah's listing of *mo'adim* in Leviticus 23, we will see that the text includes, right in the middle of its list, a lengthy description of an event that is decidedly *not* a festival. It really seems somewhat out of place. I'm referring here to the Torah's lengthy treatment of the Omer offering, which immediately follows its description of *Chag HaMatzot*:

Leviticus 23:10–11, 14–16

י דַּבֵּר אֶל־בְּנֵי יִשְׂרָאֵל וְאָמַרְתָּ
אֲלֵהֶם כִּי תָבֹאוּ אֶל הָאָרֶץ
אֲשֶׁר אֲנִי נֹתֵן לָכֶם וּקְצַרְתֶּם
אֶת קְצִירָהּ וַהֲבֵאתֶם אֶת עֹמֶר
רֵאשִׁית קְצִירְכֶם אֶל הַכֹּהֵן:
יא וְהֵנִיף אֶת הָעֹמֶר לִפְנֵי יְקֹוָה
לִרְצֹנְכֶם מִמָּחֳרַת הַשַּׁבָּת יְנִיפֶנּוּ
הַכֹּהֵן:... **יד** וְלֶחֶם וְקָלִי וְכַרְמֶל
לֹא תֹאכְלוּ עַד עֶצֶם הַיּוֹם הַזֶּה
עַד הֲבִיאֲכֶם אֶת קָרְבַּן אֱלֹקֵיכֶם
חֻקַּת עוֹלָם לְדֹרֹתֵיכֶם בְּכֹל
מֹשְׁבֹתֵיכֶם: **טו** וּסְפַרְתֶּם לָכֶם
מִמָּחֳרַת הַשַּׁבָּת מִיּוֹם הֲבִיאֲכֶם
אֶת עֹמֶר הַתְּנוּפָה שֶׁבַע שַׁבָּתוֹת
תְּמִימֹת תִּהְיֶינָה: **טז** עַד
מִמָּחֳרַת הַשַּׁבָּת הַשְּׁבִיעִת
תִּסְפְּרוּ חֲמִשִּׁים יוֹם וְהִקְרַבְתֶּם
מִנְחָה חֲדָשָׁה לַיקֹוָה:

10 Speak to the Israelite people and say to them: When you enter the land that I am giving to you and you reap its harvest, you shall bring the first sheaf of your harvest to the priest. **11** He shall elevate the sheaf before God for acceptance on your behalf; the priest shall elevate it on the day after the Sabbath.... **14** Until that very day, until you have brought the offering of your God, you shall eat no bread or parched grain or fresh ears; it is a law for all time throughout the ages in all your settlements. **15** And from the day on which you bring the sheaf of elevation offering — the day after the Sabbath — you shall count off seven weeks. They must be complete: **16** You must count until the day after the seventh week — fifty days; then you shall bring an offering of new grain to God.

What are these laws even doing here? They invade the listing of the festivals, as if they belong, somehow. But these laws don't seem to belong in Leviticus 23 at all.

However, the truth is, they *do* belong. As we noted in part 1 of our essay on **Parshat Emor**, virtually everything in Leviticus 23 is riddled with sevens and ones — *including* these descriptions of the Omer offering. When, for example, is the Omer offering brought? The text tells us "on the day after the Sabbath," which tradition understands as denoting the day after the first day of Pesach.[11] Once the offering is brought we are meant to count seven "Sabbaths," or seven weeks, bringing us to another holiday (Shavuot) celebrated a single day after these seven Sabbaths conclude.

The Omer offering's commonality with the *mo'adim* in terms of its "sevens and ones" suggests that somehow, at a deeper thematic level, this offering is of a piece with the rest of the festivals. But how?

The Omer and the Sabbath

The answer, I want to suggest, lies in what the Omer *does*. The Omer offering has a specific legal effect, which the verses themselves tell us about:

וְלֶחֶם וְקָלִי וְכַרְמֶל לֹא תֹאכְלוּ
עַד עֶצֶם הַיּוֹם הַזֶּה עַד הֲבִיאֲכֶם
אֶת קָרְבַּן אֱלֹקֵיכֶם

Until that very day, until you have brought the offering of your God, **you shall eat no bread or parched grain or fresh ears;** it is a law for all time throughout the ages in all your settlements.

Leviticus 23:14

11 Many have struggled to understand why the Torah would call the first day of Pesach "Sabbath," such that the day after it is called "the day after the Sabbath" (Menachot 65b). But in light of the explanation we advanced above, it isn't so strange after all. The Torah is explicitly referring to Pesach as a Sabbath-like event. It is, after all, the day we rest from playing God with bread.

Until the moment in the calendar year when the Omer is brought, the Torah prohibits us from partaking from the newly harvested crop of grain.[12] And, interestingly, it isn't just processed grain products like bread that we can't eat. The Torah specifically prohibits any consumption of new grain — even parched stalks, or fresh ears, newly harvested.

Newly killed, that is.

In these laws of the Omer, the Torah is, in effect, mandating another Sabbath-like event for us. But *this* Sabbath, unlike the one that preceded it (i.e., the onset of *Chag HaMatzot*), relates to the *first* cycle of life and death that accompanies the bread-making process. Recall that the first time we play God in mankind's relationship to wheat, we do so far away from the bakery. We play God out in the fields, when we plant wheat, giving it life, then kill it when we harvest it and let it dry on the ground. When we abstain from consuming any of that newly killed wheat until the Omer offering is brought, we take a pause from reaping the benefits of this creative manipulation of ours.[13] So, all in all, the offering of the Omer culminates a kind of hidden Sabbath event.

---

12 See Lev. 23:14. Namely, until the second day of *Chag HaMatzot*, when the Omer is brought, only grain harvested in previous years' crops may be consumed. The latest crop of grain is off-limits until after the Omer is offered. The prohibited new grain is called *chadash*, and the permitted old crops are referred to as *yashan*.

13 As we step out of our role of "creator" in this Sabbath-like event, the requirement to bring an offering seems to beckon us to take our recognition of the actual Creator to another level. If first we desist from the benefits of being a creator by refraining from eating the new "killed" grain, next we must acknowledge the true identity of the Creator by bringing an offering (See *Sefer HaChinuch*, mitzvah 302).

	1ST LIFE-AND-DEATH CYCLE OF BREADMAKING	2ND LIFE-AND-DEATH CYCLE OF BREADMAKING
LIFE	We plant wheat…	We add water to the flour to make dough, bringing the bread to life, through yeast's organic activity.
DEATH	…but leave it in the fields to dry and die, and then crush its seeds to make flour.	We kill the newly enlivened dough when we bake it in the oven.
	The lead-up to the Omer offering is a rest from this part of the bread-making cycle. We resume "normal life" with the offering of the Omer.	**The Sabbath of *Chag HaMatzot* is a rest from this part of the bread-making cycle: No leavened bread is made or consumed.**

Why the Pharisees Weren't Crazy

Fittingly enough, when does that culmination take place? When *is* this Omer offering brought? Just a day after the onset of the *other* Sabbath event connected to bread making: A day after the start of *Chag HaMatzot*, when we abstain from *chametz*: מִמָּחֳרַת הַשַּׁבָּת — "On the day after the Sabbath" [event, you shall bring the Omer].

Which, by the way, helps us understand one last puzzle: the curious way the Torah talks to us about when to bring the Omer offering.

The text cloaks the moment on which the Omer is to be brought in a bit of mystery. It tells us that we must bring it: מִמָּחֳרַת הַשַּׁבָּת, literally: "the day after the Sabbath." But at face value, that nomenclature seems hopelessly vague. The day after *which* Sabbath, exactly? The year has fifty-two of them. When, exactly, is the Omer supposed to be brought?

Indeed, as a matter of historical fact, the Sadducees — always ones to opt for the most literal interpretation of biblical verses — interpreted the Torah as insisting that the Omer must always be brought on a Sunday. But this interpretation was fiercely resisted by the Pharisees.[14] They were adamant that the text's mandate that the Omer is to be brought "the day after the Sabbath" meant it was to be brought the day after the onset of *Chag HaMatzot*. In other words, in this context, *Chag HaMatzot* ***itself*** was to be viewed as the "Sabbath" the text was talking about.

At face value, as heretical as it seems to say (we, today, are heirs of the Pharisees), the position of the Sadducees seemed pretty reasonable: Why would the Torah say that the Omer is to be brought the day after the Sabbath if it didn't *mean* the day after the Sabbath?

But the theory we've suggested above helps us understand the underlying logic of the Pharisees. It makes sense that the Torah was referring to *Chag HaMatzot* as the Sabbath — for it would have good reason for doing so: In the context of the Omer, *that* was the most recent, relevant Sabbath-like event the reader needed to be focused upon. As we've seen, *Chag HaMatzot* is Sabbath-like inasmuch as it involves our "rest" from the second *half* of the way we play God when we make bread (i.e., enlivening dough, then killing it). With its description of the Omer, the Torah is completing the picture. It is saying that now that the Festival of Unleavened Bread has started, and we have begun to experience a kind of Sabbath with respect to bread making, the day *after* that we are to bring the Omer, its natural counterpart: a culmination of our rest from the *first* half of the way we bread makers play God (i.e., planting the wheat and giving it life, then killing it by harvesting it).

The Genesis of Civilization

Looking back on it, bread making might seem like a small, almost trivial part of our behavior as human beings. One might question: Why bother devising "Sabbath-like events" that revolve around this relatively trivial practice? But bread making is actually the pinnacle of a very large iceberg, indeed: civilization itself.

Historically, man's domestication of wheat heralded the apex of what we now call the agricultural revolution, an event that changed human

---

14 See Menachot 65a–65b.

history forever. It was single-handedly responsible for the beginning of urban life: Suddenly, a dependable source of food existed, in a single place, that people could control. No longer would we have to embrace the nomadic life of hunters or gatherers. We could settle down now, in cities — confident that we could cultivate crops nearby that would sustain us. The agricultural revolution — the knowledge involved in planting wheat, harvesting it, and making bread from it — this little bit of know-how, surprisingly, would give birth to modern civilization itself.[15]

All in all, in our look at the laws of the mother calf, Sabbath, Pesach, and the Omer, we have begun to see how these verses in **Parshat Emor** (verses that become our common Torah reading for Pesach and Sukkot) begin to delineate a whole panoply of Sabbath-like events. These events start with a small circuit of time: The week. From there they advance to months. And in next week's **Parshat Behar**, they advance to include years (i.e., Shemittah and Yovel).

I'll leave you with a challenge: Read through the rest of the calendar of *mo'adim*, all the way into the beginning of **Parshat Behar**. Find, if you can, some of the other Sabbath-like events in these verses. As you discern more and more of these Sabbath iterations, you will come closer and closer to perceiving the full majesty of the Sabbath-centered system of holidays we call *mo'adim*.

---

15 I am indebted to Yuval Noach Harari's *Sapiens: A Brief History of Humankind* (Harper, 2015) for his analysis of the import of the agricultural revolution on subsequent world history. Harari offers a cogent treatment of what he calls three great revolutions in the history of mankind, all three of which may perhaps resonate with the *mo'adim*. The second of these revolutions, in his view, is the agricultural revolution.

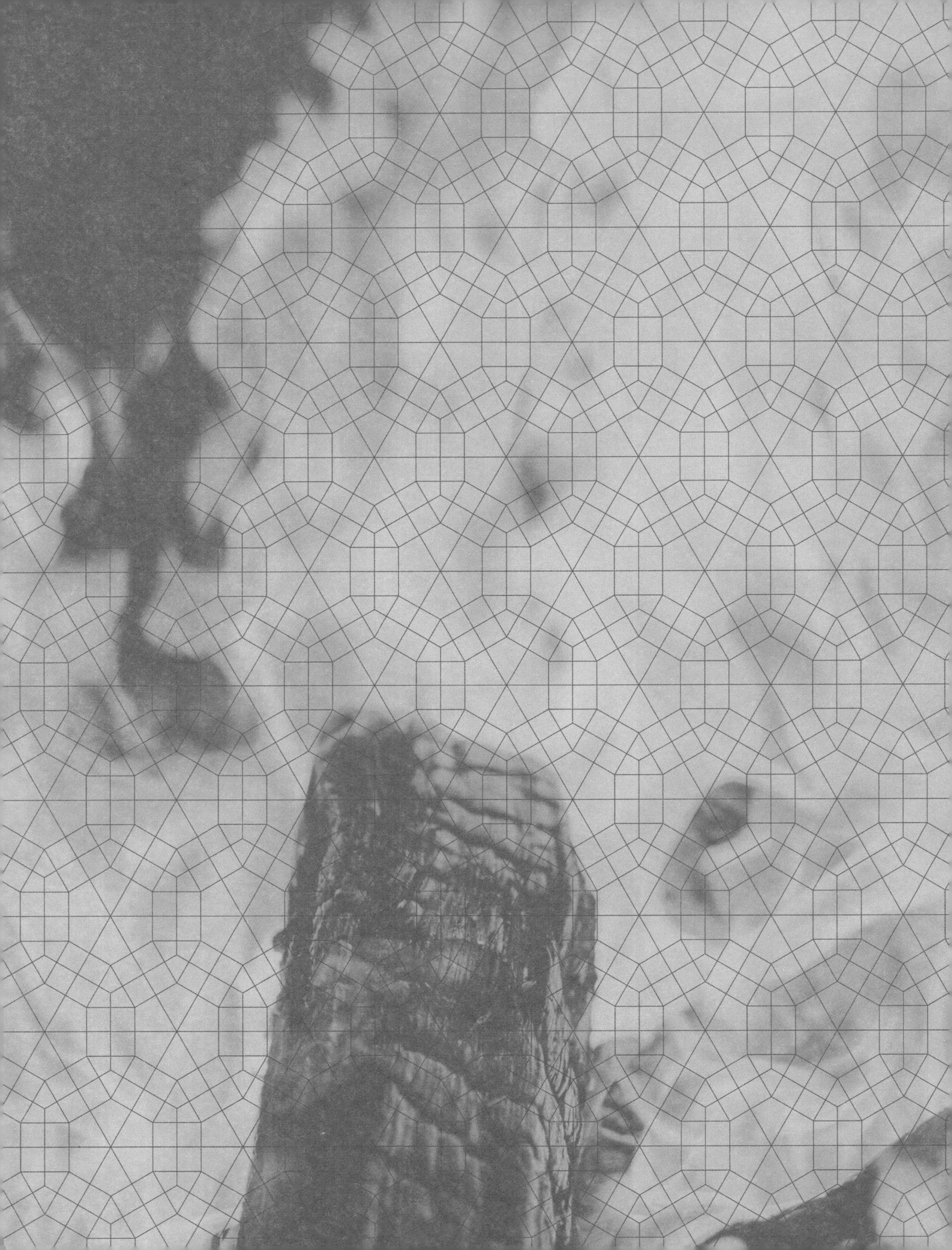

Yovel and Children of Cain

וְקִדַּשְׁתֶּם אֵת שְׁנַת הַחֲמִשִּׁים שָׁנָה וּקְרָאתֶם דְּרוֹר בָּאָרֶץ לְכָל
יֹשְׁבֶיהָ יוֹבֵל הִוא תִּהְיֶה לָכֶם וְשַׁבְתֶּם אִישׁ אֶל אֲחֻזָּתוֹ וְאִישׁ אֶל
מִשְׁפַּחְתּוֹ תָּשֻׁבוּ׃

And you shall make the fiftieth year holy, and proclaim liberty throughout the land for all its inhabitants. It shall be a jubilee for you: each of you shall return to his own ancestral land and each of you shall return to his family.

LEVITICUS 25:10

Yovel and Children of Cain

1 OF STORIES AND LAWS

TWO ENTIRELY DIFFERENT GENRES of writing make up the lion's share of the Five Books of Moses: stories and laws. But, as I mentioned earlier in this volume, it would be a mistake to see the two as entirely separate. Hidden links seem to connect many of the Torah's stories to its laws.

What do these links tell us? It isn't always easy to know. But broadly speaking, I'd like to suggest that our laws respond to our history. A law may come to rectify a historical wrong. Or, on the other side of the ledger, a law may seek to reenact a high point in our history, ensuring that its legacy continues to influence the life of the nation even after the passage of many centuries. Sometimes, it may be a little bit of both. A law may pick up on a hopeful potentiality in a story that was, tragically, never actualized.

In **Parshat Behar**, we seem to have an example of these links between stories and laws, and the explanation for that link, I believe, may fall into the last of the categories I just outlined. A legal institution in **Parshat Behar** touches on one of the earliest stories in recorded biblical history, and in doing so, it seems to pick up on and redeem a tragic, missed opportunity in that story. I'm thinking here of the institution known as Yovel, the Jubilee year.

I first became aware of the possibility that the idea of Yovel might be connected to this very early biblical episode when a remarkable email showed up in my inbox. It was from Mr. Vadim Birman, a sharp-eyed subscriber to Aleph Beta. In that email, Vadim suggested some intriguing evidence that an antecedent for Yovel — a kind of proto-Yovel, as it were — might well be lurking in one of the first generations of Adam and Eve's descendants.

If Vadim is right, it wouldn't change our understanding of Yovel's *laws*, but it might well affect how we think of Yovel's meaning. For if the Yovel idea is, in fact, grounded in one of the Torah's stories, that would give us an intriguing new perspective upon this institution. It would give us a context for Yovel, an invaluable backstory for it — and perhaps, a deeper understanding of the underlying values that emerge from it.

To be sure, even without this backstory, Yovel is clearly a game-changing institution. Every fifty years, it offers a kind of economic reset, restoring people to ancestral land they may have sold, and freeing people who had been indentured as servants, returning them to their families.[1] In this essay I want to show you, though, that textual clues seem to lead us back to humanity's first murder and to a tragic follow-up episode that destroyed what might have been an attempt to recover from that tragedy. I want to suggest that these stories and laws may be in a kind of dialogue with one another. From that dialogue, we may glean insight about some of the root causes of human suffering, and how the Torah bids us to grapple with them.

Here's a little background on the biblical story that Vadim's email referred me to.

Whispers of Yovel in the Book of Genesis

Just after Cain kills Abel, the book of Genesis introduces us to a series of generations that issue from Cain. We don't hear much about most of these people: just their names, and a single heir that they manage to father. Cain gives birth to Chanoch, Chanoch to Erad, etc., etc. But six generations

---

1 See Lev. 25:9–10. Land in Israel, of course, was apportioned to tribes, and to families within those tribes, as an inheritance. If you possessed some ancestral land, you could sell part or all of it, but the Torah declares that in the Yovel year, the land you sold would revert back to you. As for Hebrew servants, these are people who, for the most part, sold themselves into servitude as a refuge from poverty or to pay crushing debt. In rare cases, men could be sold as servants if they were found guilty of theft and didn't have the money to repay.

Servants, by Torah law, are to be set free after completing a term of six years. However, a servant who professes to love his master and who expresses a wish to remain with him, even after the expiration of his six-year term, has the right to undergo a process known as *retzia*, allowing him to stay indentured (Ex. 21:2–6). One way or another, though, once the Yovel year arrives, all Hebrew servants — those still in their first six years of service, and those who have undergone *retzia* — go free, whether they like it or not (*Mechilta DeRabbi Yishmael* 25:6).

into this list, a figure is born who stands out. His name is Lemech, and he's the first person in this chain of generations about whom an actual story is told. We will get to some of the details in that story in a moment, but for now, suffice it to say that Lemech fathers three children. Their names are Yaval, Yuval, and Tuval-Kayin.

Stop and consider those names for a moment. What Vadim suggested to me seems whimsical at first glance, like a bit of playful phonetic trivia. He suggested that all three of these names sure sound pretty reminiscent of... Yovel.

The one that sounds most like Yovel is, of course, the middle brother, Yuval. His name is spelled exactly the same way Yovel is spelled — *yud, vav, bet, lamed* — and is merely vowelized differently:

YOVEL	**YUVAL**
יוֹבֵל	יוּבָל

But it's not just this middle brother, Yuval, whose name evokes the Yovel year. It's all *three* of the brothers' names. Imagine, for a moment, that "Yovel" wasn't a noun — an institution, a name for a year — but a verb, and furthermore, that these brothers' names weren't proper nouns, but were also verbs. Seen that way, all three of these brothers' names... would be grammatical variations of Yovel, projected, intriguingly, into either the future or the past.[2]

2 Later in this essay, we will see that the story of these three brothers seems to resonate with both *past* events, and *future* events, associated with the idea of Yovel. The notion that these three brothers' names carry grammatical variations that echo these forward and backward projections of Yovel through time seems consonant with this.

IF YOVEL WERE A VERB...
THE NAMES OF LEMECH'S SONS WOULD DENOTE
THREE POSSIBLE CONJUGATIONS
IN THE FUTURE AND PAST TENSE

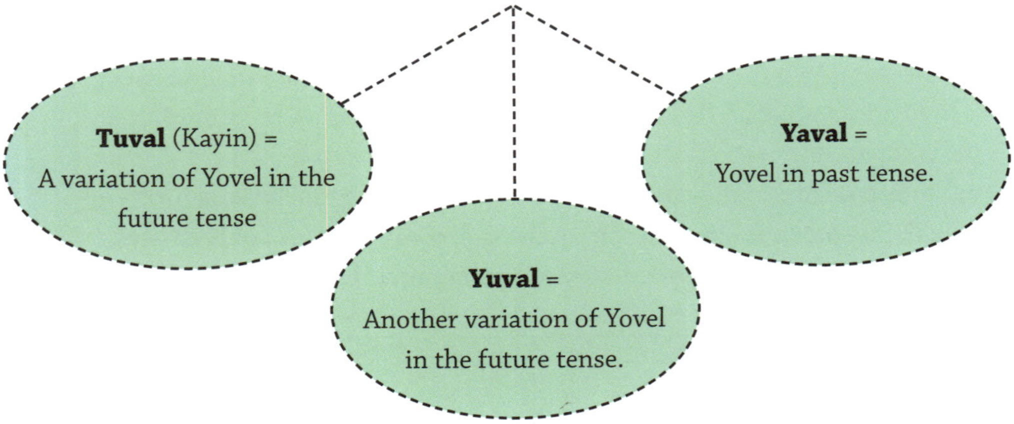

But look, all this is just imaginary wordplay, you may protest. Yovel *isn't* a verb, and neither are the names of these three brothers; they are fine and upstanding proper nouns. So while these correspondences make for an intriguing thought experiment, one might well be tempted to treat this connection as rather far-fetched and dismiss it as mere coincidence.

And I would have done that, too — except for the existence of one more, corroborating "coincidence."

You see, it just so happens that it's not just the *names* of these three brothers that remind the reader of Yovel; the *numbers* associated with the brothers — and their father, for that matter — remind one of Yovel, too. Remember how one of the distinguishing features of Yovel is that it occurs every fifty years — or, as the verse in Leviticus puts it, at the conclusion of seven times seven years?[3] Well, consider this: These three brothers, Yuval, Yaval and Tuval-Kayin, represent the *seventh* generation of descendants coming from Cain. Which is interesting, because Cain, their seventh-generation forbear, is also no stranger to "sevens": When Cain complained to God that the divine punishment for his sin was greater than he could

3 See Lev. 25:8: וְסָפַרְתָּ לְךָ שֶׁבַע שַׁבְּתֹת שָׁנִים **שֶׁבַע שָׁנִים שֶׁבַע פְּעָמִים** וְהָיוּ לְךָ יְמֵי שֶׁבַע שַׁבְּתֹת הַשָּׁנִים תֵּשַׁע וְאַרְבָּעִים שָׁנָה — "You shall count seven Sabbaths of years, **seven times seven years**; and there shall be to you the days of seven Sabbaths of years, forty-nine years."

bear, that he feared that anyone who found him would kill him — God responded with a promise involving sevens:

כל הֹרֵג קַיִן **שִׁבְעָתַיִם** יֻקָּם	If anyone kills Cain, **sevenfold** shall he be avenged![4]	Genesis 4:15

So these three brothers are seven generations removed from the man who is to be avenged sevenfold. That's an interesting seven-times-seven allusion right there. But to top it all off, Lemech — the father of Yaval, Yuval, and Tuval-Kayin — actually references that "sevenfold" vengeance of Cain in an opaque, poetic speech that he makes to his wives. And in that speech, he takes this whole idea of multiples of seven a giant step forward:

וַיֹּאמֶר לֶמֶךְ לְנָשָׁיו עָדָה וְצִלָּה שְׁמַעַן קוֹלִי נְשֵׁי לֶמֶךְ הַאְזֵנָּה אִמְרָתִי כִּי אִישׁ הָרַגְתִּי לְפִצְעִי וְיֶלֶד לְחַבֻּרָתִי: כִּי **שִׁבְעָתַיִם** יֻקַּם קָיִן וְלֶמֶךְ **שִׁבְעִים וְשִׁבְעָה:**	Lemech said to his wives, "Adah and Tzilah, listen to my voice; the wives of Lemech, heed my speech. I have killed a man for my bruise and a child for my wound. If Cain would be avenged **sevenfold**, then Lemech **seventy-seven-fold**!"	Genesis 4:23–24

Lemech's speech ends with a flourish of sevens, as if God's promise to Cain about sevens was building in orders of magnitude. So, whatever Lemech might actually mean in that puzzling speech, the reader has to ask: *Is all this just the product of one big coincidence?* You know, it is one thing for Yaval, Yuval, and Tuval-Kayin to all *sound* as if they are variations of the word "Yovel." It's quite another thing for these very same "Yovel-adjacent" children to be born seven generations after a man told he would be avenged seven times, whose father wants to up the notion of "seven

---

4 My translation here follows *Saadia Gaon, Gra,* and *Midrash Rabba* on Gen. 4:15, who see God's promise as protective of Cain, a promise that vengeance would be taken against Cain's killer. Rashi, however, translates it differently, as a promise that ultimately, Cain will be made to pay for killing Abel.

times something" by a whole order of magnitude. Add it all up and it just starts to feel a bit too similar to Yovel's culmination of seven times seven years to be the product of true coincidence. After all, at a certain point, "coincidences" cease to be the product of pure random forces. As a beloved friend once told me, coincidence is God's middle name.

As I read through Vadim's email, which touched on a few of these points, it started to feel to me that something real was going on here; that the Torah wants us to see that something in the story of these three brothers was linked mysteriously to a law, or a series of them. I started to wonder whether the very existence of these children of Lemech might somehow constitute the first whispers in the Torah of what would later become the institution we know of as Yovel.

But *why* would these particular people, at this particular moment of human history, be linked to Yovel in some way? And if this link *is* real, and not just the figment of our very possibly overactive imagination — what, if anything, would the Torah want us to learn from that?

These are the questions I'd like to explore with you here. I'd like to look with you, carefully, at Lemech's story. It is a tale that culminates with a strange song he sings to his wives about vengeance and its horrifying power. But as Lemech's own speech makes clear, his story doesn't really begin with him. It begins seven generations earlier, with an even stranger promise of vengeance made by the Almighty Himself to Cain.

In the pages that follow, I want to explore the story of Cain and the story of Lemech and try to trace the through-line between them. Eventually, this will lead us back to the Yovel ideas articulated in Leviticus. But before we begin, a word of caution: The Torah tells these early stories of Cain and Lemech in minimalistic fashion, using an extreme economy of words. We will rely, then, on reading the text closely and carefully, so that we can infer as much nuance as possible.

Let's begin our exploration with a look at Cain. We will focus, for starters, on the mysterious promise of sevenfold vengeance given to him, the very same promise referenced seven generations later by his descendant, Lemech.

2 CAIN AND THE BIRTH OF VENGEANCE

כָּל הֹרֵג קַיִן שִׁבְעָתַיִם יֻקָּם	If anyone kills Cain, sevenfold shall he be avenged!	Genesis 4:15

What a strange promise God makes to Cain! Here Cain is, the perpetrator of the world's first killing — the world's first killing of a brother, no less. God is clearly not pleased with Cain. When Cain tries to evade the question, "Where is Abel, your brother?" with the infamous words, "Am I my brother's keeper?" God retorts sharply:

מֶה עָשִׂיתָ קוֹל דְּמֵי אָחִיךָ צֹעֲקִים אֵלַי מִן הָאֲדָמָה:	What have you done? The voice of your brother's blood cries out to Me from the ground!	Genesis 4:10

From there, the Almighty goes on to level a vehement curse upon Cain:

וְעַתָּה אָרוּר אָתָּה מִן הָאֲדָמָה אֲשֶׁר פָּצְתָה אֶת פִּיהָ לָקַחַת אֶת דְּמֵי אָחִיךָ מִיָּדֶךָ: כִּי תַעֲבֹד אֶת הָאֲדָמָה לֹא תֹסֵף תֵּת כֹּחָהּ לָךְ נָע וָנָד תִּהְיֶה בָאָרֶץ:	And now, cursed are you from the ground which forced open its mouth to take in your brother's blood from your hands. When you work the ground, it will no longer give its strength to you; you will be a restless wanderer on the earth.	Genesis 4:11–12

From even a cursory reading of these words, we can readily see that God is not of a mind to buy Cain's evasions of responsibility. So why is it, then, that when Cain protests, "Whoever finds me will kill me" — claiming that his punishment is too harsh for what he did to Abel — why is it that all of a sudden, the Almighty seems sympathetic to his plight? So sympathetic that God promises him protection:

Genesis 4:15

כָּל הֹרֵג קַיִן שִׁבְעָתַיִם יֻקָּם

If anyone kills Cain, sevenfold shall he be avenged!

I don't know about you, but that seems more than a little strange. Cain, killer of his brother, merits some divine promise of sevenfold vengeance? Why does he deserve that? If I were God, and if Cain came to *me* complaining that anyone he meets might kill him for what he did to his brother, I'd probably say: *Well, that's certainly too bad for you, Cain, but that's the way the cookie crumbles. Maybe you should have thought of that before you killed Abel?*

And even if the Almighty is, for some reason, moved by Cain's pitiful protestation of vulnerability, isn't it a little much to promise "sevenfold" vengeance for anyone who manages to kill him? Not just some kind of tit-for-tat punishment for Cain's killer, but an enormous, disproportionate, sevenfold response should anyone *dare* kill Cain? That seems more than a little overboard. It seems like far more than justice would dictate. So why does God promise him this?

The Case of the Missing Avenger

To perceive the answer to this question, let's note the rather unusual grammatical construction of God's promise to Cain:

Genesis 4:15

כָּל הֹרֵג קַיִן שִׁבְעָתַיִם **יֻקָּם**

Anyone who kills Cain, sevenfold **shall he be avenged!**

Note that the verse does not promise that *God* will avenge Cain's death. Indeed, there is no active promise of vengeance at all. The verb for vengeance is curiously placed in the passive voice: Cain *will be avenged.* But the reader wonders, by whom? As for that, the verse isn't telling.

The sense of the text, therefore, is not so much that God is making a *promise* to Cain as much He's making a prediction. *You, Cain, will be avenged. It is something that will happen.*

But of course, this observation only opens up more questions. Who is the missing avenger? And if God isn't making a promise but a prediction, what are the grounds for this prediction? Is God leveraging His divine foreknowledge of the future, or is something else going on? And finally: How, if at all, is God reassuring Cain with this prediction? If Cain is worried about getting killed, wouldn't it be cold comfort for him that *after* he's dead, he will be avenged?

The answer to these questions, I think, lies in a close read of the verse that details Cain's slaying of his brother. I talked about this in an earlier essay in this book, on **Parshat Kedoshim**. Let me reproduce the relevant point for you here.

Cain's Motive

Take a moment to reread the verse that describes Cain's attack on his brother. Do you notice anything extraneous about it?

וַיֹּאמֶר קַיִן אֶל הֶבֶל אָחִיו וַיְהִי בִּהְיוֹתָם בַּשָּׂדֶה **וַיָּקָם** קַיִן אֶל הֶבֶל אָחִיו וַיַּהַרְגֵהוּ	And Cain said to Abel, his brother — and when they were in the field together, Cain **got up** against his brother, Abel, and killed him.	Genesis 4:8

That phrase, "and Cain got up" — why is it there? What more information, really, do I get from the text telling me that Cain "got up" and then killed his brother? What if the verse had just omitted this, and all we heard was that once, when Cain was in the field with Abel, he killed him. Would you have complained to me that you were deprived of the knowledge that he first "got up"? Why, then, did the text bother to include these words?

Intriguingly enough, it turns out that this apparently extraneous word, **יָקָם**, "**got up**," has an echo. It is a word composed of these very same letters, in the very same order, and it appears later in this very same story of Cain and Abel. It comes in that promise of vengeance we were talking about above:

לָכֵן כָּל הֹרֵג קַיִן שִׁבְעָתַיִם **יֻקָּם**	Therefore, anyone who kills Cain sevenfold **shall he be avenged**!	Genesis 4:15

Although the letters are the same, due to a change in vowelization, this time יקם means: *vengeance.*[5] God tells Cain that should anyone kill him for his actions, his death will be severely avenged.

Now, one might again, perhaps, chalk this echo up to mere coincidence. But there are indications that the text wants us to notice this echo. For if we widen our field of view a little bit, we will notice that it isn't just the one word יקם that connects Genesis 4:8 to Genesis 4:15. More elements of the two verses also echo one another:

GENESIS 4:15	GENESIS 4:8
לָכֵן כָּל הֹרֵג קַיִן שִׁבְעָתַיִם יֻקָּם	וַיָּקָם קַיִן אֶל הֶבֶל אָחִיו וַיַּהַרְגֵהוּ
Therefore, anyone who **kills Cain** will meet with sevenfold **vengeance.**	And he **got up, Cain** did, against his brother, Abel, and **killed him.**

The Torah seems to be inviting us to view the second passage as a kind of interpretive overlay on the first passage. The upshot is that when the verse tells us that Cain "got up" to kill his brother, we aren't just hearing about *what* Cain did; we are also hearing about *why* he did it: *It had to do with vengeance.* So much so that later, when God goes on to promise retribution to *Cain's* killer, the reader hears this as alluding to Cain's own act of violence — as if to say, *Cain, you should know something about killing in vengeance. Isn't that, after all, what you once did?*

Revenge for What?

But if the Torah is hinting to us that Cain's attack was motivated by revenge, we could be excused for asking: *Revenge for what?* What, after all, did Abel do that might warrant retribution? Sure, Cain is angry because God "turned toward" Abel's offering instead of his. But that was *God's* choice, not Abel's. When you really start to think about it, it seems as if Cain isn't really angry at Abel, he's angry at God. But you can't kill God. So he kills Abel instead.

---

5 See n. 8 on page 121, **Parshat Kedoshim**.

What I'm trying to point out here is that there is something "off" about Cain killing his brother. And that is true both qualitatively and quantitatively. Qualitatively: Cain isn't really angry at Abel, but he kills him anyway. And quantitatively: Abel brought an offering that was more pleasing than Cain's, and Cain went and killed him for it. That seems highly disproportionate, to say the least.

"Vengeance" and Its More Straightforward Cousin, "Justice"

But I want to suggest that this quality of being "off" is not incidental; it is actually in the nature of vengeance to be "off." In a strange way, that's part of its allure...

Take a step back and ask yourself this: How does the concept of "vengeance" differ from the concept of "justice"? You'll notice that the difference is subtle. An avenger usually sees themself as bringing justice to the perpetrator of some crime, almost as if they are a one-person criminal justice system. And indeed, both justice and vengeance concern themselves with the idea of repayment for wrongdoing. But the key difference is, one of these concepts has an objective quality to it, and the other is hopelessly mired in subjectivity. A court devoted to justice is a dispassionate entity. Judges don't have any skin in the game, and so they have a reasonable shot at being fair. But vengeance, not so much. Vengeance is carried out by the aggrieved person himself, or perhaps by the only person even more biased than that: their relative. Vengeance is by nature subjective. It is personal.

This quality of being personal makes vengeance sweet. But it also makes it more likely that vengeance will come off in some obtuse way, either quantitatively, qualitatively, or both. Because vengeance is personal, it is possible that the avenger will misinterpret things; will blame someone because it *feels* like they did them wrong, even if in actuality they didn't. By the same token, it is more likely that the avenger seeking justice will overdo it somehow, leading to a terrible and ever-escalating cycle of violence. Bobby taps Debby mischievously, perhaps even accidentally; but before you know it, Debby slaps Bobby back. Bobby grabs a broom and whacks her. And Debby goes and grabs a baseball bat from the garage. The cycle escalates. In the eyes of each perpetrator, their own acts are just: *I'm just getting him back!* But we tend to be blind to our own excesses. Vengeance inevitably takes things up a notch.

Opening Pandora's Box

What God is telling Cain, then, is that, for better or for worse — mostly worse — he has ushered something terrible into the world: this new way of doing things called "vengeance." Through his behavior — through his choice to kill his brother to repay a perceived slight — he has normalized the human impulse to avenge, and brought it into the world as a live option for how disputes can get settled.

What are the implications of this?

Well, on the one hand, it is deeply troubling for the world at large. It greatly increases the potential for reckless, violent escalation of disputes. But it *does* come with a certain silver lining, at least for the person willing to wield this fearsome weapon we call vengeance. For this impulse to avenge all perceived slights serves as a mighty fine deterrent. And that, I want to argue, was precisely the point of God's "prediction" to Cain:

Your own act of vengeance will become the vehicle through which you get the protection you now request — for those who might seek to harm you will shrink away from you in terror. Your willingness to use this ultimate weapon is abhorrent, but you will gain something out of it. Rightly, or most likely wrongly — it will protect you.

It is as if God is saying to Cain:

You acted both unfairly and disproportionately in taking the life of your brother. There was something obtuse about both the quality and quantity of what you did. *So now, you want protection?* What kind of protection can I offer you? Sadly, I can only offer you the prediction that your act of vengeance against your brother, in a grim and twisted way, has the potential to act as "protection" for you, in a kind of chain reaction. *People will fear you.*

Alas, you, Cain, have brought vengeance into the world. It may be a corrupt force, but it is also very powerful. It can, in an uneven kind of way, create a kind of equilibrium in the world, a period of calm enforced through the terror of intimidation. You, Cain, have shown to what length you are willing to go against your enemies, which will make people think twice before attacking you, even if they might regard themselves as justified in taking you down. Your vengeance will serve to keep an uneasy peace.

Cain's Son

We thus understand why these words of God reassure Cain. For we asked before: *Why does Cain care what happens after his death?* The answer is: He doesn't. But he gains a present-moment benefit from the threat of vengeance. That threat is a deterrent, right *now*, to all who might oppose him. People will intuit not to mess with Cain, because even if Cain goes down, his surviving allies will come after them. That's how strongman politics works.

In light of this, it is chilling that the story of Cain ends with a note about Cain's son:

וַיֵּדַע קַיִן אֶת אִשְׁתּוֹ וַתַּהַר וַתֵּלֶד אֶת חֲנוֹךְ וַיְהִי בֹּנֶה עִיר וַיִּקְרָא שֵׁם הָעִיר כְּשֵׁם בְּנוֹ חֲנוֹךְ׃	And Cain knew his wife and she conceived and bore Chanoch. [Cain] was building a city[6] and called it after his child, Chanoch.	Genesis 4:17

Chanoch: What an interesting name. Later in the Hebrew Bible, the word would come to mean "educate," or "train someone in a path for life," as in חֲנֹךְ לַנַּעַר עַל פִּי דַרְכּוֹ גַּם כִּי יַזְקִין לֹא יָסוּר מִמֶּנָּה — "**Train** a child in the way he should go, and even when he is old, he will not depart from it" (Prov. 22:6).

One wonders: Was the book of Proverbs, with its proverb about "Chanoch," making a sly reference to the very first חֲנֹךְ in the Torah, this person named Chanoch? Chanoch, we might perhaps speculate, is the first of all children "trained" as a child, by his father, in a path he is expected to follow later, when he is old. Following his father Cain's example, Chanoch is, perhaps, trained in the art of vengeance, which, in his young hands, becomes a family business. For if Cain should ever be slain, to whom, logically, would it fall to avenge him with God's predicted

---

6 Ramban (Gen. 4:17) notes that the language of the text is not that Cain "built" a city, in the past tense, but that he builds, in the present tense. Cain, as we shall see below, was cursed to be a wanderer all the days of his life, never to settle down anywhere. Ramban posits that Cain attempted to build a city, but found himself incessantly building and building, never able to finish it, never able to settle down.

sevenfold retribution? Wouldn't it be his son? If the time ever comes to avenge an attack on him, Chanoch can be counted on to do what he needs to do.

If we are right in these musings, it emerges that, by the end of Cain's story, the impulse to vengeance is no longer limited to Cain. A generation later, that impulse has spread to another. Generations later, it will infect the lives of many.

The Revulsion of the Earth

The truth is, though, that vengeance is even more insidious than this. For it co-opts others, too, besides children, family members, or even their friends and allies. In Cain's case, God seems to speak of Cain's vengeance as having co-opted the most unlikely of collaborators: *The earth itself.* God laments that it, too, has been pulled into the role of unwitting accomplice to Cain's crime:

Genesis 4:11

אָרוּר אָתָּה מִן הָאֲדָמָה אֲשֶׁר פָּצְתָה אֶת פִּיהָ לָקַחַת אֶת דְּמֵי אָחִיךָ מִיָּדֶךָ׃	Cursed are you from the land, that forced open its mouth to accept your brother's blood from your hands.

As God puts it, Cain — in spilling the blood of his brother — has forced the land to do something abhorrent: accept the blood of Abel. As Cain, a sower of crops, might well be in a position to know, blood makes good fertilizer. But land, the verse insists, doesn't want that kind of fertilizer. To the contrary, the earth finds it utterly abhorrent to be an accomplice to fratricide. It is as if Cain had to "force open" its mouth to accept his brother's blood.[7]

Why is the land so revolted by Cain's deed? Land is just a thing. But in the Torah's world, land is far more than a "thing." *We come from land.* Recall that, in creating human beings, God breathed into Adam the breath of life, but fashioned Adam's body from earth. The earth, then, is a parent of ours — a parent of Cain as well as Abel — along with God. And what do parents do? *Why, they care for their children, of course.*

---

7 See Netziv, and Rabbi David Tzvi Hoffman on Gen. 4:11.

As a parent of humanity, land is predisposed to nourish us, to give its bounty to its human children. We get our basic needs met through land. Our nutrition comes from the earth in the form of crops and fruits. But even beyond that, land provides a home for humanity. We get from land what any child gets from any parent: food and shelter. But Cain perverted his relationship with this parent of his. He forced the earth to do what it didn't want to do: to take an abominable form of nutrition from his hands, the blood of a brother.

A Curse in Kind

We thus begin to understand the nature of the punishment God metes out to Cain. Yes, he brought vengeance into the world, and to some extent, that offers him a twisted benefit in the form of protection. But the earth itself is repelled by what Cain has forced it to do. And so, God says to him, the earth will have a kind of revenge of its own:

Genesis 4:11–12

וְעַתָּה אָרוּר אָתָּה מִן הָאֲדָמָה אֲשֶׁר פָּצְתָה אֶת פִּיהָ לָקַחַת אֶת דְּמֵי אָחִיךָ מִיָּדֶךָ: כִּי תַעֲבֹד אֶת הָאֲדָמָה לֹא תֹסֵף תֵּת כֹּחָהּ לָךְ נָע וָנָד תִּהְיֶה בָאָרֶץ:	And now, cursed are you from the land that forced open its mouth to accept your brother's blood from your hands. When you work the ground, it will not continue to give its strength to you; you will be a restless wanderer on the earth.

The land itself becomes a source of curse to Cain. Mother Earth, disgusted, will now recoil from providing that which is natural for it to provide — food and shelter — to Cain. Cain will have to wrestle the ground to obtain crops, for the land, newly disinterested in Cain's welfare, "will not continue to give its strength" to him. And the earth will withhold a home from Cain, too. Cain will become a wanderer, never able to settle down, never able to really call any place on this earth "home."

3 THE ADVENT OF THE SEVENTH GENERATION

And so, for six generations after Cain killed Abel, that's the way things were. The curse of the land remained in place. Cain's progeny remained doomed to try to wrest nutrition from a recalcitrant earth through their paltry efforts at subsistence farming, and the earth continued to truly deny Cain's children a home upon it. Until ... the seventh generation came. And with it, the first whispers of change arrived.

In the seventh generation, a man named Lemech — remember him? — fathers three sons. And curiously, the names of these brothers don't *only* evoke Yovel, a concept the Torah hasn't yet mentioned. They also seem to evoke ... the names of children born seven generations ago:

Genesis 4:19–22

וַיִּקַּח לוֹ לֶמֶךְ שְׁתֵּי נָשִׁים שֵׁם
הָאַחַת עָדָה וְשֵׁם הַשֵּׁנִית צִלָּה:
וַתֵּלֶד עָדָה אֶת **יָבָל** הוּא הָיָה
אֲבִי יֹשֵׁב אֹהֶל וּמִקְנֶה: וְשֵׁם
אָחִיו **יוּבָל** הוּא הָיָה אֲבִי כָּל
תֹּפֵשׂ כִּנּוֹר וְעוּגָב: וְצִלָּה גַם
הִוא יָלְדָה אֶת **תּוּבַל קַיִן** לֹטֵשׁ
כָּל חֹרֵשׁ נְחֹשֶׁת וּבַרְזֶל

Lemech took two wives. The name of the first was Adah and the name of the second was Tzilah. Adah bore **Yaval**; he was the first of those who dwell in tents and tend livestock. His brother's name was **Yuval**; he was the father of all who play the lyre and pipe. And Tzilah, she, too, bore **Tuval-Kayin**, forger of all instruments of copper and iron.

ADAM'S CHILDREN	LEMECH'S CHILDREN
קַיִן, הֶבֶל *Kayin, Hevel*	יָבָל, יוּבָל, תּוּבַל קַיִן *Yaval, Yuval, Tuval-Kayin*

Not only did Lemech's sons have *names* that, in Hebrew, sounded like Cain and Abel, their choice of livelihood also seemed to mimic the very same choices Cain and Abel made, respectively. Abel (Hevel) was a shepherd; his namesake, Yaval, tended sheep, too. Likewise, Cain (Kayin) worked the land as a farmer. Tuval-Kayin, his seventh-generation namesake, forges iron implements — quite useful for working the land, one might say.[8]

What are we to make of this? Does the text wish us, the reader, to view these children of Lemech as ... some sort of latter-day version of Cain and Abel? It is hard to see exactly what this would mean, though. Seemingly, the link between the children of Lemech and their seventh-generation namesakes would have to be more than skin-deep. It can't all be about their names and professions. So what *is* it about, then?

Redeeming Cain's Curse

Well, to answer this, let's start by reviewing what else we know about these brothers. The text tells us that each was an innovator of the highest order: one invented tents, another musical instruments, and a third figured out how to smelt iron and turn it into tools. I want to suggest that each of these innovations was particularly important to the kind of world these brothers found themselves inhabiting. Their inventions brought hope, where none could be found before.

To explain: These three brothers lived in the world of Cain. It was a cursed environment, a world in which land, revolted at Cain's crimes of vengeance, had alienated itself from human beings. But, suddenly, with the advent of these three children, representing the seventh generation removed from Cain, the first glimmers of redemption began to appear. The curse of the land began to be mitigated.

Two key technological innovations launched this process, each brought into the world by these children of Lemech:

---

8 This interpretation follows Abarbanel on Gen. 4:17 and Mizrachi on Gen. 4:22, who pick up on iron implements having obvious utility to farmers. However, Rashi (ibid.), quoting the Midrash, links Cain to Tuval-Kayin by understanding that the iron implements were weapons of war. Either way, Tuval-Kayin seems to innovate the technology that underlies the plow and other farm tools. We will have a bit more to say about this later.

Genesis 4:19–22

יָבָל הוּא הָיָה אֲבִי יֹשֵׁב אֹהֶל וּמִקְנֶה...תּוּבַל קַיִן לֹטֵשׁ כָּל חֹרֵשׁ נְחֹשֶׁת וּבַרְזֶל

Yaval: he was the first of those who dwell in tents and tend livestock.... Tuval-Kayin, he was the forger of all instruments of copper and iron.

Until now, in the wake of Cain's curse, humankind had failed to settle down and find themselves a true home upon land. But Yaval begins to change that, ever so slightly. He is the father of all "who dwell in tents." That is, Yaval, the shepherd, seems to have innovated a new form of domicile: tents. Thus, the land may not allow itself to become truly settled by humanity yet — but still, life is more bearable now that Yaval's tents are in the world. His newly invented form of temporary domicile is a technological salve for one aspect of Cain's terrible curse.

Tuval-Kayin, for his part, offers a technological fix for the other aspect of Cain's curse. Until now, a farmer would work the fields from morning until night, by the sweat of his brow, and have almost nothing to show for his efforts. As the text tells us, the earth would stubbornly refuse to give "its strength" to humans in the nascent field of agriculture. But Tuval-Kayin starts to change things. He becomes the first forger of iron tools. He creates the technology that underlies the creation of the plow.

With the tools of Lemech's children, the horrors of the land's curses begin, ever so slightly, to recede.

Precursors of Yovel

We can now understand, perhaps, why the names of Lemech's children sound so much like Yovel. Through these very innovations, these brothers really *did* bring a kind of primal Yovel into the world. Because, think about it: The Yovel year... what does it do, after all? Two things, mainly: It brings freedom to servants, and it returns ancestral land to its owners. And now ask yourself: Who was the first person who was forced to relinquish any sense of permanence on his own land — the first one to lose his ancestral land, so to speak? Who was the first person to pour his sweat and tears into his labor and get almost nothing out of it — who, like a slave, reaped no economic gain from all his efforts? Wouldn't the answer to both these questions be… *Cain*? Cain, and by extension, all his progeny, doomed to live in the shadow of his curse?

Sure, Cain wasn't a slave to a person; he had no external master that he served. But the earth was master enough for Cain. And to travel incessantly from place to place, never finding a home? If Adam had been promised dominion over the earth, Cain, his son, had all but lost that prized ancestral heritage. Cain couldn't even find a place on earth to call his home. He was the first one to really lose ancestral land.

But when it comes to these twin aspects of loss, things started to get just a bit brighter in the generation of Lemech's children. It was as if the curse of the land held, unabated, for six generations, but in the seventh — courtesy of these brothers, the land finally relaxed its grip. The technological innovations of Lemech's sons held within them the first whispers of redemption. People would feel less enslaved because of the invention of iron tools to help them work the ground. People incessantly traveling the earth would feel more at home once they figured out how to pitch tents to at least create temporary domiciles.

In the days of Lemech's children, the terrible alienation between mankind and its terrestrial parent, the land, began, tentatively, to recede. Thus, in truth, in the days of Lemech's children, a first, primal Yovel came to the world: a moment when the first slaves the world ever knew were able to shed their bonds, a moment where a homeless humanity began to reassert their lost claim of domicile upon earth itself.

LEMECH'S CHILDREN REDEEM TWO ASPECTS OF CAIN'S CURSE IN A KIND OF PROTO-YOVEL

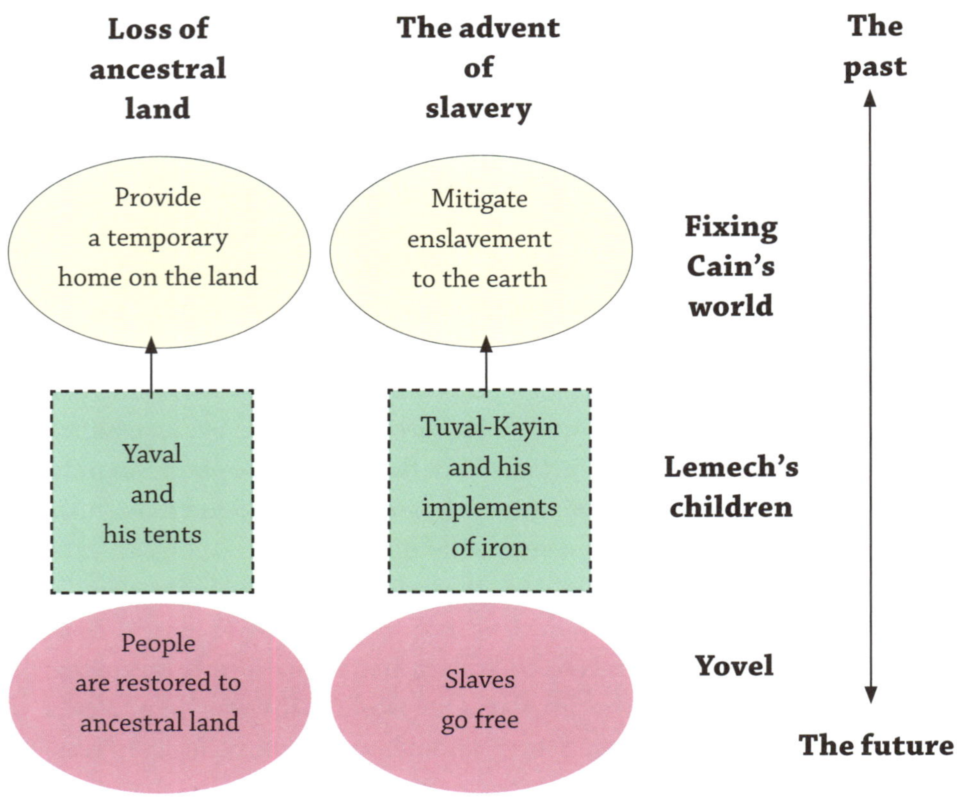

Yuval's Invention

The question that remains to be solved, though, is: *Why?* Why, all of a sudden, would land abide a loosening of its curse? In other words, it seems fair to ask why God would allow for the children of Lemech to be... so successful. After all, later in history, in the story of the Tower of Babel, God showed Himself quite willing to impede man's technological march of progress, when He deemed such progress incompatible with His designs for humankind. Why, then, in the case of Lemech's children, did God permit technological solutions to mitigate His divinely ordained curse?

To find the answer, we need to look a little more carefully at these three brothers. For until now, we've spoken only of the innovations of two of Lemech's children. But there was a third brother, too: Yuval. And he, too, brought an innovation into the world. Yuval's invention, though, was categorically different from the others. It wasn't directly focused on utility, on mitigating the effects of Cain's curse. Instead, it spoke to something far more essential: the spiritual rot that caused the curse of the land to haunt mankind in the first place.

יוּבָל הוּא הָיָה אֲבִי כָּל תֹּפֵשׂ כִּנּוֹר וְעוּגָב׃	Yuval: he was the father of all who play the lyre and pipe.	Genesis 4:21

Yuval, according to the text, was the first to bring musical instruments into the world. Among them were wind instruments, like the musical pipe.[9]

Why was this of such dramatic import? Well, consider how Yuval's name interacts with that particular innovation. We mentioned before that Lemech's children seem to remind us of their seventh-generation forebears, Cain and Abel. In matching the three brothers to the two ancestors, we'll find that one of Lemech's children reminds us, predominantly, of Cain,[10] whereas two seem to directly echo Abel, Hevel in Hebrew:

LEMECH'S SONS, SEVEN GENERATIONS LATER	ADAM'S SONS
Yaval Yuval	Hevel
Tuval-Kayin	Cain

Above, we theorized that the children of Lemech might play similar roles to Cain and Abel, perhaps channeling the respective legacies of their seventh-generation ancestors. But the fact that *two* of Lemech's sons — Yaval and Yuval — *both* seem to echo Abel's name (Hevel), gives rise to an

9 See *Bereishit Rabba* 23:3 and Talmud Yerushalmi Sukkah 5:6 which seem to identify עוּגָב as a type of water pipe or organ.

10 As noted earlier, "Tuval-Kayin" contains a (less obvious) grammatical variation of "Hevel," but it also contains a direct reference to Cain. The other names of the brothers do not.

intriguing possibility. Might these brothers "split" Abel's legacy somehow? We saw above how Yaval seemed to channel one aspect of Abel: Herding sheep and livestock. Perhaps that suggests there is another aspect of Abel's legacy that we are overlooking. Might Yuval, this creator of musical instruments, channel that other, phantom piece of Hevel's legacy?

A Silenced Voice Comes Alive

Well, come to think of it, in the Cain and Abel narrative, there *is* another aspect of Abel that we hear about. It is, indeed, easily overlooked, since in real time, as the Cain and Abel story was unfolding, no one paid any attention to it...

I'm thinking of Abel's voice:

Genesis 4:10	קוֹל דְּמֵי אָחִיךָ צֹעֲקִים אֵלַי מִן הָאֲדָמָה:	The voice of your brother's blood cries out to Me from the ground!

In fact, the notion of voice is related to Abel's very name, since in Hebrew, *hevel* is not just a name but a word that means "breath" — or more precisely, the ephemeral vapor that dissipates into the air when someone exhales.[11] Tragically, as Abel's story plays out, his breath coalesces into a voice — a cry that goes unheard by his brother, as Abel's lifeblood seeps into the ground from his mortal wounds. Somehow, Cain found it within himself to remain impervious to that voice, convincing himself that Abel's cries were not his business:

Genesis 4:9	הֲשֹׁמֵר אָחִי אָנֹכִי	Am I my brother's keeper?

Seven generations later, though, the lost breath of Abel seems to return, in a new form. *Hevel*, mere breath, which would ordinarily just dissipate once it leaves one's lips, now resolves itself, via the medium of a special wind instrument, into a magical, beguiling voice, a sound of such beauty

---

11 See Ecclesiastes chapter 1.

it is nearly impossible to ignore. In creating wind instruments like the pipe, Yuval — Abel's namesake — finds a way to take mere breath and make music out of it. Abel's dissonant scream reemerges as a beautiful melody. Now, perhaps, the ancient voice of Abel is no longer ignored by brothers. Instead, it has become music they can't help but delight in.

Yuval resurrects the lost breath of Hevel.

Music as an Antidote to Toil

If the other two brothers, Yaval and Tuval-Kayin, bring technological innovations into the world — *material* ways of coping with the curse of the land (i.e., the ability to build tents and implements of iron), Yuval, the middle brother, brings an innovation of a different sort altogether. He brings music into the world, a way of allowing humanity to experience something transcendent and ethereal in this otherwise very material world of ours.

Perhaps because it seems to reach beyond our material world, we humans experience music as soothing. We use music instinctively to take the edge off of pain and hardship. Slaves would famously sing in the fields to make their grueling labor bearable. Music even takes an exhausting workout in the gym and transforms it into something we might actually look forward to. If Yaval and Tuval-Kayin took the edge off Cain's curse through tents and implements of iron, Yuval showed us a different salve for the hardship that working the earth imposed upon us. He gave us the transcendent experience of melody, taking our breath and turning it into an instrument of tranquility.

And speaking of tranquility, here we arrive at another crucial contrast between Cain and Abel and their seventh-generation descendants, the children of Lemech. Cain and Abel descended into competition with one another, with the life of one brother ended by the violent vengeance of another. Yaval, Yuval, and Tuval-Kayin, though, are apparently at peace with one another. We have no record of competition between them, despite their apparent use of a single, common resource — land — for competing purposes (farming versus the raising of animals). Somehow, these brothers found a way to live at peace with one another. We can't know why for sure, but perhaps Yuval and his soothing music had something to do with that. Perhaps the willingness of other brothers to listen to the breath, the *hevel,* of a fellow sibling helps explain why humanity's parents, the earth and God, allowed humanity's relationship with land to begin to heal. These brothers, between them, paved the way for the possibility that land could reconcile itself to the presence of humanity upon it, and could begin to nurture its human children once again.

A Poison Returns

What became of this nascent détente between the earth and mankind?

Something tragically interrupted it. And that something was a resurgence of Cain's vengeance. Seven generations after Cain, the poison he brought into the world would return. But this time, it would increase in potency by an order of magnitude. Now, it would become an ensconced feature of statecraft. And now, it would be truly terrifying.

4 THE REIGN OF LEMECH

Cain's vengeance makes its return, ironically, through the father of the very three brothers we've been talking about. Lemech takes a violent emotional outburst by Cain and sharpens it into a deliberate and devastating political weapon. Immediately after we hear about the renaissance of Yaval, Yuval, and Tuval-Kayin, the next verse picks up the thread of Lemech's story:

Humanity's First Song

Genesis 4:23–24

וַיֹּאמֶר לֶמֶךְ לְנָשָׁיו עָדָה וְצִלָּה
שְׁמַעַן קוֹלִי נְשֵׁי לֶמֶךְ הַאְזֵנָּה
אִמְרָתִי כִּי אִישׁ הָרַגְתִּי לְפִצְעִי
וְיֶלֶד לְחַבֻּרָתִי: כִּי שִׁבְעָתַיִם
יֻקַּם קָיִן וְלֶמֶךְ שִׁבְעִים וְשִׁבְעָה:

Lemech said to his wives, "Adah and Tzilah, listen to my voice; the wives of Lemech, heed my speech. I have killed a man for my bruise and a child for my wound. If Cain would be avenged sevenfold, then Lemech seventy-sevenfold!"

In these verses, we get the first poetry — the first song, really[12] — ever recorded by the Torah. But it is a curious song. Its theme is threatening and dark. It extols vengeance, of all things. What is the meaning of Lemech's song? Why did he sing it — and why did he feel a need to sing it to his wives, of all people? Why are *they* his primary, intended audience?

If we pay attention to what Lemech is singing about, we will have our answer.

How Lemech Rolls

After his preamble, in which he asks his wives to listen to his voice, the first thing Lemech tells the women in his life is this:

אִישׁ הָרַגְתִּי לְפִצְעִי וְיֶלֶד לְחַבֻּרָתִי׃	I have killed a man for my bruise and a child for my wound.	Genesis 4:23

Lemech's words, being poetry, are somewhat opaque, and there are many ways to interpret them. Some commentators, such as Rashi, interpret Lemech as asking a rhetorical question (Have I *really* killed a man or a

---

12 I take the liberty of calling Lemech's words not just poetry but "song," because of the way Lemech's words at the beginning of Genesis so clearly form a template for words the Torah explicitly calls a "song" at the end of Deuteronomy — *Shirat Ha'azinu*. The language of the two would indicate that this very last "song" of the Torah is, somehow, an echo of the Torah's first "song." Consider for example, Lemech's preamble: לֶמֶךְ נְשֵׁי קוֹלִי עָדָה וְצִלָּה **שְׁמַעַן** **הַאְזֵנָּה** **אִמְרָתִי** — "Adah and Tzilah, **listen** to my voice; the wives of Lemech, **heed** **my speech**," and its resonance with *Ha'azinu*'s opening words: **הַאֲזִינוּ** הַשָּׁמַיִם וַאֲדַבֵּרָה **וְתִשְׁמַע** הָאָרֶץ **אִמְרֵי פִי׃** — Heed [me] O heavens and I will speak, and **listen** O earth to **my speech**. (Deut. 32:1)

Other aspects of the *Ha'azinu* song likewise resonate with Lemech's words. Lemech closes his song with an assurance about taking vengeance, and, chillingly, *Ha'azinu* likewise closes with a promise of vengeance. The larger meaning of these parallels still remains a mystery to me.

child?). But a more straightforward approach is advanced by Yosef Ibn Kaspi, a lesser-known classical commentator, and I want to present it for your consideration here. Ibn Kaspi asserts that Lemech is speaking in direct, declarative sentences, which means, essentially, that Lemech is confessing to a crime. Confession, though, maybe isn't the best word for it, since there is no hint of remorse in his little song. Instead, Lemech's speech is boastful and dripping with malice. He seems to be casually telling his wives what happened on his way home from work one day:

A man bruised him, and he, Lemech, responded by killing him in return; a child wounded him, and so he killed the child, too.

What's more, Lemech is *singing* about all this.

Let's come back to the question: Why is Lemech addressing his wives in particular? Well, think of it this way: What would any wife naturally seek from her powerful husband? Many things, probably, but perhaps protection looms larger than them all. Lemech is reassuring his wives that they have nothing to fear. No matter how great his crimes, no matter how over-the-top his violent acts of reprisal, they will be safe. No one will dare come after him, because...

Genesis 4:24

כִּי שִׁבְעָתַיִם יֻקַּם קָיִן וְלֶמֶךְ
שִׁבְעִים וְשִׁבְעָה׃

If Cain would be avenged sevenfold, then Lemech seventy-seven-fold!

Lemech's calling card is Cain's vengeance, but seven generations later, that vengeance has morphed itself into something truly terrifying. Lemech takes Cain's penchant for retribution up an order of magnitude. Sevenfold retribution has turned into payback that is seventy-seven-fold. Thus, to fight Lemech is to risk everything: Not just your own death, but the deaths of all whom you love. Vengeance to the nth degree, in all its utter disproportionality.

What is going on in Lemech's inner world? Is he a man totally without any moral sensibilities? That, of course, is certainly possible. But his song to his wives suggests a different motivation, one that carries with it the possibility of rationalizing the terror he would unleash. His willingness to make a calling card out of unrestrained vengeance... isn't really about violence for the sake of violence. To the contrary, that terrifying threat *is precisely what's going to keep the peace.* Who, after all, would dare oppose him?

Lemech is the world's first fully developed strongman, a proto-tyrant. Indeed, transpose the letters of his name, and look what you get:

למך = מלך transposed

It is *melech,* the Hebrew word for "king."

The Student of Cain

Just as Lemech's three children began to redeem the earth's revulsion at humanity, just as Yuval's lyre and pipe began to whisper that harmony was possible between brothers, the efforts of Lemech's children were snuffed out by the power grab of their own father. Cain's spirit of vengeance remained dormant for seven generations. But Lemech reached for the dying embers of Cain's rage and rekindled them. Lemech picks up the gauntlet of Cain's vengeance and runs with it. He makes a policy out of it. He truly *is* the student of Cain, not just in this, but in several other terrifying ways.

First, just as with Cain, there's something "off" about Lemech's boasts of vengeance.[13] But whereas with Cain you could chalk that up to mere impulsiveness, for Lemech, the subjectivity inherent in vengeance has become a policy. It is a feature, not a bug.

A kid runs over Lemech's toe with a tricycle. Lemech kills him in return... and Lemech is willing to casually sing an anthem about that? Why? *Because this is how Lemech rolls.* He kills to avenge any perceived slight against him. Just as Cain killed Abel even though Abel may not have intended to slight him, Lemech boasts that he will kill anyone who *seems* to offend him, whether the offense was real or not. Just as Cain responded with extreme disproportion when he killed Abel, so will Lemech. Lemech seems like a crazy man, but there are advantages to being perceived that way. Lemech publicly demonstrates that he is willing to use violence without restraint. Because Lemech rules by intimidation, the more impulsive and out-of-proportion his retribution, the better.

---

13 Imagine someone kills Lemech — justly, one would imagine, for his crimes. But Lemech contorts any attempted violence against him and turns *that* into a crime, one that will be "justly" avenged seventy-seven-fold. Lemech takes his own culpability and projects it outward.

In line with this, Lemech is also Cain's student when it comes to how much violence is necessary to "keep the peace." As God told Cain, there is something darkly protective about using violence disproportionately to settle grievances. People will think twice before they kill him, if they fear "sevenfold vengeance" from Cain's children. But seven generations later, the threat of sevenfold vengeance isn't enough to repel would-be attackers anymore. Lemech, the new strongman on the block, laughs at sevenfold retribution. His vengeance would multiply any violence against him seventy-seven-fold.

Under Lemech, the gold standard for deterrence must climb ever higher, for the world has become desensitized to violence. As Lemech proudly sings to his wives, the dynamics of vengeance *can* create a fragile peace. But only for a while. All it takes to upset the applecart is one person who is willing to take the threat of violence up one notch further, up yet *another* order of magnitude. All it takes is one person who is willing to bring a gun to a knife fight. Seven generations after Cain, Lemech was that person.

Lemech and the Apocalypse

It shouldn't surprise us, then, that Lemech and his children represent the last generation before the Great Flood. For once vengeance gets fully normalized; once it takes hold as simply the way business gets done; once seventy-seven-fold retribution is the *new* level of threatened destruction necessary to impose a fragile calm — *that's* when you know you've reached the end of the line. That's when the world has become so "full of violence" that it reaches a point of no return:

Genesis 6:6, 11

וַיִּנָּחֶם יְקוָה כִּי עָשָׂה אֶת הָאָדָם בָּאָרֶץ וַיִּתְעַצֵּב אֶל לִבּוֹ... וַתִּשָּׁחֵת הָאָרֶץ לִפְנֵי הָאֱלֹקִים וַתִּמָּלֵא הָאָרֶץ חָמָס:	God regretted that He had made man on earth, and He was saddened to His heart.... The earth had become corrupt before the Almighty, and the earth was filled with violence.

Lemech's boast to his wives, his gleeful power grab, became emblematic of a world that had crossed the Rubicon into an ever-accelerating spiral of violence. And thus, the earth once again recoiled in disgust from humanity. If sevenfold vengeance was enough to consign Cain and his children to a life of wandering the face of the earth, in the days of Lemech, when seventy-seven-fold vengeance became the norm, the earth would *fully* expel man from its environs. Land would not suffer to provide man shelter anywhere in its dominion.

And the Flood came.

5 YOVEL AND THE CHILDREN OF LEMECH

One of the lessons of Cain's first furtive experiments with violence is that vengeance always co-opts unwitting bystanders. In Cain's case, the bystander the text most directly references is the land. Forced against its will to accept the blood of Cain's brother, the earth becomes a passive accomplice in the matter of Abel's death. We suggested, though, that others must have been co-opted as well. Most particularly, this would have involved Cain's progeny. Should anyone dare to kill Cain, it would be up to Cain's son Chanoch to avenge his father's death. The implicit pact of family loyalty would demand that of him. As the name Chanoch perhaps implies, to be Cain's child is to be "schooled" in this, just by being part of the family.

Let's extend that argument, then. Seven generations after Cain, when, in his song to his wives, Lemech resurrects Cain's stance of vengeance as the way he will do business, notice that Lemech's promise to them also implicitly co-opts others. *He* acted with vengeance when he killed a man for a wound, a child for a bruise. But should he ever be killed in retribution, it would fall to *others* — his loyal children, presumably — to avenge him, in a seventy-seven-fold riot of violence.

Whether they like it or not, a familial duty has been thrust upon Yaval, Yuval, and Tuval-Kayin.

The Corrupting of Lemech's Children

There is a terrible tragedy here — a tragedy that perhaps might be illustrated viscerally with a modern analogue from the world of fiction. The twin themes of vengeance and loyalty that so animate Cain and Lemech's story have reverberated through the centuries in many forms of art and literature, among them one of the most universally acclaimed films ever produced, Francis Ford Coppola's 1972 classic, *The Godfather*. Why did that film leave such a powerful impression on so many? It's not just the acting, I would suggest to you, or even the great music. It's the way the film expertly appropriates a theme as old as time: how loyalty and vengeance can work together to snuff out the nascent virtue of those caught in a strongman's vortex.

A dapper Michael Corleone appears early on in the film as a returning American war hero. His father is a Mafia don, and his brothers are part of the "family business" — but Michael is the exception. He is the one who opts for a different life, a chance to fulfill the American dream of prosperity in pursuit of legitimate business opportunities. But all that falls away once his father falls ill and later dies. He feels duty-bound by honor to step into his father's shoes. And, in one of the final scenes of the film, he wreaks vengeance upon his family's enemies in a paroxysm of violence so explosive as to make the menace of his father's era seem like child's play by comparison. The man who always envisioned a different life for himself becomes the emblem of seventy-seven-fold vengeance, as the quiet but imperious demands of family loyalty swallow the remains of his virtue.

The film is powerful precisely because it illustrates a heartbreaking truth: There is a credible path through which a good person can become transformed into a purveyor of terror. Family loyalty, usually a virtue, can co-opt the innocence and idealism of children, and pave a path to the abyss.

The final tragedy of Lemech, in the interpretation I've suggested above, is the role he implicitly expects those loyal to him, principally his children, to play in the preservation of his protection racket. He co-opts his kids, like it or not, into the family business. Should anyone have the courage to step forth and justly kill Lemech for his crimes, it would be up to Yaval, Yuval, and Tuval-Kayin to do what they know they must do.

Thus, while these brothers did, perhaps, manage to quell the impulse toward vengeance and violence within their own family, it will be nearly impossible for them to preserve this stance toward others, outside the family, in light of their father's choices. Father has asked them to arm themselves with the power of vengeance-as-policy against the onslaught of any outsider. If they are good kids, predisposed to honor their fallen father, what are they to do? The insistent demands of family loyalty will, in all likelihood, eventually swallow their nascent virtue whole. They will become the point of Lemech's spear.

Yuval's Melody and Lemech's Song

Lemech's willingness to corrupt his children in this way is evident in an ironic twist highlighted by the verses of his story. For right after we, the readers, hear of Yuval's innovation, his creation of the musical pipe — an instrument that transforms breath into a beautiful melody — we next hear of a song that is sung. But it is *not* the song of Yuval, the one who created musical instrumentation. It is the song of his father Lemech:

Genesis 4:23–24

עָדָה וְצִלָּה שְׁמַעַן קוֹלִי נְשֵׁי לֶמֶךְ הַאְזֵנָּה אִמְרָתִי כִּי אִישׁ הָרַגְתִּי לְפִצְעִי וְיֶלֶד לְחַבֻּרָתִי׃ כִּי שִׁבְעָתַיִם יֻקַּם קָיִן וְלֶמֶךְ שִׁבְעִים וְשִׁבְעָה׃	Adah and Tzilah, listen to my voice; the wives of Lemech, heed my speech. I have killed a man for my bruise and a child for my wound. If Cain would be avenged sevenfold, then Lemech seventy-sevenfold!

Lemech co-opts his son's invention of music. If Yuval's song may have helped bring harmony internally, within the family, Lemech's appropriation of that invention brings discord into the larger family of man. Yuval's voice came into the world through his music. But Lemech turns a deaf ear to that voice. Instead, he has other ideas about whose voice should get listened to:

עָדָה וְצִלָּה שְׁמַעַן **קוֹלִי** נְשֵׁי לֶמֶךְ הַאְזֵנָּה אִמְרָתִי	Adah and Tzilah, listen to **my voice**; the wives of Lemech, heed my speech.

Lemech's voice drowns out the voice of his son, as the reconstituted flame of Cain's vengeance steals the day.

Yovel and the Children of Lemech

The reader of Genesis, absorbing this tragedy, is left to ask: What legacy do these children of Lemech really have, then? They, with their father, were wiped out in the Great Flood. Their innovations, their tentative attempts to redeem mankind's broken relationship to the earth, have all but vanished into oblivion. In the long march of human history, do the three sons of Lemech really matter?

They do.

It turns out there is a life raft, as it were, for the legacy of these three children. For the Torah creates an institution out of their innovations. It makes a law out of their story: the law of the Yovel year.

Linguistically, the law emerges from their names: Yaval, Yuval, and Tuval, all grammatical variations of the common "Yovel." Conceptually, it emerges out of a merger of their three innovations. Through the institution of the Jubilee year, the Torah takes the proto-Yovel of the children of Lemech, and transforms it into a working institution meant to help regulate life in the society Israel will set up in the Land of Israel. As we shall see, Yovel, as an institution, is designed to help make certain that the vengeance that bedeviled the children of Cain will not snowball, as it once did, into ever-increasing suffering for the masses. It is designed to take what Yuval, Yaval, and Tuval-Kayin were trying to bring to the world — innovations that would mitigate loss of ancestral land and slavery — and transform them into something new, something that would help Israel salve a latter-day version of Cain's curse.

Let me explain what I mean by this.

A Socioeconomic Version of Cain's Curse

Loss of ancestral land and slavery: These two scourges are still with us. Back in Cain's world, both were expressions of God's curse, which mandated that land would become alienated from us humans. Intriguingly, in the post-Flood world, one can argue whether Cain's original curse is still with us, but one way or another, an updated version of alienation from land — a socioeconomic version of it — conspires to keep these two maladies with us.

How so? Well, in the Torah's depiction of things, how does someone usually get to be a slave? More often than not, it happens when and if someone down on their luck becomes so hard-pressed to come by food and shelter that they agree to indenture themselves as a servant in return for food by day, and a place to sleep by night.[14]

---

14 See, for example, Lev. 25:39. The Torah discusses a few "classes" of slaves in the

Because slavery is primarily a function of lack of access to food and shelter, the greatest historical bulwark against slavery has always been... land ownership. For even if I am very poor, still — if I retain a little plot of family land, passed down from parent to child over the generations — I have a safety valve. If things ever get so bad that I have no money left, I can always come by my basic necessities through my little patch of Mother Earth. I can, if necessary, do some subsistence farming and feed myself. I can, if necessary, roll out a sleeping bag on my land and spend the night. Land's security keeps the prospect of servitude at bay.

Should I ever lose that ancestral land of mine, though, all bets are off. If I am ever forced to sell it... suddenly, I live life only a step away from the specter of slavery. I make one catastrophic financial mistake, and nothing, anymore, stands between me and an unyielding creditor. My freedom is only as fragile as the next downturn in the economy. One false move and I'm a slave.

Cain's Curse for a Modern Age

That's Cain's curse for a modern age. In our world, alienation from land, with its twin ramifications, arises naturally as a by-product of human transactions as civilizations develop normal, basic systems of commerce. Let people engage in financial transactions enough, and sooner or later, there will be poor people and rich people. There will be those who sell their ancestral land and those who don't. There will be those sold as slaves and those who remain free. The point is that, even in modern times, a fundamental reality persists: When humans become alienated from the earth they call their own, homelessness and slavery lurk right around the corner.

But, it turns out, the Torah has something to say about this state of affairs. And that something is detailed at the end of **Parshat Behar**.

To Be Your Brother's Keeper

At the end of **Parshat Behar**, the Torah sets forth its preferred solution to this latter-day version of alienation from land. The Torah directly references here both examples we've been speaking about: The person who,

---

subsequent verses. However, here, I am focusing on the Israelite slave who is set free by the Yovel year.

burdened by crushing debt, sells himself as a slave; and the person who sells his ancestral land.

What to do about this? Here is what the Torah tells us:

ONE WHO SOLD HIS ANCESTRAL LAND	ONE WHO SOLD HIMSELF INTO SLAVERY
כִּי יָמוּךְ אָחִיךָ וּמָכַר מֵאֲחֻזָּתוֹ וּבָא גֹאֲלוֹ הַקָּרֹב אֵלָיו וְגָאַל אֵת מִמְכַּר אָחִיו׃	אַחֲרֵי נִמְכַּר גְּאֻלָּה תִּהְיֶה לּוֹ אֶחָד מֵאֶחָיו יִגְאָלֶנּוּ׃ אוֹ דֹדוֹ אוֹ בֶן דֹּדוֹ יִגְאָלֶנּוּ אוֹ מִשְּׁאֵר בְּשָׂרוֹ מִמִּשְׁפַּחְתּוֹ יִגְאָלֶנּוּ
If your brother becomes poor and sells some of his ancestral land, then his relative, his redeemer, shall come and redeem that which his brother has sold (Lev. 25:25).	After he is sold [into slavery] he should be redeemed. One of his brothers should redeem him, or his uncle, or his uncle's son, may redeem him too, or any who is a close relative to him of his family may redeem him (Lev. 25:48–49).

In each case, the Torah ordains an urgent imperative: If your brother sold his ancestral land, or went further and actually sold himself as a slave — it is up to *you*, his relative — brother, uncle, cousin, doesn't matter — to step forward and redeem him. The Torah then devotes the better part of a chapter to explaining how this would work. It ordains that a person has a right to bargain with the buyer of his relative's ancestral land or his relative's master (if he was sold as a slave), and redeem each for less than the original price of sale.

That's the optimal solution. But what's Plan B? What if the optimum solution never takes place? What if no relative — no brother, son, uncle, or cousin — ever steps forward to help the person who sold his ancestral land or indentured himself into servitude. What then?

Later verses in **Parshat Behar** give us the answer… in the form of Yovel. When the Yovel year arrives, society at large must ensure that all land returns to its original ancestral holder. And when the Yovel year arrives, society must ensure that all those who are indentured return to their families:

וְקִדַּשְׁתֶּם אֵת שְׁנַת הַחֲמִשִּׁים שָׁנָה וּקְרָאתֶם דְּרוֹר בָּאָרֶץ לְכָל יֹשְׁבֶיהָ יוֹבֵל הִוא תִּהְיֶה לָכֶם וְשַׁבְתֶּם אִישׁ אֶל אֲחֻזָּתוֹ וְאִישׁ אֶל מִשְׁפַּחְתּוֹ תָּשֻׁבוּ׃	You shall make the fiftieth year holy, and proclaim liberty throughout the land for all its inhabitants. It shall be a Yovel to you: Each of you shall return to his own ancestral land, and each of you [who has been indentured] shall return to his family.	Leviticus 25:10

A Cry from the Ground

But pay attention to the mechanism by which all this happens. How, exactly, does this Yovel year begin? What must society do to launch it?

Parshat Behar tells us:

וְהַעֲבַרְתָּ שׁוֹפַר תְּרוּעָה בַּחֹדֶשׁ הַשְּׁבִעִי בֶּעָשׂוֹר לַחֹדֶשׁ בְּיוֹם הַכִּפֻּרִים תַּעֲבִירוּ שׁוֹפָר בְּכָל אַרְצְכֶם׃	You shall sound the calling-shofar on the tenth day of the seventh month. On the Day of Atonement you shall sound the shofar throughout all your land.	Leviticus 25:9

The Torah decrees that a shofar, one of the most primal musical instruments we humans possess, shall herald the onset of Yovel. This shofar blast will usher in a last-ditch solution to our civilization's socioeconomic version of Cain's curse. It shall return people to their family's land and shall set servants free.

If we think back to the Cain and Abel story, the origin point of Cain's curse, we might be excused for imagining that this shofar blast is channeling a latter-day version of Abel's desperate but ignored cry. For, you will recall, the text describes that brother's cry as a scream that emanated specifically *from the earth*:

קוֹל דְּמֵי אָחִיךָ צֹעֲקִים אֵלַי מִן הָאֲדָמָה׃	The voice of your brother's blood cries out to Me from the ground.	Genesis 4:10

Well, the socioeconomic maladies that **Parshat Behar** seeks to mitigate are also versions of cries "from the ground"; they come about when someone quite literally loses the ground beneath his feet, or becomes enslaved because he no longer possesses any ground to call his own. And what, according to **Parshat Behar**, is Yovel positioned to do? It is there as a final remedy, when a person's "cry from the ground" is ignored by his closest relatives. When the enslaved person's brother doesn't respond, nor his uncle, nor his cousin...then *society* must respond, galvanized by the cry of the shofar.

In ordaining that Yovel begins specifically with the shofar's call, then, it is as if the Torah is echoing the ignored cry of Abel. The Torah is taking that cry and transforming it into a sound that heralds freedom throughout the earth. At the moment of Yovel, the Torah offers a kind of music to desperate ears.

Yes, Abel's cry was ignored by a vengeful brother. Yes, the harmony of Yuval's pipe was silenced by the malicious song of Lemech. But in the cry of the Yovel shofar, the sound of Yuval's pipe shall finally be given new life. It will be heard anew throughout the land. In that blast of the shofar, the Torah provides an eternal legacy for the lost music of Yuval.

To Be a Brother's Keeper

What is the motivation of the person who stands silently by and refuses to redeem his brother's lost ancestral land, or, even worse, refuses to redeem his brother from the clutches of servitude?

It might be that they don't have the money. But it also might be they just can't be bothered. *My relative got himself into trouble; why is it my responsibility to help?* One discerns in that the faint echo of another person, long ago, who argued it wasn't his responsibility to help:

Genesis 4:9

I don't know; am I my brother's keeper? לֹא יָדַעְתִּי הֲשֹׁמֵר אָחִי אָנֹכִי׃

One could plausibly argue that, even in the story of Cain, it is Cain's passive-aggressive response, "Am I my brother's keeper?" that is his truest act of malice. As we discussed in the second part of our essay on **Parshat Vayikra**, no one had ever died before. Cain was angry and he hit his brother. You could argue he didn't exactly know what would happen. But after Abel is dead, to simply not *care* about his fate, to imagine that what happened to his brother is none of his concern, *that's* when God really becomes angry with Cain. Likewise, in the post-Flood age, imagine someone who sensed himself as his brother's rival, as Cain did. Imagine he experienced misfortune at someone else's hands, but in a misplaced way, like Cain, always blamed his brother for it. Well, if you want to get even, modern economic realities mean you don't have to actually get up and strike your brother to lash out at him vengefully. You can be much quieter about it. Actually, you don't even have to do *anything*. You can just stand by passively when your brother faces the extremes of socioeconomic privation. You ignore his plight when, and long after, he becomes homeless or gets sold as a slave. By doing so, you get to settle your scores, and afterward, like Cain, you get to shrug and say, "*Who? Me?*" It's a kind of subtle vengeance, cloaked in the respectable garb of deniability.

The insidious part about it is that the relative may not even recognize vengeance as his motive at all. Blinded by his own subjectivity, he might see his silence as a form of…justice. *Sure, my brother is suffering terribly. But isn't he suffering for his own economic sins? Isn't he just the victim of a modern curse of Cain? If he's allowed himself to get alienated from land, that was his choice. Should I really get involved?* One might therefore argue to oneself that justice demands an attitude of stoic indifference toward the cry of a brother dispossessed of the earth. But then again, vengeance always seems like justice in the eyes of its own purveyors.

Who Gets Drawn In Now?

So let's follow this thread and see where it takes us. Let's say the person described in **Parshat Behar** who won't redeem his brother from slavery, or won't help him redeem his ancestral holding, is guilty of a latter-day form of failing to act as "his brother's keeper." In Cain's instance, that passive-aggressive attitude was a subtle expression of vengeance, a quality that, as we have seen, tends to pull unwitting co-conspirators into its orbit. So let us inquire: *What about here, much later in the Torah, in **Parshat Behar**?* The person who rationalizes to himself that he is not his brother's keeper and stands by while his brother languishes in slavery — if that, too, is a subtle expression of passive vengeance, who, if anyone, does *he* co-opt? Who, if anyone, is in danger of becoming the Michael Corleone of **Parshat Behar**?

The uncomfortable answer is: *all of us.*

When society turns its back on the neediest among us, when it just goes about its business and chalks up the ills of slavery and homelessness to the mere dispassionate workings of market economics, it may not be acting out of malice — but it *has* become an accessory to the malice-tinged indifference of others, of the neediest nearest kin. Society can thus easily become a co-conspirator in a relative's stony silence.

Just Say No

But the Torah, in innovating the institution of Yovel, asks the society of Israel to resist getting co-opted. Instead, it insists that if individuals won't act in the face of alienation from land, society will. If individuals won't be their brother's keeper; if they won't redeem the land of their kin, then once every fifty years, society will act collectively to return family land, unilaterally, to its original owner. And if individuals won't redeem their own kin from slavery, then once every fifty years, society will act collectively to annul the bonds of servitude and return people to their families.

The children of Lemech tried to counter slavery and loss of ancestral land. But their efforts were thwarted by a father whose vengeance swallowed whatever benign intentions they might have had, and co-opted them. At all costs, society must refuse to be similarly co-opted. It must not allow itself to remain a passive bystander in the face of cold indifference. Yovel, with its shofar blast — part scream, part music — gives voice to the lost breath of Abel, and new life to the instruments of Yuval. That voice, the voice of a brother finally *heard,* galvanizes society's reset, triggering the return of all ancestral land and freedom from all slavery. That voice, finally heard, makes real the lost dreams of Yaval the tent maker and Tuval-Kayin the ironsmith. The children of the earth will come home. The children of the earth will no longer be enslaved.

Leviticus 25: 9–10

וְהַעֲבַרְתָּ שׁוֹפַר תְּרוּעָה
...וְקִדַּשְׁתֶּם אֵת שְׁנַת
הַחֲמִשִּׁים שָׁנָה וּקְרָאתֶם
דְּרוֹר בָּאָרֶץ לְכָל יֹשְׁבֶיהָ

You shall sound the calling-shofar…and you shall sanctify the fiftieth year and proclaim liberty throughout the land to all its inhabitants. It shall be a Yovel to

יוֹבֵל הִוא תִּהְיֶה לָכֶם וְשַׁבְתֶּם
אִישׁ אֶל אֲחֻזָּתוֹ וְאִישׁ אֶל
מִשְׁפַּחְתּוֹ תָּשֻׁבוּ׃

you; each of you shall return to his own ancestral land, and each of you shall return to his family.

The Yovel shofar does all this. For it declares emphatically that we all, after everything is said and done, are our brothers' keepers.

THE LEGACY OF LEMECH'S CHILDREN BECOMES IMMORTALIZED IN YOVEL

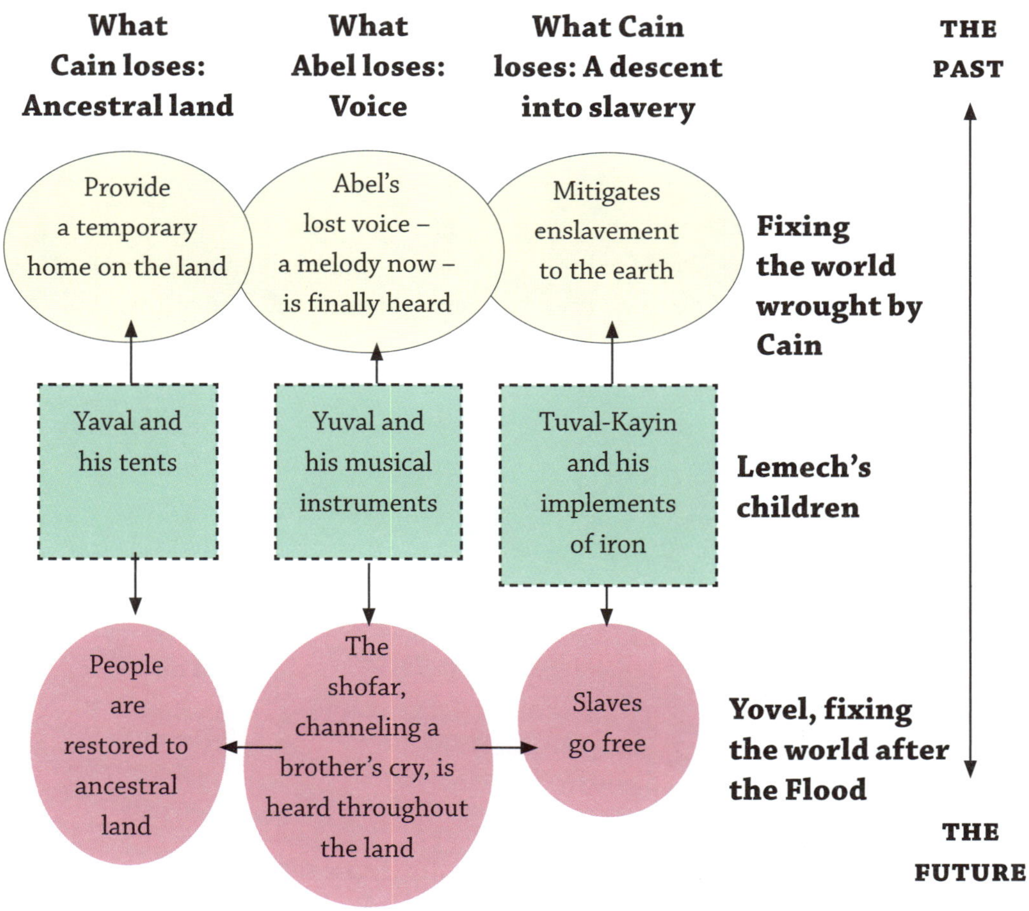

BECHUKOTAI

Back to the Future

וְהִתְהַלַּכְתִּי בְּתוֹכְכֶם
וְהָיִיתִי לָכֶם לֵאלֹקִים
וְאַתֶּם תִּהְיוּ לִי לְעָם׃

I will walk among you; I will be your God, and you will be My people.

LEVITICUS 26:12

יִרְדְּפוּ וְנָפְלוּ אֹיְבֵיכֶם לִפְנֵיכֶם לֶחָרֶב: ט וּפָנִיתִי אֲלֵיכֶם וְהִפְרֵיתִי אֶתְכֶם וְהִרְבֵּיתִי אֶתְכֶם	**8** Five of you shall chase a hundred, and a hundred of you shall chase ten thousand; and your enemies shall fall before you by the sword. **9** I will turn toward you, and make you fruitful, and multiply you.

In these words, the Almighty assures us that, once we enter the land, if we follow His statutes, we can be assured of divine blessing. But it's not just *any* divine blessing that **Parshat Bechukotai** has in mind. The blessings it speaks of seem to hark all the way back to the dawn of mankind, all the way back to the sixth day of Creation. Because once you look at these verses closely, you start to notice that just about every element here reminds us of God's blessing to humans on Creation's sixth day.

Take, for example, the very end of this section of text, where we find these words:

וְהִפְרֵיתִי אֶתְכֶם וְהִרְבֵּיתִי אֶתְכֶם	And I will **make you fruitful, and multiply you**.	Leviticus 26:9

The two verbs used here in **Parshat Bechukotai** — וְהִפְרֵיתִי and וְהִרְבֵּיתִי — should sound familiar to any reader of the Creation story. Together, they are versions of the iconic blessing that God issues to the very first humans, Adam and Eve:

וַיְבָרֶךְ אֹתָם אֱלֹקִים וַיֹּאמֶר לָהֶם אֱלֹקִים פְּרוּ וּרְבוּ	God blessed them and said to them, "**Be fruitful and multiply**."	Genesis 1:28

And the connections don't stop there. Go back to **Parshat Bechukotai** and look at the words right before this. Just before the text promises that the Almighty "will make you fruitful and multiply you," we find a promise that if Israel follows His statutes, the nation will enjoy military success in war:

Leviticus 26:6–8

וְחֶרֶב לֹא תַעֲבֹר בְּאַרְצְכֶם: וּרְדַפְתֶּם אֶת אֹיְבֵיכֶם וְנָפְלוּ לִפְנֵיכֶם לֶחָרֶב: וְרָדְפוּ מִכֶּם חֲמִשָּׁה מֵאָה וּמֵאָה מִכֶּם רְבָבָה יִרְדֹּפוּ וְנָפְלוּ אֹיְבֵיכֶם לִפְנֵיכֶם לֶחָרֶב:	The sword shall not go through your land. You shall chase your enemies, and they shall fall before you by the sword. Five of you shall chase a hundred, and a hundred of you shall chase ten thousand; and your enemies shall fall before you by the sword.

That, too, seems to echo the blessing that God had given to Adam and Eve. For back in Eden, right after God blessed the first humans with fertility, that they should be fruitful and multiply, the next word has an unmistakably militaristic connotation:

Genesis 1:28

וְכִבְשֻׁהָ	And conquer [the earth].

In this verse, God promises this new race of humans that in the end, it will be people that put bears in zoos, rather than the other way around. Why? Because humans, using their ingenuity and superior skills in communication and tool making, would dominate the competition and come to rule the earth. They would have success in their first great war of survival.

Parshat Bechukotai's promise of military success in defending the nation's land seems to carry an echo of mankind's first promise of success in "conquering" the land.

A Third Echo

Thus far, we've discerned two echoes of Genesis's sixth day in **Parshat Bechukotai**'s opening blessing. But the echoes don't stop here. Here's a third echo:

Just before **Parshat Bechukotai** promised fertility to the people of Israel, and just before it promised military success, it promised something else:

וְהִשְׁבַּתִּי חַיָּה רָעָה מִן הָאָרֶץ	I will remove wild animals from the land.	Leviticus 26:6

The idea that we, Israel, will dwell safely in the Land of Israel without fear of wild animals is, in fact, the third-to-last element of **Parshat Bechukotai**'s blessing. And guess what? If you go back to Genesis, right after we hear a promise of fertility to Adam and Eve, and right after people get this very militaristic promise that they will "conquer" the earth, we get an element of blessing that mentions beasts of the animal world, of all things.

וּרְדוּ בִּדְגַת הַיָּם וּבְעוֹף הַשָּׁמַיִם **וּבְכָל חַיָּה הָרֹמֶשֶׂת עַל הָאָרֶץ:**	Dominate the fish of the sea, the birds of the sky, and **every animal that roams on the earth.**	Genesis 1:28

First to Last

So at this point, we've seen three connections between the blessing of **Parshat Bechukotai** and the original blessing to mankind, just as the human species was first created. But it's not just the number of connections that is significant here. It is also the order in which they appear. Back in Genesis, the *first* element of God's blessing to mankind is echoed by the *last* element of **Parshat Bechukotai**'s blessing. And then, the *second* element in God's Genesis blessing, is echoed by the second-to-last element of **Parshat Bechukotai**'s blessing. The same holds for the next echo: The third element in Genesis is echoed by the third-to-last in **Parshat Bechukotai**:

GOD'S BLESSING TO ISRAEL IN PARSHAT BECHUKOTAI	GOD'S BLESSING TO MANKIND ON THE SIXTH DAY
	Be fruitful and multiply
	Conquer the earth
	Dominate the animals
God will remove wild animals	
You will vanquish your enemies	
I will make you fruitful and will multiply you	

So maybe you're a skeptic, and you say to yourself: "*Well, that's intriguing — but maybe it's all just a coincidence. To be convinced I'd have to see more. Does the pattern continue?*"

Well, as a matter of fact, it does. Remarkably, the pattern embraces a fourth and fifth element, too.

A Fourth and Fifth Element

Back in Genesis, after Adam and Eve were blessed with fertility; after they were told about conquering the earth; after they were told about dominating the animal world — they were next told that plant life would be given to them as a source of food: Herbs and vegetation were to be theirs to enjoy:

Genesis 1:29

וַיֹּאמֶר אֱלֹקִים הִנֵּה נָתַתִּי לָכֶם
אֶת כָּל עֵשֶׂב זֹרֵעַ זֶרַע אֲשֶׁר עַל
פְּנֵי כָל הָאָרֶץ

God said, "Behold, I have given you every herb which yields seed that is on the face of the earth."

Lo and behold, in **Parshat Bechukotai**'s blessing, the fourth-to-last element *also* revolves around our ability to harvest the bounty that the plant world provides for us:

Leviticus 26:5

וְהִשִּׂיג לָכֶם דַּיִשׁ אֶת בָּצִיר
וּבָצִיר יַשִּׂיג אֶת זָרַע וַאֲכַלְתֶּם
לַחְמְכֶם לָשֹׂבַע וִישַׁבְתֶּם לָבֶטַח
בְּאַרְצְכֶם׃

Your threshing shall [be so plentiful] that it will reach to the vintage, and the vintage shall [be so plentiful] as to reach to the sowing time; and you shall eat your bread to the full, and dwell in your land safely.

Wine and bread, the products of grapes and grain, all these, **Parshat Bechukotai** tells Israel, will be theirs in abundance.[2]

And after that? You guessed it: The two blessings correspond in a fifth way, too. The fifth element of the Genesis blessing revolves around trees:

Genesis 1:29

וְאֶת כָּל הָעֵץ אֲשֶׁר בּוֹ פְרִי עֵץ
זֹרֵעַ זָרַע לָכֶם יִהְיֶה לְאָכְלָה׃

And every tree which has fruit and yields seed; these will be yours for eating.

And, right in line with the pattern we've been seeing, the fifth-to-last element of Bechukotai's blessing corresponds perfectly:

2 Interestingly, a difference appears here with respect to how the blessings of bounty from the plant world manifest themselves in Genesis and in Leviticus. In Genesis, the emphasis is on the raw, whole foods that are the direct and immediate product of plants themselves: כָּל עֵשֶׂב זֹרֵעַ זֶרַע אֲשֶׁר עַל פְּנֵי כָל הָאָרֶץ וְאֶת כׇּל הָעֵץ אֲשֶׁר בּוֹ פְרִי עֵץ זֹרֵעַ זָרַע לָכֶם יִהְיֶה לְאָכְלָה — "every herb which yields seed that is on the face of the earth, and every tree which has fruit and yields seed; these will be yours for eating" (Gen. 1:29). In Leviticus, however, the emphasis changes to derivative products of plants — wine and bread. The latter are products that humans make with their own ingenuity; they are not the direct products of vegetation or trees. This progression has its own internal logic, though. In Genesis, God was speaking to humanity in its infancy, just as people were first created. The first humans would, in fact, consume the direct products of plant life. Leviticus, though, addresses humans at a much later stage of their development. At this point, humans would be practiced in creating derivative products from plants. Hence, their blessing would revolve around wine and bread.

Leviticus 26:4

וְעֵץ הַשָּׂדֶה יִתֵּן פִּרְיוֹ׃ The trees of the field shall yield their fruit.

All in all, **Parshat Bechukotai**'s blessing seems to be an exact image, backward, of God's original blessing to mankind:

GOD'S BLESSING TO ISRAEL IN PARSHAT BECHUKOTAI	GOD'S BLESSING TO MANKIND ON THE SIXTH DAY
	Be fruitful and multiply
Fruits of the trees are given to you	Conquer the earth
The bounty of the land is yours for the taking	Dominate the animals
God will remove wild animals	Herbs and vegetation are yours for the taking...
You will vanquish your enemies	...as are fruit trees
I will make you fruitful and will multiply you	

A Sixth Element: The Seventh Day

So far, all five elements of God's blessing to humankind on the sixth day have found echoes in **Parshat Bechukotai**. And now I want to consider one more crucial piece of evidence with you. I believe this additional point may help us begin to unlock the meaning behind all these parallels. Let's return to the Genesis-Leviticus connection, and ask if we can extend the links between these passages one more step. Could there possibly be a *sixth* element in common here?

To see if the pattern continues, we need to go back to Genesis, and consider what happened after God issued that blessing to mankind on the sixth day. *What happened next?*

The answer is: The Sabbath — Creation's primal, seventh day:

Genesis 2:1–3

וַיְכֻלּוּ הַשָּׁמַיִם וְהָאָרֶץ וְכָל צְבָאָם: וַיְכַל אֱלֹקִים בַּיּוֹם הַשְּׁבִיעִי מְלַאכְתּוֹ אֲשֶׁר עָשָׂה וַיִּשְׁבֹּת בַּיּוֹם הַשְּׁבִיעִי מִכָּל מְלַאכְתּוֹ אֲשֶׁר עָשָׂה: וַיְבָרֶךְ אֱלֹקִים אֶת יוֹם הַשְּׁבִיעִי וַיְקַדֵּשׁ אֹתוֹ כִּי בוֹ שָׁבַת מִכָּל מְלַאכְתּוֹ	The heavens and the earth and their entire array were completed. On the seventh day, God completed His work that He had done, and on the seventh day, He ceased from all His work that He had done. God blessed the seventh day and made it holy, because on it He ceased from all His work.

Having established this, let's fast forward to **Parshat Bechukotai** to see whether there is anything there that reminds us of the Sabbath. We would be looking for something "Sabbath-like" that *precedes* the five elements of the blessing here:

GOD'S BLESSING TO ISRAEL IN PARSHAT BECHUKOTAI	THE SIXTH AND SEVENTH DAYS OF CREATION
???	Be fruitful and multiply
Fruits of the trees are given to you	Conquer the earth
The bounty of the land is yours for the taking	Dominate the animals
God will remove wild animals	Herbs and vegetation are yours for the taking...
You will vanquish your enemies	...as are fruit trees
I will make you fruitful and will multiply you	The Sabbath

As it happens, just before all five elements are mentioned, we get the following words. They appear just before the blessings that follow:

Leviticus 26:2–3	אֶת שַׁבְּתֹתַי תִּשְׁמֹרוּ וּמִקְדָּשִׁי תִּירָאוּ אֲנִי יְקוָה: אִם בְּחֻקֹּתַי תֵּלֵכוּ וְאֶת מִצְוֹתַי תִּשְׁמְרוּ וַעֲשִׂיתֶם אֹתָם:	**You shall keep My Sabbaths,** and have reverence for My sanctuary. I am God. If you walk in My Statutes, and keep my commandments, and do them.

Indeed, there we have it. We found our sixth parallel, and it fits the pattern remarkably.

Diving into the Sabbath Connection

I think we've seen enough to establish that the pattern we've been investigating isn't the product of our overactive imagination. To the contrary, it seems very real. But it's one thing to find a pattern. It is entirely something else to understand its meaning. So let's turn our attention to that question. What are we, as readers, meant to take away from this connection between **Parshat Bechukotai**'s opening and its connections to Genesis?

To begin to parse the meaning of all these connections, let's begin with this last one — that of Sabbath. In pondering the language in Leviticus, the reader notices an interesting quality in the Torah's description of the Sabbath Israel is meant to keep:

Leviticus 26:2	אֶת שַׁבְּתֹתַי תִּשְׁמֹרוּ	You shall keep **My** Sabbaths.

What a strange thing to say! God seems rather possessive about His Sabbath, wouldn't you say? Is there a difference between "the" Sabbath and "My" Sabbath?

I think there is. Let me explain.

A Personal Sabbath

Generally speaking, the Bible is not really a theological book, in the sense that its purpose is not really to describe what it is like to be God. The Torah normally focuses on the *relationship* between humans and God, which is another thing entirely. There is, however, a notable exception to that, and it comes in the Genesis account of the very first Sabbath. There, and there alone, we learn something about what it is like to be God. We learn that, after God finished creating the world, He devoted a day of creation to His rest and to nothing else. And it turns out that God was positively *thrilled* with the Sabbath.

וַיְבָרֶךְ אֱלֹקִים אֶת יוֹם הַשְּׁבִיעִי וַיְקַדֵּשׁ אֹתוֹ כִּי בוֹ שָׁבַת מִכָּל מְלַאכְתּוֹ	God blessed the seventh day and made it holy, because on it He ceased from all His work.	Genesis 2:3

The Almighty was so very pleased with His new Sabbath, that He blessed it and sanctified it, for He wished to celebrate His rest.

That first of all Sabbaths was God's very own. Notice that this celebration of the Sabbath by God doesn't involve any humans, nor do humans, at the time, even know about it. We, the readers of the text, many years after Creation, know about it. But at the time, God didn't command Adam and Eve to observe that Sabbath or even tell them that He was resting. For all we know, Adam and Eve were entirely unaware of the Sabbath's existence. That first Sabbath was God's, and God's alone. No one else shared in its experience.

By the time we get to Leviticus, though, all that changed. God had since commanded Israel to join Him in the celebration of these phenomena we call Sabbaths. And these Sabbaths come in all shapes and sizes (see our essay on **Parshat Emor** for details). One such Sabbath occurs in the realm of years — the Sabbatical or Shemittah year. For six years we work the land, but during the seventh year — the one we proclaim a Sabbath — we refrain from working the land or exhibiting dominion over it.

The laws of this Sabbatical year are the main focus in the Torah leading into **Parshat Bechukotai**. And in the verse just before the parsha begins, the Torah concludes its discussion with the admonition that Israel is to observe "*My* Sabbaths" — which in context, is clearly a reference to these Sabbatical years. So, it is almost as if, when we read those words, we are meant to conjure, in our minds' eye, the *personal* Sabbath in Genesis, the one in which the Almighty, alone in His numinous solitude, celebrated His completion of a universe. It is as if the text wants us to conflate the two. Almost as if the text was telling us: *That* Sabbath was experienced by God alone; but now — now that we are commanded to observe these Sabbatical years, now that we are bidden to join with the Master of the Universe in the experience of Sabbath... now, the Divine Being would have some company in His rest. Israel would join and be a part of it.

And to further buttress this sense of conflating the two, consider how this admonition to keep "My Sabbaths" just happens to match up with God's original, personal Sabbath in the Creation story, as the final element in a series of correspondences between Leviticus and Genesis:

GOD'S BLESSING TO ISRAEL IN PARSHAT BECHUKOTAI	THE SIXTH AND SEVENTH DAYS OF CREATION
Keep "My" Sabbaths	Be fruitful and multiply
Fruits of the trees are given to you	Conquer the earth
The bounty of the land is yours for the taking	Dominate the animals
God will remove wild animals	Herbs and vegetation are yours for the taking
You will vanquish your enemies	...as are fruit trees
I will make you fruitful and will multiply you	The advent of God's Sabbath

Are We at the End of the Line?

So let's take stock of where we are at.

All in all, we have seen six elements that seem to connect a broad swath of text in Leviticus and Genesis, respectively. For the most part, it connects the blessings promised to Israel should they observe God's commands when they enter the land, to the blessings given to humankind during the primal sixth day of Creation. But this pattern extends just a bit further, as well: It goes on to encompass the Sabbath of the seventh day of Creation, and the Sabbatical years of Leviticus.

In the interests of rounding out our picture and seeing what it all might mean, I believe we actually need to extend our exploration just a bit further. Might it be possible that the parallels between these two sections of text extend still further?

At first, the answer to that question seems to be no. To this point, the parallels between Leviticus and Genesis have unfolded in reverse order. Every step *forward* in Genesis took us another step backward in the Leviticus text. Well, the next thing we hear about in Genesis is the Garden God plants in Eden, which means that, if the parallels continued following that same pattern, we would expect to find some sort of analogue to the Garden of Eden earlier in Leviticus, right before the mention of keeping God's Sabbaths. And nothing at this point in Leviticus presents itself as a likely candidate for such a parallel. So it seems like we are at the end of the line.

But... maybe not.

Because it just so happens that right after all these parallels we found in **Parshat Bechukotai** — the promise of fruits, of vegetation, of the removal of wild animals, vanquishing of enemies, and fertility — right *after*[3] all of that, we *do* hear of something that reminds us suspiciously of the original Garden:

---

3 What I'm suggesting here is that the last step of the pattern is the advent of the Garden and its analog in Leviticus. And, for some reason that remains somewhat mysterious to me, this last step of the pattern diverges from all the prior steps. Instead of the Leviticus analogue to the Garden of Eden appearing at the *beginning* of all the Leviticus elements, it appears at the end of them. Why might the pattern proceed in this unusual way precisely at this point? I don't have a fully worked-out theory — but I would proffer a speculative theory.

Perhaps, seen in its totality, the Torah may be treating the various elements that comprise the blessing to Israel in **Parshat Bechukotai** as a single unit. Likewise, it may be treating the analogous elements that comprise the blessing to humankind in Genesis as a single unit. Each of the elements of each blessing parallel one another as well, but these are viewed as subunits within the larger, parallel unit.

Leviticus 26:11 וְנָתַתִּי מִשְׁכָּנִי בְּתוֹכְכֶם I will have My Presence dwell among you.

Why, you might ask, does this sound like a Leviticus analogue to the primal Garden that God planted in Eden? Well, stop and think about the significance of that original, paradisiacal Garden. What, really, was the point of it? God had just made an entire world, full of forests and lush vegetation. What was the special Garden for?

One might perhaps surmise: the Garden was there for the newly created people. Maybe the Lord wanted to make somewhere especially pretty to put these new humans He created. The Garden was a gift to them, with its manicured trees and lush ferns.

Could be. But I think the truth of the Garden extends beyond this, too. The Garden wasn't just a place for humans. It was a place for God, too.

I don't think it is a coincidence that the verses in Genesis telling us of God's creating the Garden immediately follow the advent of God's Sabbath. These two events, I'd suggest, are juxtaposed for a reason: What the Sabbath is to time, the Garden is to space.

Finding Parker

To explain: God is a non-corporeal, non-time-bound being. When we say that He created the world, we don't just mean that He created all the *stuff*, all the matter and energy, that exists in the universe. We also mean that He created the environment in which all this stuff exists. Which is to say, the Almighty created time and space itself. But, as the Creator of time and space, God's natural abode is *outside* of time and space. The Divine Being exists in a realm that is entirely beyond these constraints.

I remember a conversation I once had with a self-professed atheist who wondered why, if God really exists, we don't see Him all the time in this world of ours. The analogy I gave by way of reply came from the

---

Thus, while the subunits in Leviticus proceed in backward order relative to the subunits in Genesis, still, the larger units themselves — that is, (a) the blessings in *totality* in Genesis and Leviticus and (b) God's subsequent choice to create a kind of Garden in each story — these larger units *do* appear in order: First, the blessing, and then the Garden.

game Monopoly. Imagine a conversation between Little Hat and Little Shoe, these two Monopoly icons. They are making their way around the board, and somewhere between Tennessee Avenue and Park Place, Little Hat asks Little Shoe if he believes in Parker.

"Parker." replies Little Shoe, "Who's that?"

"Well, it says right over here on the side of the board, made by Parker Brothers. So...do you believe in Parker?"

Little Shoe is taken aback. "Well, I guess so," he stammers.

But Little Hat is not so sure: "Me, I don't know. Look, I've been around this board dozens of times. Every week I pass Go and collect two hundred dollars. I've seen it all. Baltic Avenue, Boardwalk, you name it. Hey, I've even been to jail. But I never see Parker!"

What would you say to Little Hat?

The answer is: *He's been looking for Parker in all the wrong places.* Parker doesn't live on the board. He *made* the board.

It's the same way with God. The Almighty is the author of time and space. The author doesn't live in our world, the world of His own making.

Except... that there's a problem with this.

Two Exceptions to the Parker Rule of Thumb

The problem is: loneliness. *We humans would be lonely without our Creator around.*

God's desire in making a world, ultimately, isn't simply to achieve a great feat of engineering. That engineering feat had a purpose. God wished to have a place where beings created in His own image could live, and where He could relate with them. But ultimately, if God were to be limited to His own world, and humans, these carbon-based life forms, would be relegated exclusively to their own separate domain — well, sure, a relationship is possible from afar; but wouldn't it be better if there was some way that these two beings, God and humans, could really connect? Could they actually share an environment together? It's pretty lonely living all alone. How could God and humans actually share one another's company?

We can think of Sabbath and Eden as two attempts, on the part of God, to do just that.

The Sabbath was a place, in our very human world of time, in which God would reside.[4] He would "rest" there. The word "to be at rest" in Hebrew seems related to the phonetically similar word "to settle": *shav*. God, having been involved in a relentless flurry of creative activity, rests and comes to "settle" or "reside," in the Sabbath.

But if the Sabbath is a place for God to reside in *time*, Eden would be the counterpart to that in the realm of *space*.

Consider for a moment that according to the verses, Adam and Eve were not created in the Garden. They were formed, dust from the earth, *outside* the Garden and then brought by God into the Garden: וַיִּטַּע יְקוָה אֱלֹקִים גַּן בְּעֵדֶן מִקֶּדֶם; וַיָּשֶׂם שָׁם אֶת הָאָדָם אֲשֶׁר יָצָר — "And God planted a Garden eastward, in Eden; and there He put the man whom He had formed" (Genesis 2:8). The Garden was God's domain first, and He invited mankind to join Him there.

This notion of God's "space" may help us better understand the following verse, which appears halfway through the story of Adam and Eve, situated, as they were, in the Garden of Eden:

Genesis 3:8	וַיִּשְׁמְעוּ אֶת קוֹל יְקוָה אֱלֹקִים מִתְהַלֵּךְ בַּגָּן לְרוּחַ הַיּוֹם	And [the humans] heard the voice of God, strolling in the Garden in the breeze of the day.

The text conveys a remarkable scene here: The voice of God, strolling through the Garden in the afternoon…. The ethereal aspects of the metaphor jump out at you: God, personified only by a voice without a body, is doing what one normally needs a body to do: stroll around a garden. But by making use of this metaphor, the text conveys to us something important about God's relationship to that special place on earth. For who, exactly, strolls through a garden in the afternoon? It's something… the Garden's owner might do. After all, how better to get some rest than to stroll through the grounds of one's garden on his premises after a long

4 For more detailed explorations of the Sabbath and its connection to the idea of a "place" for God in our world, see two of my essays in *Exodus: A Parsha Companion* (Maggid Books, 2020): "Vayakhel II: An 'Apartment' in Our Everything" and "Pekudei: A Tale of Two Clouds."

day's work? So too, here is God walking through His summer home in the realm of space, His special garden.

All in all, just after the Torah tells us about the Almighty's rest in the realm of time, we are told about His "resting place" in the realm of space. God wanted to enjoy the company of these humans He created. So God made a little "summer home" in space for himself. He planted this Garden, rested there, and invited humans to join Him.

A Summer Home in Space

As we might expect by now, all of this has echoes in **Parshat Bechukotai**, too.

וְנָתַתִּי מִשְׁכָּנִי בְּתוֹכְכֶם	I will have My Presence dwell among you.	Leviticus 26:11

The promise in **Parshat Bechukotai** that God would have His Presence "dwell among you" suggests that the Land of Israel could become what Eden once was: a special place in this world where God and a community of people could dwell in proximity to one another.

To be sure, mankind's sojourn in the Garden didn't last long. Humans, in the wake of their choice to eat of the forbidden fruit, had been expelled from the Garden, the place God had made for Himself in this world. But, **Parshat Bechukotai** suggests enticingly, we don't have to take that banishment as destiny. We can do something about it. Sure, the God-made summer home called Eden remains off-limits to us, but we humans can still try to construct a replacement: A *man-made* place for God. It turns out, Israel can develop itself into a nation that can serve as a domicile for the Divine Presence, and we can invite God in.

Who Is God Walking With?

If the Land of Israel had the potential to house a new Eden, how would man and God relate to one another in this new Garden? How would they "enjoy one another's company," so to speak?

Here too, **Parshat Bechukotai** offers an answer; an answer drawn from the language of Eden:

Leviticus 26:12

וְהִתְהַלַּכְתִּי בְּתוֹכְכֶם   I will walk among you.

That particular form of the root *heh-lamed-chet* is unusual. It is formulated in the *hitpa'el* form, *vehit'halachti,* and is a direct and unmistakable echo of that mysterious "stroll in the afternoon" that the Master of the Universe took back in Eden:

LEVITICUS	GENESIS
וְהִתְהַלַּכְתִּי בְּתוֹכְכֶם I will walk among you (26:12).	וַיִּשְׁמְעוּ אֶת קוֹל יְקֹוָה אֱלֹקִים מִתְהַלֵּךְ בַּגָּן לְרוּחַ הַיּוֹם They heard the voice of God strolling in the Garden in the breeze of the day (3:8).

What are the particular connotations of *heh-lamed-chet* when it is conjugated this way, in *hitpa'el*?

Well, typically, *hitpa'el* indicates action that is reflexive, when a certain subject is doing something to him or herself. So, for example, if you take the verb *lamed, vav, shin,* which means to dress or to wear, and you make it *lehitlabesh* — that is, you put it in *hitpa'el* form — then, all of a sudden, it's going to mean: *To get oneself dressed.* But that doesn't quite seem to work in either the Genesis or the Leviticus version of the text describing God's "walking." Because if *hey, lamed, chet* means to walk, what would *lehit'halech* mean? How do you even think about that reflexively? Was God "taking Himself for a walk" in the Garden? Possibly, but that's a pretty awkward notion.

There is, however, another intriguing possibility.

It turns out that *hitpa'el* forms of verbs occasionally connote something else, besides reflexive action. Sometimes, *hitpa'el* describes actions that two people, or two beings, do together with one another. Like, for example, when the text in Genesis relates that Rebecca is pregnant with twins, the Torah uses the *hitpa'el* form of the verb "to run"[5] and states: וַיִּתְרֹצְצוּ הַבָּנִים בְּקִרְבָּהּ (Gen. 25:22) — "the two *ran at one another* in the womb." We find a similar use of *hitpa'el*, in Modern Hebrew, where *lehitkatev* means that two people are pen pals, that they correspond with one another; and where *lehitkasher* means that I reach out and talk with you on the phone. In all of these cases, *hitpa'el* connotes mutual action.

The Unifying Idea of *Hitpa'el*

And we might pause and ask: How strange of Hebrew grammar to do that! Why is there a particular grammatical form, *hitpa'el*, that does two entirely different things? Why does it on the one hand connote reflexive action (a subject acting on itself) and on the other hand connote mutual action (two beings doing something together)?

The answer might be: When people do something together, there is a hidden aspect of what they are doing that can well be viewed as reflexive action, as a unit acting upon itself. To explain:

Let's imagine two people are doing something together. How should we view that? One way to see it is to look at each individual person and their actions toward the other. But one might also look at both *together*. That is, one might say: When two people engage in mutual action, there's a kind of new *unit* that's formed between the two of them, a kind of "we." Above and beyond each person's individual activity, the unit — the "we," as it were — is acting on itself.

Walking Together

How does this understanding impact the way we interpret God's being *mit'halech* in Genesis and Leviticus?

Let's take Genesis first. It provides the backdrop, I think, against which we need to understand Leviticus.

---

5 There is actually a debate among the classical commentators as to precisely which Hebrew root וַיִּתְרֹצְצוּ comes from. Rashi, quoting the Sages of the Midrash, understands the word as deriving from *resh-vav-tzadi*, "to run," while others say that it comes from the root *resh-tzadi-tzadi*, "to crush" (see, for example, Bechor Shor, Rabbi Avraham ben HaRambam). However, regardless of which root the word comes from, the idea being conveyed is one of mutual action.

Back in Genesis, the text signifies to us a kind of tragedy in how events unfolded there:

Genesis 3:8	וַיִּשְׁמְעוּ אֶת קוֹל יְקֹוָה אֱלֹקִים מִתְהַלֵּךְ בַּגָּן לְרוּחַ הַיּוֹם וַיִּתְחַבֵּא הָאָדָם וְאִשְׁתּוֹ מִפְּנֵי יְקֹוָה אֱלֹקִים בְּתוֹךְ עֵץ הַגָּן׃	They heard the voice of God walking in the Garden in the breeze of the day, and the man and his wife hid themselves from the Presence of God among the trees of the Garden.

Just before God's "stroll," just before His being *mit'halech* in the Garden — something had gone wrong. The people had eaten from the forbidden fruit, and they were now hiding from God in fear. They seem to have perceived this as a gotcha moment: *Here comes God to castigate us for what we've done.*

But were they correct? Remember the *hitpa'el* in that sentence. They didn't just hear the voice of God "walking." They heard that voice walking in ... *hitpa'el.*

What, then, did they *really* hear? They didn't hear God "taking Himself on a walk." The *hitpa'el* seems to imply mutual action — two beings, God with humans, walking together. God wasn't coming *at* them; God was coming to walk *with them. That* was His intention. There was an invitation issued to the humans to engage with God in mutual action.[6] *Come walk with Me...*

But at that very moment, Adam and Eve chose to hide. God was inviting the humans to join Him on a stroll through the Garden ... but there was no answer to the invitation. God was ready to go on a stroll with His precious humans but they were nowhere to be found.

One can detect the mournful overtones of God's question to them:

Genesis 3:9	אַיֶּכָּה	Where are you?

---

6 Indeed, the *hitpa'el* form of *heh-lamed-chet* is regularly used to describe walking with God. (See Gen. 5:22–24, 6:9, 17:1, 24:40, and 48:15.)

It is as if God was saying to them: *I am here. I am ready to enjoy a walk with you. But you... where did you go? How come you aren't here?*[7]

The added tragedy of Eden is this: *Not only did we humans sin, but we hid afterward.* We misinterpreted a moment of love, of joyful togetherness, for a moment of castigation. This was a chance to be together with God. It was God reaching out with an affirmation of our essential humanity and worth, even in the face of our sin. But it was a chance we were too afraid to take. When God reached out to us, seeking to go walking with us, we were nowhere to be found. We recoiled from that invitation, thinking ourselves unworthy of it; thinking that God could be nothing other than disgusted with us. It was then that we truly withdrew from God. It was then that we all but chose exile from the Garden. And a few verses later, that exile in fact comes to pass.

An Invitation That Still Stands

But that exile wasn't the last word.

These Genesis parallels that we've detected in **Parshat Bechukotai**, they are meant to be the backdrop for understanding the verses in

---

7 There are two Hebrew words for "where." The far more common one is *eifoh*. *Eifoh* is an ordinary kind of "where"; it is the word we use when I actually want to know where you are, and I request to know your location. The less common word for "where" is the one used here in Genesis, *ayeh*.

If you look carefully at how *ayeh* is used in the Torah, you'll find that it actually is never, really, a request for location. It doesn't actually mean "where" at all; it means "where did you go?" For example, in the story of the Binding of Isaac, Abraham is going up the mountain with his son and Isaac engages him in conversation. He says: הִנֵּה הָאֵשׁ וְהָעֵצִים וְאַיֵּה הַשֶּׂה לְעֹלָה — "Here is the fire and here is the wood; but where is the lamb for the offering?" (Gen. 22:7)

When Isaac asks that, he's not really requesting the location of the lamb. He doesn't mean: *I want to know exactly where the lamb is! Did we leave it by the woodshed or by the barn?* It wasn't *eifoh* that Isaac was asking, it was *ayeh*. He was talking about a lamb that was supposed to be there, but wasn't: *I see the wood, I see the fire, but there's no lamb. Dad, what happened to the lamb?*

It's the same thing with the original *ayeh*, back in the Garden. The Master of the Universe wasn't requesting Adam and Eve's location. This was instead a plaintive cry: *We were supposed to go walking together! How come you're not here with Me?* It is the original lament in the Torah.

Leviticus. And they suggest that the broken *hitpa'el* of God's invitation back in Eden wasn't the last word. For in **Parshat Bechukotai**, we have an echo of that invitation in a new promise God holds out to us:

Leviticus 26:3; 12

אִם בְּחֻקֹּתַי תֵּלֵכוּ...וְהִתְהַלַּכְתִּי בְּתוֹכְכֶם	If you walk with My commands...I will walk with you.

Parshat Bechukotai tells us that God's voice will be back. In the Land of Israel, we will hear a version of what we once heard back in the Garden: God's voice, issuing an invitation. That invitation will come to us in the form of commands, statutes that God makes known to us through instruction that we can *hear*. God's promise in **Parshat Bechukotai** is that His age-old invitation from Eden… *still stands.* This, I think, is what the Sages meant by that enigmatic comment quoted by Rashi: What does it mean that God will walk with us? *[It is as if] He will stroll with us together, in the Garden of Eden.*

As Israel stands ready to enter the land, it stands poised to recreate a version of Eden. It stands ready to realize the blessings that accompanied man's entrance to the original, mysterious summer home of God's on earth. Some of those blessings were material — success in conquest, dominion over animals, abundant produce. But one aspect of those blessings was transcendent in nature: The chance to go walking with God's voice.

How do we go walking with God's voice in the Land of Israel, God's new summer home? What does it mean, in concrete terms, to stroll with that voice? The prologue to **Parshat Bechukotai** tells us:

Leviticus 26:3

אִם בְּחֻקֹּתַי תֵּלֵכוּ	If you walk with My commands.

If you walk with My commands, these expressions of My voice — then you've taken Me up on My invitation. And then וְהִתְהַלַּכְתִּי בְּתוֹכְכֶם, then I will stroll with you. When we walk with God's voice, God's voice, too, will walk with us, and togetherness with the Master of the Universe can be had once more.

Maggid Books
The best of contemporary Jewish thought from
Koren Publishers Jerusalem Ltd.